3/24/93

D0025333

UNDERSTANDING WAR

UNDERSTANDING WAR

ESSAYS ON CLAUSEWITZ AND THE HISTORY OF MILITARY POWER

Peter Paret

PRINCETON UNIVERSITY PRESS

PRINCETON, NEW JERSEY

LIBRARY OF CONGRESS CATALOGING-IN-PUBLICATION DATA

PARET, PETER.

UNDERSTANDING WAR : ESSAYS ON CLAUSEWITZ AND THE HISTORY OF
MILITARY POWER / PETER PARET.

P. CM.

INCLUDES INDEX.

ISBN 0-691-03199-1

1. WAR. 2. CLAUSEWITZ, CARL VON, 1780–1831. 3. MILITARY ART AND
SCIENCE—HISTORY. 4. MILITARY HISTORY, MODERN. I. TITLE.

U21.2.P32   1992   355.02—DC20   91-37491   CIP

THIS BOOK HAS BEEN COMPOSED IN LINOTRON SABON

PRINCETON UNIVERSITY PRESS BOOKS ARE PRINTED
ON ACID-FREE PAPER, AND MEET THE GUIDELINES FOR
PERMANENCE AND DURABILITY OF THE COMMITTEE ON
PRODUCTION GUIDELINES FOR BOOK LONGEVITY
OF THE COUNCIL ON LIBRARY RESOURCES

PRINTED IN THE UNITED STATES OF AMERICA

10 9 8 7 6 5 4 3 2

TO MY COLLEAGUES

IN THE SCHOOL OF HISTORICAL STUDIES

CONTENTS

ACKNOWLEDGMENTS

I SHOULD LIKE to express my thanks to David Nelson Blair for imposing a reasonable consistency on texts that first appeared at different times in a variety of publications, to Carol Starnes, who handled the design of the book, to Don Hatch, who designed the jacket, and to Harriet Hitch, who gave such matters as the jacket and catalog copy the attention they deserve. As so often before I am especially indebted to Joanna Hitchcock for the interest and care with which she watched over the manuscript and guided it toward publication.

৯

The following essays are reprinted by the kind permission of their original publishers:

Essay One from the *Journal of Military History* 53, no. 3 (1989); first given as a lecture at a symposium on power at the Shelby Cullom Davis Center for Historical Studies, Princeton University, in 1989.

Essay Two from *Reconsiderations on the Revolutionary War*, ed. Don Higginbotham, copyright (c) by Don Higginbotham, Greenwood Press, Westport, 1978; first given as a lecture at a symposium on the American Revolutionary War at the United States Military Academy, West Point, New York, in 1976.

Essay Three from *Military Affairs* 34, no. 1 (1970).

Essay Four from *Geschichte als Aufgabe: Festschrift für Otto Büsch*, ed. Wilhelm Treue, Colloquium Verlag, Berlin, 1988; first given as a lecture at the Lawrence Gipson Symposium on the End of the Ancien Régime at Lehigh University in 1981.

Essay Five from *Proceedings, the Consortium on Revolutionary Europe, 1983*, ed. Clarence B. Davis, University of Georgia, Athens, 1985; first given as a banquet address at the 1983 meeting of the Consortium.

Essay Six from *Great Military Battles*, ed. Cyril Falls, Weidenfeld and Nicolson, London, 1964.

Essay Seven from *Makers of Modern Strategy*, ed. Peter Paret, Princeton University Press, Princeton, 1986.

Essay Eight from Carl von Clausewitz, *Two Letters on Strategy*, eds. Peter Paret and Daniel Moran, copyright (c) by Peter Paret, U.S. Army War College Foundation, Carlisle Barracks, 1984.

Essay Nine from Carl von Clausewitz, *Historical and Political Writings*, eds. Peter Paret and Daniel Moran, Princeton University Press, Princeton, 1992.

Essay Ten from *Journal of the History of Ideas* 49, no. 1 (1988).

Essay Eleven from *Festschrift für Eberhard Kessel*, eds. Heinz Duchhardt and Manfred Schlenke, Wilhelm Fink Verlag, Munich, 1982; first given as a banquet address at the annual meeting of the German Studies Association in 1979.

Essay Twelve from *Freiheit ohne Krieg?* ed. Ulrich de Maizière, Dümmler Verlag, Bonn, 1980; first given as a lecture at a symposium of the Clausewitz Gesellschaft in 1980.

Essay Thirteen from *Jahrbuch für die Geschichte Mittel- und Ostdeutschlands*, 26 (1977).

Essay Fourteen under the title "An Anonymous Letter by Clausewitz on the Polish Insurrection of 1830-1831," from the *Journal of Modern History* 42, no. 2 (1970).

Essay Fifteen from the *Journal of Military History* 55, no. 2 (1991).

Essay Sixteen from *Daedalus*, Journal of the American Academy of Arts and Science, 100, no. 2 (1971), and *Parameters* 31, no. 3 (1991); the second part was first given as a banquet address at the annual meetings of the American Military Institute in 1991.

The human mind . . . has a universal thirst for clarity, and
longs to feel itself part of an orderly scheme of things.
Carl von Clausewitz

❧

INTRODUCTION

WAR HAS its own characteristics but is linked to all other areas of society and culture. It is both unique and subsumed in the generality of the human experience. This dualism, which it shares with everything else in life, imposes a fundamental choice on historians who take war as their subject. They can interpret war in its context, or they can concentrate on its instrumental center—the phenomenon of violence—and pay less attention to the nonviolent elements that surround and penetrate war. The alternatives need not be absolute, of course; but it is surprising how often interpretations of the second kind leave out the nonviolent context altogether or address it only in passing. Treated in this manner, their subject takes on the appearance of a contest fought in a vacuum, an agonistic drama played out by opponents whose strength, courage, and cunning are all that matters.

Both approaches have advantages as well as weaknesses, and both have led to good history. Historians who are mainly interested in tracing the course of battle may feel that a narrow focus serves them best. A broader perspective—though of necessity it will still be selective—runs the danger of obscuring the violent core or of reducing its significance. But that need not be the case. There have always been historians who link their narratives of operations in the field to discussions of the political circumstances that gave rise to them and continue to affect them, and of the other countless elements—ranging from social conditions to the management of economic resources—that shape the fighting and help determine its outcome. On the whole I find this approach more interesting. Not only does it address matters that historians of war too often ignore although they are of great importance to their subject, usually it also holds the key for a full understanding of the fighting.

No one would claim that a strategic plan is based on military factors alone. The political motives and consequences of the plan are only some of the many nonmilitary elements involved. But it is equally true that every segment of military policy and action, down to the level of small-unit tactics, is influenced by any number of factors beyond the strictly military. To understand why men fought in a certain fashion we must know something of their circumstances before they heaved the first rock or fired the first shot. The Duke of Wellington recognized his own worth too clearly, and was far too clever, to have said that the battle of Waterloo was won in the playing fields of Eton. But if we enlarge this fictional homage to the

English gentleman to encompass all aspects of the society in which he assumed a major place, the statement makes a valid point. The background, schooling, attitudes, and regimental traditions of the officer; the social antecedents, motives for serving, treatment, and drill of the rank and file; the bonds of deference and duty that held the common soldier firmly in his assigned place—all these help explain the specific tactical behavior of the British forces at the time and the ways in which it differed from the methods of their Dutch and Prussian allies and their French opponents. Of course, the actual clash of opposing armies and the movements that led to it form only a part of any battle, and the battle of Waterloo, above all, can hardly be understood if we limit ourselves to the actions of commanders and men between 15 June and 18 June 1815.

ða

If the essays in this volume share a defining motif, it is that without losing sight of the unique nature of war they treat the history of war as part of history in general. That many of the essays discuss a man who placed the interaction of war and politics at the center of his career and of his theories could only expand their orientation. Even on those rare occasions when Clausewitz was nothing but a soldier, it would be ludicrous to discuss him in purely military terms.

The essays are divided into three parts. The first part is primarily about war from the ancien régime to the early decades of the nineteenth century. Several essays analyze issues that begin earlier and end later—if they can be said to have ended at all—but their center of gravity remains in this period. Together they outline some of the fundamental conditions of the military world into which Clausewitz was born and which provided the starting point for his efforts to understand not only war in his time but war in general. The first part of the book forms the backdrop for the second part, which consists of nine essays on Clausewitz himself. They begin with a general account, continue with discussions of particular aspects of his life and thought, and end with two studies on the last year of his life. The third part, with which the book concludes, consists merely of one essay. It is neither about a historical episode or problem nor—except in passing—about Clausewitz, but about the history of war as an academic discipline.

Nearly all of these essays were written in response to invitations to take part in a conference or to give a talk. Nevertheless they represent steps in a fairly coherent scholarly enterprise. War from the Frederician to the Napoleonic era and Clausewitz's life and work were areas in the history of war that held my interest for two decades or more. During these years I also wrote a biography of Clausewitz, and the essay that here appears under the new title "Reactions to Revolution" was a preliminary study for a section of the book. The remaining essays on Clausewitz were written after the biography had appeared. They either interpret newly discovered documents or analyze aspects of Clausewitz's work that I had not discussed in the book, or explore such issues as his methods of analysis or his political views from a different perspective.

Except for small corrections and some updated references, thirteen of the essays are reprinted without substantial changes. Two I originally wrote in German. In the process of translating them into English, I somewhat revised one and considerably shortened the other. The last essay, "The History of War and the New Military History," combines parts of a paper I wrote in 1970 with a talk I gave in the spring of 1991. A brief introduction to each essay suggests the circumstances under which it was written.

❧

Clausewitz lived at a time when war in the Western world radically changed. What is sometimes called the revolution in war at the end of the eighteenth century replaced the assumptions and practices of the ancien régime with new methods of raising and organizing armed forces and of employing them in ways that could add tremendous power to the policies of the state. Out of these innovations a pattern emerged that in general terms was to last for a century and some parts of which continue to affect war to this day. Clausewitz was not only an observer of this process, he took part in it. He was just old enough to serve in the last campaigns waged in the spirit of eighteenth-century maneuver warfare, but sufficiently young to fight in the reformed Prussian army, which he himself had helped to modernize.

That Clausewitz lived during this transition undoubtedly played a great part in the development of his theories. Not that the conjunction of theorist and military revolution was in itself sufficient to bring about *On War*. Many of Clausewitz's contemporaries drew the wrong conclusions from the military revolution. They saw the old ways as a necessarily inferior preparatory stage for Napoleonic war, and most assumed that from this time on the norm would be the climactic battle, which destroyed or at least severely weakened the enemy's capacity to fight on. Clausewitz, on the other hand, took for granted that like every previous form of warfare, the Napoleonic pattern, too, was subject to change. Consequently it lacked universal authority, either as a model for a campaign or as the basis for a general theory of war. Instead of thinking exclusively in terms of the present—overwhelming though the present was—he took the past seriously and tried to understand it on its own terms. He looked beyond the surface appearance of Frederician and Napoleonic war and asked what these two types might stand for. His answer was that they did not represent an inferior and a superior way of fighting but expressed different political and social conditions, one of which was conducive to more limited operations, the other to the more extreme use of force. Each might be valid, depending on the motives of the particular conflict and the circumstances in which it occurred.

The relationship of Clausewitz to the physical and intellectual world in which he lived is important and deserves study for its own sake. But its exploration also opens a useful perspective on his writings. It is true that Clausewitz sought to detach his hypotheses from an overly close reliance on the events of his day and that their analytic strength is great enough to make *On War* into a work that is far more than a historical document. But his complex ideas and the often similarly complex methods he employed to express, develop, and test them become clearer when they are seen in historical context.

That may seem an odd statement to make about writings whose author was praised in the national press during the recent Gulf War as "the man of the hour." In recent years the view has become widespread in this country and in much of the world that Clausewitz's theories are relevant to modern war. The exact nature of their relevance is not always clear; too often his ideas are cited as though they constitute a doctrine, a set of laws, instead of the analytic, sometimes speculative observations Clausewitz meant them to be. His theories offer us a way of looking at the day-to-day events of a conflict from the perspective of its underlying dynamic; they help us to identify the significant elements of any particular war and to form our own conclusions. *On War* is a work of analysis, not of advocacy. But however it has been interpreted, *On War* seems to have had something to say to every generation since it was first published over a century and a half ago. It has demonstrated staying power and a degree of timelessness. Do readers of such a work need the perspective of history to follow its arguments?

"Need" is surely too strong a term. We don't need to master the literature on Renaissance Florence to follow Machiavelli as he penetrates rhetoric, pretense, and custom to lay bare the realities of political power. Nor—to move closer to Clausewitz's period and culture—must we study the conditions of East Prussia in the eighteenth century to recognize the logic and authority of Kant's ethics. But because knowledge is not essential should it be unwanted? Even if ideas often seem to exist on their own, they come from somewhere—the mind of a particular individual, living at a given time, in a specific environment. Some recognition of the historical and biographical conditions that lay at the source of the ideas can only help us to understand them. The essays in this volume discuss specific aspects of the history of war. But most—some more directly than others—also address the development of Clausewitz's ideas, and the logic, historical accuracy, and more than temporary relevance of his conclusions.

PART ONE

WAR AND ITS INSTITUTIONS

1

MILITARY POWER

ARMED FORCES are employed not only for war and the threat of war, whether for purposes of aggression or defense. Throughout history they have had other political and social functions as well. For this reason it may be useful to distinguish between the history of war, the history of military institutions, and even the history of military thought; although if the distinctions are drawn sharply and permanently the historical interpretation suffers. Operational history—which is what most people mean by the history of war—is shallow unless it is supported by the study of the relevant institutions and theories. It is equally apparent that military institutions and ideas about how they are to be used cannot be studied in isolation. Eventually their entire political and social context must be taken into account.

In 1989 I was offered an opportunity to attempt an integrated analysis of these elements. Lawrence Stone organized a symposium on the theme of "power" at the Shelby Cullom Davis Center for Historical Studies of Princeton University, and he invited me to write the paper on military power, which together with papers on political and economic power would serve as basis for the discussion. I used the occasion to trace a number of general features of military institutions and war through European history, as they changed under the pressure of other forces and changed these forces in turn. In particular I wanted to outline the function of violence and the state-creating and state-maintaining function of military power, as well as the development of special interests in the institutions in which military power rests. When I revised the talk for publication, I added a brief final section, which shifted the perspective from military power as such to its historical interpretation. Here, too, I thought the main need was to understand military power for what it is and at the same time to recognize its constant interaction with other forces. The concluding essay in this volume returns to the historical interpretation of war, a matter that has posed difficulties to historians over the past two centuries.

❧

The purpose of this paper is to suggest starting points for a broader discussion of military power and its links with other kinds of power. It identifies some general features of military institutions and of the use of military force, and illustrates their characteristics with examples drawn from the history of the early modern period, the French Revolution, and nineteenth-century Europe. Of course, in historical analysis no less than in reality, political, economic, and military power are not easily separated. In peace and war they depend on each other, nurture and exploit but may also diminish each other, and act on and react to the societies that gave rise to them. If we study any one of these different but interlocking kinds of power, we must be prepared to isolate them; but although this is a necessary expedient, misinterpretations often follow. They seem to occur most often in the historical literature on military power which, despite a number of important recent works, continues on the whole to be less satisfactory than current studies of economic and political history, perhaps because of its pronounced concentration on war, which is merely one aspect of its subject.

The following pages treat military power in early modern and modern Europe both as an institutional process of applying physical force and as an expression of political power, especially the power of the state. It goes without saying that political energy is generated not only by the state, and that military power is often associated with other political interests or factions. Armed force may be a component of resistance to the state or a manifestation of economic or religious crises during which the state stands apart, at least initially, as in the German peasant wars of the early sixteenth century. But whether it supports or opposes the state or is present in conflicts between segments of society, military power always has political implications. It may therefore be useful for the first part of this paper to address military power primarily from a point of view that emphasizes its links to the dominant political force of our period, the emerging centralized state, which gradually becomes the European norm. The second part outlines changes brought about by the French Revolution, industrialization, and the rapid population increase of the nineteenth century; and the third discusses the relationship between political and military power as illustrated by conflicts between Bismarck and Moltke during the Franco-Prussian War. A final section offers some observations on the approach to the subject used in the paper, followed by a few general comments on the historical study of military power.

I

Military power expresses and implements the power of the state in a variety of ways within and beyond the state's borders, and is also one of the instruments with which political power is originally created and made permanent. Holders of political power do not invariably wish to increase it. When they do, the threat or use of force becomes an important element of their policy. In medieval Europe armed men in the service of whatever central authority exists in an area will seek to destroy or immobilize the resources for organized violence of rival bases of power within the territory that acknowledges a measure of allegiance to the central authority. The aim is to impose first a preponderance of the armed power of the central government, and then its monopoly. This is achieved not only by the threat or actual use of violence against internal opposition and whatever outside support it can call on, but also by combining administrative and military measures to extend the reach of the central authority. Toll collectors protected by a few armed men station themselves by a river crossing or mountain pass; an agent of the crown and a small garrison are admitted within city walls; men-at-arms accompany census takers and surveyors into the countryside. By such means soldiers expand and strengthen government control, and as their numbers increase and they place heavier demands on economic resources and administrative support, their needs further stimulate growth of government. The impact of this process is intensified as a proportion of the armed forces changes from levies raised for brief periods, often still as the result of feudal obligations, to permanent and increasingly hierarchically structured contingents, which require an equally permanent organization of administrative specialists of all kinds. Interaction between soldiers and administrators, not only in the field but also—and primarily—on institutional levels, leads to the standing army and to the proliferating professional bureaucracy.

Once these forces are in place, the stability of the government they serve is significantly increased. They provide a new and more resilient basis for political power; in particular, they have far greater capacity than did former practices to tap the human and economic potential of society for war. Interests opposed to the central authority, either because they wish to limit its power or—as in the Revolt of the Netherlands or in the English Civil War—because they want to assume power itself, need to develop or adopt the same kinds of regular and permanent bureaucratic military institutions to achieve their aims.

The reciprocal process of creating and employing political and military power in early modern Europe followed a pattern often encountered at other times and in other parts of the world. Wherever and whenever it occurs, it responds to similar considerations, must solve similar problems, and is usually made up of identical elements. Among the military factors that are always present, five that were highly significant in the emergence of the centralized state and its wars in Europe might here be singled out for brief comments: (1) the constitution of armed forces; (2) their ways of fighting; (3) military technology and its economic implications, including the division of resources; (4) the institutionalization of command and the coordination of political and military leadership; (5) the social role of military elites.

Under feudalism the greater part of armed power usually consisted of mounted vassals and their retainers, of groups of armed men provided by urban communities, religious centers, and rural associations, and often of some form of local home defense. Retainers permanently in the service of the crown—their social position ranging from privileged to unfree—formed only a small part of the whole. As feudal service obligations were replaced by money payments, a new mixed system developed, made up of men permanently under arms—still a minority but becoming more significant—and mercenaries for shorter periods. This new type of force permitted a more differentiated organization and made possible greater versatility in action. For the first time since the Roman Empire, the tactical training of units took the place of the individual fighter's practice of arms, it was more amenable to central control than its feudal predecessor, could be mobilized and could react more rapidly, and usually proved a more predictable instrument of policy and of a continuous strategy than had the feudal host.

The military practices of certain peasant societies in which feudalism had not fully taken hold—Frisia, for instance, or the territories north and south of Lake Lucerne—favored this development. Men fighting on foot, usually in terrain that inhibited horsemen, learned the value of rudimentary discipline and of acting in unison. The victories they achieved by translating social cohesion into its tactical equivalent contributed to the decline of the armored knight, and their forms of organization and ways of fighting eventually became a part of the new mixed system. These two related lines of development, which gradually merged, led in the course of several centuries to the standing armies of the ancien régime, commanded by local and international elites, their rank and file made up of long-serving foreign or native mercenaries and of natives forcibly enrolled, while in most societies home defense forces and militias now existed only on paper and in the minds of military reformers and political theorists. The disciplined, drilled units of eighteenth-century armies and their linear tactics reflected the ideals of rationalism and absolutism as accurately as the fragmented knightly forces had reflected the political and social characteristics of feudalism.

The expense of armor and horse had played a role in dividing medieval society into armed and unarmed segments, and the economics of military technology continued to be a defining factor in the early modern period. The cost of artillery, of firearms, of new types of fortification, the need for large-scale manufacture, all worked to the disadvantage of the centrifugal forces in political society—the upholders of local autonomy, breakaway factions, rebels, and the dispossessed. If as late as the 1620s it was still possible for the Huguenots in western France or for a military entrepreneur like Wallenstein to maintain important military forces, at least for a time, the twin requirements for money and for technical expertise inevitably benefited the larger government entities.

It is difficult to generalize about the political decisions that determined the percentage of resources made available to the armed forces and how it was distributed among their various components, except to note the obvious: political and military power are never two unitary partners advancing together toward a common goal. Not only are different points of view and conflicting interests at work in each, the relationship between the two is constantly at issue, even in systems that in reality and not only formally are dominated by a single individual. At any one time in the seventeenth and eighteenth centuries, the military's share of the budget, the use made of it, and the relationship between political and military authority varied greatly between the states.

This diversity is exemplified by the conditions in Great Britain and Prussia during the eighteenth century. In the United Kingdom crown and Parliament shared control of the armed forces and strategic policy was the work of many hands. The need for a strong navy as well as for a substantial army further increased the potential for political strife and economic rivalry. Political and budgetary considerations kept the army too weak to carry out its missions in Europe and overseas on its own, although the services consumed a significant share of the budget even in peacetime. Between 1788 and 1790, the sums spent on the army, navy, and ordnance ranged from nearly 28 percent to 31 percent of the government's total net expenditures.[1] But the same imperial responsibilities that placed heavy burdens on the armed forces also made it possible to limit their size: subventions were paid to allies when a crisis arose, the army found useful auxiliaries in native contingents and quasi-private British forces, as in India, and throughout the century the Hanoverian army provided London with a permanent if not especially strong foothold on the continent. A sizable militia complemented the regular establishment. It had strong local roots, and as the armed force of the nation rather than of the crown, it enjoyed broad political support. Its contribution to the

---

[1] These totals, derived from B. R. Mitchell, ed., *The Abstract of British Historical Statistics* (Cambridge, 1971), 391, are surely less than what was actually spent. They do not, for instance, include such items as pensions paid from the Privy Purse. But for our present purpose of drawing a general comparison between the United Kingdom and Prussia, where the royal purse also contributed to cover expenses associated with the armed forces, a rough approximation of the services' share of total expenditures will suffice. See also note 3 below.

military power of the state was nevertheless slight, apart from helping to maintain public order at home and bolstering defense against invasion from abroad. The complex organization of the armed services and the fragmentation of authority into competing boards and agencies, not only at subordinate levels but also at the top, made the army a cumbersome and expensive instrument of policy; but this did not prevent it from solving the difficult problems of fighting major campaigns on the continent and overseas, thousands of miles from its home base, and usually winning them.

In Prussia the administration and command of the armed forces (which meant the army, the navy consisting merely of a few coast guard vessels) were in the hands of the crown, which also controlled strategic policy and domestic and foreign affairs. After the death of Frederick I the influence of the king's advisors and of the provincial estates faded to such an extent that it is appropriate to speak of one-man rule. In the administration, civil and military functions became integrated to an unusual degree with the establishment in the 1720s of the War and Domain Chambers and of a supreme financial administrative General Directory. The country was divided into conscription districts, operated jointly by the civil and military authorities, which provided the quota of native recruits demanded by the crown. The remaining manpower needs were filled by foreign mercenaries who, in the last years of the old monarchy before 1806, amounted to 37 percent of the army's rank and file.[2] By the standards of the times, the Prussian system was simple and efficient, even if it bore the marks of a corporative society with its many gradations of privilege and of a state in the process of being united out of various territories. Taxation was not uniform. The greater part of the population was legally exempt from conscription, or in practice immune to it. The crown nevertheless periodically asserted its power to call on all able-bodied men to serve in the army, a principle that was converted to policy at the end of the Napoleonic era.

This system, together with expenditures for the army that at times rose above two-thirds of the entire budget, made possible the exceptional military exertions that in the reign of Frederick William I became a permanent characteristic of the state.[3] In the last years before the French Revolution, Prussian and French armies were approximately equal in strength, although the population of France was between four and five times that

---

[2] I discuss the relationship of foreigners to natives in the Prussian army in "Conscription and the End of the Old Regime in France and Prussia" below.

[3] See, for instance, the figures for the last decades of Frederick the Great's reign in Reinhold Koser, *Geschichte Friedrichs des Grossen* (Stuttgart and Berlin, 1913), 3:360–66, especially 365.

of Prussia. It was her disproportionate military power that gave Prussia new political weight in Germany and in Europe.[4]

Prussia's wars were fought as the expression of one man's political and strategic will. Frederick the Great's occupation of Silesia in 1740 and his determination to retain the province shaped his entire reign. The superior strength of his opponents in the three Silesian wars should have resulted in Prussia's defeat; but the advantages of political and military power concentrated in one man, who determined to fight basically defensive wars in an extremely aggressive manner and was prepared to take the greatest risks, allowed Prussia to survive. To revert to the theme of state-building, it was also during the Silesian wars that in the mind of many inhabitants the concept of a common Prussian state began to join if not yet supercede the sense of allegiance to a particular territory.

During the centuries in which the new mixed system of armed forces evolved into the standing army, commanders and subordinate officers in most parts of Europe came from every social group. Inevitably with an element as significant as military power, the political and social elites sought to control it not only indirectly by political and economic means but also directly by themselves assuming positions of authority in these forces. That such transitional types as the Condottieri and the bands of Swiss lancers and German Landsknechte for hire escaped much of this social control contributed to their reputation of dubious reliability. But it was by no means the case that the feudal military elites simply carried over their past dominance to the new institutions. Descendants of the old military nobility became officers in the new armies, but they shared their authority with men of very different social backgrounds. Throughout the early modern period, military institutions were avenues of upward social mobility, as they have continued to be to the present.

By the end of the seventeenth century, nevertheless, a time of social consolidation set in. As armed forces became permanent and the states they served gained stability, the social character of the officer corps also became more sharply defined. In many countries the old and new military elites, often with the support of the crown, sought to establish a monopoly of officer positions for themselves and their descendants. In some countries—France, Hanover, and Prussia, for example—they largely succeeded, although ennoblements by the crown and the widespread practice of undocumented claims of noble status prevented a completely closed system. Elsewhere—Bavaria is an example—the former open conditions survived. But whether or not particular social groups obtained privileged

---

[4] An extended comparison of the Prussian and French armies in the later 1780s may be found in my *Clausewitz and the State*, rev. ed. (Princeton, 1985), 24–29.

status in the armed forces, the issue is a further illustration of the interdependence of military institutions, society, and politics. The specific social character of an army might benefit or detract from its military effectiveness, but it is always an integral element of military policy.

II

The French Revolution and subsequently nationalism, industrialization,
and the rapid increase of the population throughout Europe intensified
and speeded up the techniques and application of military force and their
interaction with politics. But not every element of military power was
equally affected. If the Revolution did away with noble privilege in the
French armies once and for all, that was not the case everywhere. In many
countries the appropriate relationship between social elites and military
status remained an issue up to the First World War, and policy based on
social considerations more than once affected the strength of armed
forces.[5] In short, the revolution in war that occurred at the end of the
eighteenth century did not take the same form throughout Europe. In
France it quickly meshed with the social and political revolution. Elsewhere military institutions might incorporate innovations—even such
radical measures as conscription—without adopting the social changes
that had preceded or accompanied them in France. Some even remained
largely untouched by the revolution and nevertheless functioned effectively—the British army in the Napoleonic era for one. As the century
progressed it also became apparent that new technological and political
forces diminished the close correlation that once had existed between social and political conditions on the one hand and tactical characteristics
on the other. Flexibility and initiative even at the lowest levels might be
shown by troops serving in a system as autocratic as the Prussian; citizen
soldiers of a republic might fight like automatons in stolid masses.

The major components of the revolution in war were above all a great
increase in the number of soldiers, provided by one or another form of
conscription. Far larger, more sophisticated administrative services
equipped and maintained the new forces. Innovations in infantry tactics
and technical improvements in artillery for the first time made possible

---

[5] One example among many: It was not only for political and financial reasons but also
on ideological and social grounds that in the first years of the twentieth century the German
government failed to conscript all eligible males. Enlarging the army would have necessitated reaching into the lower middle classes for additional officers. Revealing statements of
concern over the danger of lowering social barriers are cited in Gerhard Ritter, *Staatskunst
und Kriegshandwerk* (Munich, 1960), 2:262 and notes 24 and 25; and Karl Demeter, *Das
Preussische Ofizierkorps* (Frankfurt a.M., 1964), 20–23.

the close coordination of infantry, cavalry, and artillery in all phases of combat. The system of living off the country with its attendant damage to civilian society enabled very large forces to operate without the absolute reliance on the supply services that until then had inhibited the size and mobility of armies. Finally, armies that had been essentially undifferentiated masses of more or less interchangeable regimental building blocks were broken up into large and relatively permanent segments—brigades, divisions, corps—made up of the three arms and support units, which could function independently. The new, more articulated organization speeded up operations, made them more flexible, and expanded the supreme commander's strategic possibilities. It also greatly complicated the tasks of command and control.

Financial crises, social pressures, and political conflicts ushered in the great upheaval at the end of the eighteenth century, but beyond a certain point, violence, whether legal or not, was essential for setting in motion processes that led to change. The illegal assumption of military power recurred throughout the course of the French Revolution, from the storming of the Bastille and the Great Fear to the counterrevolutionary movements of 1793 and the *journées* after Thermidor. Military power also helped define the place of the Revolution in the international community. It was by war that France in the Revolutionary and Napoleonic period nearly destroyed the European balance of power. Eventually the inappropriate use of military force—the invasions of Spain and Russia—weakened the empire that the threat and use of force had created; but it still required a further round of wars before the European balance could be restored. If we revert to the nonmilitary origins of this quarter century of nearly unremitting strife, we encounter a second and in its own way equally profound impact of military power. The war that the Girondins began in 1792, primarily for reasons of domestic politics, at once became an integral part of the Revolution. It helped bring about, and justified, the increase of violence at home as well as the vast expansion of governmental authority into all areas of life. Put differently, war helped create the militant Revolution that French armies soon carried to the rest of Europe.

The most significant long-term effects that the revolution in war had on the forms that military power assumed in the course of the nineteenth century were the professionalization of military institutions and the growing importance of the concept that service in the armed forces was a duty the citizen owed to the larger political community. The expansion of military institutions, the complexity of modern technology, and the proliferating specialization of tasks demanded professional training, examinations, and systems of promotion that took technical expertise into account, not only in such fields as communications or military engineering but also in the working out of mobilization timetables, the administration of very large forces, or strategic and operational planning. The creation of large police forces was another significant phenomenon of specialization, which provided the holders of political power with a new type of paramilitary force. The traditional military-social elites either adapted themselves to the new demands or lost their privileged positions in the armed forces. At the same time many governments sought to attach a new meaning to service in the ranks. The sense of military obligation as part of the relationship between the individual and the state was advanced as the basis for conscription and its ethical message was gradually acknowledged even in societies that continued to rely on volunteer forces.[6] The French Revolution had justified the *levée en masse* with the principles of liberty and equality. The Prussian reformers pressed for conscription as an obligation voluntarily undertaken by men who were no longer passive subjects but active citizens of a state that served the material and ideal needs of the community. Here again, however, the revolutionary concept could be adapted to the status quo. Autocratic systems did not find it difficult to substitute deference and apolitical patriotism for a freer political life as justification for compulsory military service.

Two further results of the changes in war that began with the French Revolution became apparent only toward the end of the nineteenth century but since then have acquired universal significance. One is militarism—the transfer of soldierly concepts, values, and ways of acting to society as a whole, even their adoption by important segments of society and in extreme cases by its political leadership. The other is the tendency of the instruments of military power to escape from rational control. This does not refer to the failure of armed forces to defeat their opponents. Defeat has always been possible, even if the resources available for war have been used intelligently and for a reasonable purpose. But there may be times when military techniques are extremely destructive without achieving changes in the opponent's political behavior—as happened for four years on the western front during the First World War. The military instruments of the opposing sides worked with awesome efficiency, but the links that joined political and military power and turned both against the enemy had loosened, for a time had almost broken. Of a different order is the more recent development of nuclear weapons. Since 1945 military technology has reached a level of destructive power that defensive measures cannot fully neutralize and the effects of which may be far out of proportion to the motives of the antagonists. Consequently, that part of military power made up of nuclear weapons has so far been ex-

---

[6] I outline the development of this issue in European history in "Nationalism and the Sense of Military Obligation" below.

pressed by the potential rather than the actual use of force. Even in these conditions, however, military power remains more flexible than many people expected. The advent of nuclear weapons has not yet brought an end to war. Dozens of conventional wars have been fought since 1945, and irregular wars and domestic and international terror have flourished under the nuclear umbrella.

III

The relationship between the holders of political and military power is central to all societies and helps determine their character. It may be useful to illustrate this universal issue with a brief case study that outlines the collaboration and conflicts between Bismarck and Moltke during the Franco-Prussian War.

In the 1820s Clausewitz had defined the relationship between the two kinds of power by declaring that war is the continuation of politics by other means. This dictum told neither the statesman nor the soldier anything new. Everyone recognized that wars were fought not for their own sake but for a political purpose, although in the course of the war this purpose might fade far into the distance or change, and the soldiers taking part generally did not know what they were fighting for. What was unusual about Clausewitz's statement was, first, that it was made by a soldier—that a soldier emphasized the political nature of war—and, second, the conclusions he drew from his assertion.

In his view, the political nature of war affected both the actions of the armed forces and the relationship between the political and military leadership. Because wars were fought to achieve a political purpose, every action in war should, if possible, accord with this purpose. A purely military act did not exist. To give an example; from the perspective of a soldier engaging the enemy, the extreme use of force regardless of later consequences might be desirable. But if extreme measures increased the determination of the opposing side to continue fighting, they were counterproductive even if they momentarily weakened the enemy. The choice of military objectives, the level and intensity of force used to achieve them, the treatment of prisoners and civilians—everything had political implications and therefore should, if possible, be decided not only on military but also on political grounds. That, at least, was the reasonable approach to the problem. Clausewitz conceded that it was neither easy to achieve nor the way soldiers usually proceeded. He also acknowledged that the political leadership might place unrealistic demands on its armed forces and that its policies might not always coincide with the true interests of society and the state. Nevertheless, he believed that a theoretical inquiry that sought to understand the nature of war and define its limits among other activities of society should presuppose rational intentions and behavior on the part of the political leadership.

Moltke took a more expansive view of military authority. He agreed that war was an instrument of state policy and was therefore ultimately controlled by the head of government. The armed forces must work only for the political purpose, but their actions must be totally independent of politics. Once war was declared, the soldiers were autonomous in their operations against the enemy until they presented the head of government with the victory that would enable him to conclude an advantageous peace. Moltke, who held to this view even after the experience of three wars, was by no means a narrow military specialist. He had broad cultural and intellectual interests, his pronounced monarchism did not blind him to contrary positions, and he had a sophisticated understanding of domestic politics and international affairs. That such a man could nevertheless wish for the extreme separation of war and politics—and, indeed, think it possible—may indicate the intensity of the differing, even opposing concerns of the two constituencies that at any particular moment possess and represent military and political power.

The constitutional vacuum in which Moltke functioned afforded his views considerable scope. The Prussian king was head of state and supreme commander of the armed forces. Bismarck, the head of the Prussian ministry and chancellor of the North-German Confederation, had no independent authority but governed in the king's name. From a monarchical perspective he was merely the king's first advisor in domestic and foreign affairs, just as Moltke as chief of staff was the king's senior advisor in military matters once the army was mobilized. Moltke, too, could issue orders only in the king's name and needed his approval for major decisions. Each was the king's advisor in his particular area; beyond that their relationship was left undefined, but Bismarck neither was considered nor believed himself to be Moltke's superior.

The two men were in close touch during the crisis over the Hohenzollern candidacy in the summer of 1870, one basis of Bismarck's diplomacy being his complete confidence in Moltke and the army.[7] Once war was declared both men joined royal headquarters in the field. By the beginning of September, one French army was isolated before Metz, another had surrendered at Sedan, and the Second Empire was about to be replaced by a provisional republican government of national defense.

The first serious difficulties between Bismarck and Moltke arose over

[7] The relationship between Bismarck and Moltke during the Franco-Prussian War has been frequently analyzed. Particularly enlightening seem to me the discussions in Rudolf Stadelmann, *Moltke und der Staat* (Krefeld, 1950), 197–264; and in Eberhard Kessel's remarkable biography, *Moltke* (Stuttgart, 1957), 541–91.

Bismarck's interest in the possible survival of the empire, which could still rely on Bazaine's army, enclosed in Metz. Moltke regarded this prospect as chimerical and saw no reason to spare Bazaine on the remote chance that a revived imperial system would sue for peace. Soon it became apparent that the two men had different aims. Moltke worked toward the complete destruction of French fighting power. Bismarck hoped for a peace settlement that would not unduly embitter German-French relations and consequently favored a quick war, which need not end with the total defeat and humiliation of France. By the third week of September, Paris was encircled, and the fate of the capital became a key issue in the intermittent negotiations between the two governments. In his eagerness to end the war and to avoid the diplomatic intervention of other powers, Bismarck began to press for the speedy bombardment of the city. Although some senior officers rejected the shelling of civilians on principle, Moltke did not, but he refused to give the order until the remaining French field armies had been defeated and enough material was at hand to shell the city effectively and for an extended period.

Disagreement over this particular issue fed into Bismarck's general complaint that he was not kept informed on military developments. On 5 December Moltke sent a communication to the commander of the French forces in Paris without giving the chancellor the opportunity to discuss the letter's political implications with the king. Bismarck used this incident to demand that henceforth he be present whenever Moltke's daily briefing to the king touched on political issues. He also insisted on the right to ask the general staff for information on all military matters of political significance. The king had not yet announced his decision when it became clear that the fall of Paris was imminent, and the terms of capitulation became a new object of conflict between the chancellor and the chief of staff, Bismarck arguing for flexibility and Moltke insisting on harsh terms. On the morning of 18 January, shortly before Paris surrendered, Bismarck proclaimed the German empire; that afternoon he denounced to the new king-emperor the military's continued interference in political matters and again demanded adequate information from the general staff as well as the right to review the daily military communiques, and if necessary to revise their texts in line with political requirements.

After a week the emperor at last decided that Bismarck should receive all information he requested but did not give him authority to edit the communiques. Moltke drafted a letter asking the emperor to dismiss either him or the chancellor, then agreed to provide the chancellor regularly with information on everything that had taken place but not on operations that were being planned, a compromise Bismarck accepted because the war was winding down.

The concerns and methods of political and military power are never easily reconciled, and the conflict we have just traced may suggest the intractability of the problem beyond the specific historical situation and the personalities of the two protagonists. Some elements of their clash recurred in many of the complex relationships between political military authority elsewhere in Europe, and indeed in the United States, but its outcome went against the tendency of the nineteenth century, which on the whole was moving toward greater institutionalization of the links between the two kinds of power and toward the subordination of the military to the political leadership. In another sense the episode does carry a general meaning; the conflict between Bismarck and Moltke reflected the character of their society and significantly influenced its subsequent history.

The two men never again disagreed on a major policy issue. But the limits Moltke placed on the information he was prepared to reveal—restrictions in which the emperor silently acquiesced—meant that the chief of staff remained the chancellor's equal. The institutional methods of cooperation between the political leadership and the services, which even then were felt to be inadequate, were not altered. In peacetime the chancellor almost of necessity held greater power, the more so because the chief of staff's authority over the army was limited until mobilization began. From the 1890s on, it was further compromised by the strong naval building program. The army was deprived of resources, and the planning of the two services could never be effectively coordinated. But in a crisis the position of the chief of staff changed. In the summer of 1914 he became the key figure in German policy. He, a few other senior officials, and the emperor, acting in what was almost an institutional vacuum, reached the ultimate decisions, without the support of a comprehensive system of joint planning, efficient exchange of information, and coordinated execution of policy. After the war began, the power of the chief of staff climbed steeply, until four years later the former separation between military and political power had been significantly reduced and the army had grown from a state within a state to a point where in many respects it had become the state itself.

IV

Our analysis has outlined some general elements of military power, their relationships to each other, and their connections with other kinds of power. The discussion followed a broadly chronological and developmental approach, which ties the exploration of military power to a specific historical phenomenon—the rise of the centralized state in Europe.

This link undoubtedly affects the shape of the elements we are studying, but it does so only to some extent. Their essence is not compromised
or distorted by being placed in a particular historical context. On the
contrary, the context allows us to see their essential nature as they act and
react in a dynamic state rather than as abstractions. Still, other quite different ways of discussing the same phenomena are also conceivable. We
might draw up taxonomies and categories and engage in model building.
Or we might continue to rely on the explanatory power of the specific but
choose different historical epochs or different cultures, or we might remain in the same centuries of European history from the Middle Ages to
the First World War, but consider the subject from another perspective,
for example that of the history of ideas. One possible line of enquiry runs
from late medieval teachings on the just war through Machiavelli, who
insists we recognize what is rather than debate what should be, and such
late Renaissance neoscholastics as Victoria and Suarez, to Grotius and the
Enlightenment theorists of war and the political and moral order. Such
an approach would emphasize ethical and legal ideas about military
power, which are interesting and sometimes significant aspects of its history; but history has also shown that they lie at the margin rather than at
the center of our subject. In a brief discussion they might obscure its sa-
lient features.

Yet another approach would be to consider military power as it was
employed not for the state but against it. This paper briefly refers to this
side of military power, but much more could and should be said about it,
although once again it seems that the essence of the various components
of military power is best revealed in their association with the state—if
only for two reasons. One has to do with the role of force in domestic
and foreign affairs, which presupposes some kind of political base. Revolutionary movements will seek to turn themselves into revolutionary
governments. The other, perhaps more fundamental reason is that although military power may suddenly emerge as though out of nowhere—
examples mentioned earlier are Parisians arming themselves and besieg-
ing the Bastille and peasants destroying manorial archives during the
Great Fear—as soon as people want to make this transient force and their
control over it permanent, they adopt the institutional and bureaucratic
techniques developed and practiced by the state. In essence the armed
companies of the Paris sections in 1793 and the first half of 1794 were
the same kinds of force as the royal army before the summer of 1792 and
the republican army afterwards, and stood in a similar and often ambiguous relationship to their political partners and superiors.

The primary task of this paper was to bring out some functions of two
different though interlocking aspects of our subject: military power as the
institutionalized process of applying physical force; and military power

as a way of creating, maintaining, and in other respects expressing political power. These functions are subject to many limitations, on the part of those they represent as well as on the part of their antagonists. Each function has a potentially negative side. The process of applying physical force may fail; the process of creating and maintaining political power may go awry and destroy what it means to support. Throughout history the possibility of failure has been a prominent characteristic of military power, which does not, of course, eliminate military power as a historical force or as an object of historical investigation.

V

It may be appropriate to conclude with a few observations on the writing of the history of military power. Some readers may have gained the impression that this essay implicitly argues for the primacy of the kind of military history that addresses civil-military relations or analyzes the interaction of war with its social, economic, political, and cultural context. That was not the intention. If the opening paragraph criticized the undue concentration on war that characterizes much of military history, it did not favor an equally exaggerated emphasis on any other aspect of military power. The claim that only certain parts of the subject are important, that history concerned with other parts is marginal and old-fashioned, is destructive of scholarship and inhibits genuine understanding. What does seem desirable when writing about military power is to take account of the particularity of the specific phenomenon under investigation, while noting its constant interaction with other military and nonmilitary factors. A history of a campaign will never tell us very much if it is limited to the events of that campaign. We ought to know at least something and often quite a lot about such matters as the recent history of the two belligerents, their positions in the international community, their political conditions and the impact these may have on strategic planning, their economies and technologies, as well as such more strictly military aspects as the strengths of the opposing forces, their structure, methods of training, doctrine, promotion practices, and the personalities of the senior commanders.

That is asking a good deal of the military historian, even if in practice the demand is not for universal expertise. It is enough if we are aware of the more important links between our immediate subject and the wider world and familiarize ourselves with some of its related areas so that we can raise our interpretations from the one-dimensional. Extreme, unreconstructed specialization will always have a place, but it can rarely reach more than limited goals, and when studied in a broader perspective its findings will usually need to be corrected.

The pioneers of the modern history of war and of military institutions were in no doubt about the need for breadth. In some of his campaign histories, especially in his study of Prussia and the War of 1806 and in such sections of *On War* as Book VIII, chapter 3B, Clausewitz tried to work out the links between the minutiae of tactics and bureaucratic techniques with such general forces as political theory, popular attitudes, and the history, economy, and society of the belligerent states. In their research into widely differing aspects of military power in history, Otto Hintze, Hans Delbrück, and Jean Colin combined the specific with the general, convinced that only by tracing the interactions between them could each be understood. The work of these scholars is marked by a further characteristic that seems particularly appropriate to the study of potential and actual conflict—the comparative method. It was the comparative historical study of wars that helped Clausewitz propose his revolutionary distinction between absolute and limited war. Comparisons of military and civil institutions defined each more precisely; comparisons of earlier with later ideas and practices made it possible to formulate hypotheses of change and development; the comparison of belligerents revealed itself as the only adequate basis for historical studies of combat.[8]

A good example of the strength of this approach is Michael Howard's *The Franco-Prussian War*, which thirty years after its first appearance continues to be a satisfying and instructive work because of the even-handedness with which the author described and interpreted the concerns, intentions, and actions of both the French and the Germans. And yet even in the study of campaigns where its usefulness is most readily apparent, this approach continues to be widely ignored. Archival restraints, personal predilections, limitations of time and energy help explain the frequent practice of concentrating on only one side of a conflict; but combat is more than shadow boxing. No single pattern or set of patterns should be imposed on the historical study of any subject; but the comparative method in its many forms seems to offer one important possibility for the further development of the history of military power in our time.

[8] See, among many possible examples, Otto Hintze, "Military Organization and the Organization of the State," in Felix Gilbert, ed., *The Historical Essays of Otto Hintze* (New York, 1975), 178–215; Hans Delbrück's comparison of Frederician and Napoleonic battle and strategy in his *Geschichte der Kriegskunst im Rahmen der politischen Geschichte*, new ed. (Berlin, 1962), 4:487–521; and the beautifully clear concluding analysis of line and column in Jean Colin's *L'Infanterie au xviiie siècle: La Tactique* (Paris-Nancy, 1907), 276–82.

2

THE RELATIONSHIP BETWEEN THE AMERICAN
REVOLUTIONARY WAR AND EUROPEAN MILITARY
THOUGHT AND PRACTICE

TOWARD THE END of the eighteenth century a revolution in thought and practice swept over great areas of warfare and its institutions, from the organization and administration of armies to their manpower policies and ways of fighting. Soldiers at the time were confronted with the intellectual and practical challenge of recognizing the nature of the changes taking place and of learning how to adopt or oppose them effectively. To Clausewitz the contrast between the cataclysm of the Napoleonic wars and the relatively limited warfare of an earlier generation helped reveal the range of apparently contradictory phenomena that a true theory of war must accommodate. Since then the revolution in war has challenged historians to separate its interlocking components, study the workings of each and how they worked together, understand the political as well as military dynamic that their interaction produced, and rid the process of the mistaken interpretations and legends in which it was soon enveloped. This essay and the five that follow address various aspects of the revolution.

One of my early explorations of the subject was a lecture, published in 1964, that explored the extent to which colonial warfare, particularly the war of the American Revolution, contributed to the breakup of eighteenth-century linear tactics and to the development of new, more flexible ways of fighting. A study of operations in Europe and America and a survey of the contemporary literature concluded that colonial wars had little if any impact on the wars of the French Revolution and of Napoleon, and that the world historical significance of the American rifleman had been greatly exaggerated. Instead I suggested that a gradual coming together of various European military practices led to the changes in infantry tactics, which formed an important—but only one—element of the new warfare. Fourteen years later I took up the subject again with this more systematic comparison between the fighting in America and European campaigns, in the hope that it might contribute to a more accurate appraisal of the developments that led to the revolution in war.

≥◆

I want to compare the war in America with other conflicts of the period, consider these wars as discrete military episodes—separate entities that combine into a broad stream of military experience—and ask what these wars attempted to do, how they went about doing it, and how we might characterize the relationship between effort and achievement in each. By comparing the Revolutionary War with other conflicts, we not only fit it more accurately into the overall picture of eighteenth-century warfare, but we may also come to understand some of its unique phenomena more clearly than we would if we were to immerse ourselves in its particulars to the exclusion of what soldiers and governments were doing elsewhere.

Let me begin with two statements that in one form or another pervade the literature: First, in essential respects the Revolutionary War differed from other wars of the period; and, second, the elements that differentiated it from other conflicts were of seminal significance—that is, the Revolutionary War, at least as it was fought on the American side, pointed toward the future. Don Higginbotham, in his book *The War of American Independence*, expressed the idea in this way: "The American Revolution did more than prove the validity of Enlightenment ideals; it ushered in yet another revolution—in the aims and nature of warfare."[1] It should be added that the passage in which this statement occurs contrasts wars waged by mercenaries for aims to which they are indifferent—dynastic or state policy—with wars fought by patriots, defending, in Washington's words, "all that is dear and valuable in life." The English historian Piers Mackesy, in his book *The War for America* states that "the struggle that opened at Lexington was the last great war of the *ancien régime*."[2] That sounds like a contradiction of Higginbotham's statements; but it need not be one. Mackesy may merely be saying that Great Britain fought the war in a traditional manner, or perhaps he uses the term *ancien régime* not to characterize behavior but to define a period of time—as a synonym for the eighteenth century before the French Revolution. He continues with a statement that certainly seems to be in complete accord with Higginbotham's views: "In the American War there first appeared the fearful spectacle of a nation in arms." But the second part of his sentence imme-

[1] Don Higginbotham, *The War of American Independence* (New York, 1971), 103. See also ibid., 57.
[2] Piers Mackesy, *The War for America, 1775–1783* (Cambridge, Mass., 1964), 4.

diately qualifies and restricts this assertion: "In the American War there first appeared the fearful spectacle of a nation in arms; and the *odium theologicum* [for present purposes, this might be translated as the 'bane of ideology'] which had been banished from warfare for a century returned to distress the nations." I don't mean to go on with textual analyses of recent scholarship; I have cited these passages from two admirable works simply to illustrate the difficulty historians face in bringing out the particularity of a specific event while giving an accurate account of its larger context. And furthermore, the second half of Mackesy's sentence points to a not unimportant analytic failing that is frequently encountered in the literature on the American Revolution. Mackesy rightly observes that the bane of ideology, which had been banished for a century, returned. That is, ideologically motivated war, in which many of the participants even at the lowest levels are emotionally involved—rather than detached impassive professionals—was not introduced at Lexington, but *re*introduced.

That suggests that the Revolutionary War should be compared to the European military experience of the seventeenth, rather than of the eighteenth, century; to the Dutch struggle for independence; to certain phases of the Thirty Years' War; to the English Civil War. I say that because it might be useful to resist the tendency of bracketing Revolutionary War with the conflicts of the mid-eighteenth century, a time when Europe had temporarily shed the *odium theologicum*, when many states had achieved relative political stability, and when the European community had devised a nonideological balance-of-power system as the basis for its international relations. Political development proceeded at different rates of speed on the two sides of the Atlantic; and rather than contrast the military behavior of an emerging nation with those of developed states, it might be more appropriate to compare the Revolutionary War with some seventeenth-century episodes and then perhaps compare the Mexican War, which was hardly waged "for everything that is dear and valuable in life," with the War of the Austrian Succession or with some other eighteenth-century attempt at territorial aggrandizement. I am not suggesting that we disregard differences in time in favor of constructing historically disembodied models of civil and military behavior. The passage of time and the uniqueness of the specific event must always be the first determinants of historical analysis; but I do want to raise the question whether comparisons should be based solely on proximity in time or whether stages of social, ideological, and political development should not be taken into account as well.

Let me return once more briefly to the statements quoted above in order to trace one or two of their implications further. It is, of course, true that European armies in the eighteenth century were essentially mercenary and professional in character—at least so far as the rank and file are concerned. But many—including the Prussian, Austrian, and Russian armies—were in fact made up of a mix of mercenaries, who might be foreign or native volunteers, and of native conscripts.[3] Certainly the Prussian conscript or the Austrian inductee from the military frontier was not a free citizen who fought for a policy that he understood or in some manner identified with: he was a peasant, more likely than not illiterate, who was forcibly enrolled. But there can be no question that he was not only motivated by compulsion and, after a period of service, by esprit de corps but also by loyalty to his local environment—the patriarchal conditions of his existence—and by a regional patriotism. Soldiers may not yet have been conscious of fighting for a nation—Frederick the Great's grenadiers thought of themselves as Pomeranians, Silesians, men of the Mark Brandenburg, rather than as Prussians; their peers across the Rhine may already have dimly sensed that beyond their native Normandy or Poitou there was a more comprehensive abstraction called France—but everywhere in Europe the idea of nation was announcing itself. And here and there it was already cracking the shell of the absolute monarchy and of corporate society. Governments and commanders employed the concept of nation to justify their actions, appealed to their men in its name, and in turn were influenced by it. The military institutions of eighteenth-century Europe contained within their native cadres the seed of the future nation in arms.

But just as we cannot regard the armies of the ancien régime simply as institutions of uninvolved mercenaries, so we should not assume that the military future belongs wholly to the nation in arms. Once more we must ask what time frame should contain our analysis. Fifty years ago it was easier than it is today to view modern history as a process toward the nation-state and the nation in arms. Now, with separatist movements at work in such ancient political entities as Great Britain and Spain and with the apparent dissolution of the Russian multinational empire, we

---

[3] Some Prussian examples: In 1776 the rank and file were evenly divided between natives and foreigners (most of whom were non-Prussian Germans)—78,767 to 78,280—a relationship that remained unchanged to the end of Frederick's reign. In 1787 new regulations called for a slight preponderance of natives in all branches except the hussars, where natives and foreigners were to be equal in number. At the outbreak of the Wars of the French Revolution natives outnumbered foreigners by some 20,500 men in the infantry and by some four thousand men in the cavalry. In the officer corps the percentage of natives was still higher, although as late as 1805, as many as one-third of all infantry officers holding the rank of lieutenant colonel or higher were foreigners. For additional statistics, and remarks on the politically significant appeal that Prussian service had for foreigners, see my *Clausewitz and the State*, rev. ed. (Princeton, 1985), 59. Austrian manpower policies of the period are analyzed in Jürg Zimmerman, *Militärverwaltung und Heeresaufbringung in Österreich 1806*, vol. 3 of *Handbuch zur deutschen Militärgeschichte* (Frankfurt, 1965).

can no longer be quite so certain. And even in the early stages of the process that may now have passed its peak, the trend was far from uniform. In the wars of the French Revolution and of the Napoleonic Age we can, on the one hand, point to what might be called the "sentiment of military nationalism" in the French armies and at least to the force of military patriotism—if not yet nationalism—in the reformed Prussian army and the modernized Austrian army, though to a lesser extent. But such developments scarcely affected the rank and file of the British and Russian armies, which do not differ radically from their eighteenth-century predecessors. The English and German professionals who were defeated in America decisively beat the Grande Armée and the Grande Nation in Spain and at Waterloo three decades later. The European military future was mixed; and so, of course, was that of the United States.

I have made these comments, which go over familiar ground, merely to suggest the kind of evidence that ought to be considered when we try to fit the Revolutionary War into its historical environment—that is, place it among the wars that immediately precede and follow it. When we come to analyze the war in America as one conflict among several, we will find it useful to divide our inquiry into two parts: first we must take a closer look at the hypothesis of the war's seminal nature, which on the one hand refers to motivation and organization. Having sorted out the matter of influence, we should then consider some other elements in the war—number of men involved, size of the theater of operations, the relationship between effort and goal—and compare these with analogous factors in the three major wars that were waged in Europe between 1756 and the 1790s.

To begin with—motivation. The politico-military characteristics of the Revolutionary War find no parallel in eighteenth-century Europe. Part civil war, part struggle against an external opponent, the conflict was waged by a political authority organized as an assembly representing states each of which possessed a measure of sovereignty. Its army was composed of state militias and of a central force, the Continental army, originally made up of volunteers enlisting for varying periods of time but soon enrolling some men through a compulsory quota system, which, however, accommodated a range of exemptions. Except for the ill-conceived Canadian expedition, the policy of the colonies was one of enduring, of maintaining an independent political authority and an armed force in being, regardless of territorial losses. In this they succeeded magnificently; but it is equally impressive that in the course of the war they consolidated the political resources of their society and created a new system of government.

Nothing similar can be found in Europe in the hundred years preceding Lexington: "A revolutionary struggle which involved an armed insurgent population was unique in the memory of the age."[4] And, indeed, a significant element of American resistance consisted not in regular operations but in thousands of episodes of civil disobedience and active opposition throughout the vast area of the thirteen states—what we today mean when we use the term "revolutionary warfare" in a generic sense.[5] And it was entirely appropriate that as a counterstrategy the British repeatedly chose a policy of pacification—long-range penetrations, breakup of the rebel infrastructure, reestablishment of a loyal administration and society.

But the American Revolutionary War was not only highly innovative in its political features, it was also unique in the sense that it did not set a trend. It inspired some Europeans, but it was not a model that European societies followed. The political and military upheavals of the age of the French Revolution and of Napoleon contained nothing like it. The French Revolution itself was from the start a highly centralized movement whose task was not to create a new nation, but to replace one social system and ideology with another and a relatively inefficient system of centralized government with a stronger one. After a brief transitional period its military institutions, too, progressed from a lower to a higher level of standardization and uniformity and fought in support of policies that almost immediately changed from the defense of the revolution to aggressive national expansion on the order of Louis XIV's assault on the balance of power.

Other revolutionary movements, such as the Polish insurrection of 1794, followed a different pattern: they neither possessed America's relative social homogeneity, her economic and diplomatic resources, or her strong yet flexible political traditions, nor were they able to pursue a strategy of delay and attrition because of the size of their territories and the distance separating them from the enemy base. The occupation of one or two urban centers meant the end of the struggle in Poland. Nor, finally, can we trace similarities in the popular movements against French imperialism during the second half of Napoleon's reign. Resistance in Spain, in the Tyrol, in Russia was characterized not by democratic tendencies but by traditional loyalties and hatred of the foreigner. In 1823 the Spanish peasant, who had helped make life unbearable for the French between 1808 and 1813, welcomed a French expeditionary force, which occupied Madrid with the blessing of the other major powers and overthrew the constitutional, mildly liberal, anticlerical system that had gained power by a coup d'état.

[4] Mackesy, *War for America*, 31.

[5] On this aspect of the war, see John Shy, "The American Revolution: The Military Conflict Considered as a Revolutionary War," in *Essays on the American Revolution*, ed. Stephen J. Kurtz and James H. Hutson (Chapel Hill, 1973), 121–56.

Probably the closest European parallel to the American Revolutionary War was provided by the antirevolutionary movements in France during 1793 and 1794; the insurrection of Lyon, that of Toulon, and the uprising in the Vendée.[6] These were true armed insurrections, incorporating a significant proportion of the population, fighting for such traditional liberties as freedom of worship and freedom from conscription, against the double tyranny of centralization and a hostile, activist ideology. The comparison doesn't bear too much weight, but in passing let me refer to the difficulties England experienced in supporting her allies in the French civil war of the 1790s. The troubled course of naval operations off Toulon and in Quiberon Bay, both relatively near to major British bases, suggests that waging a war across the Atlantic posed almost insuperable obstacles to the command structure and technology of the period and to the social and economic preconceptions on which all eighteenth-century logistic systems were based.[7]

Let me now turn to the area of tactics and of operational organization. The view that in the revolution Americans pioneered a new type of warfare that influenced the next generation of European soldiers, once widely accepted among American historians, is no longer tenable today.[8] Again we must look both at what came before and what followed the Revolutionary War. The assertion of American tactical and operational innovation rests almost entirely on the issue of infantry tactics. But it is a misconception to hold that eighteenth-century armies fought only in tightly packed linear formations. Since the beginning of the century each major force had units trained for reconnaissance and combat patrols, raids, ambushes, outposts—for the so-called war of detachments, or the little war, and the relative proportion of these units increased in each generation. A crucial element of the military revolution that occurred in the 1790s was the fusion of these specialists of the light service with specialists of the line, the heavy infantry, so that henceforth at least in some armies—first in the French, then particularly in the Prussian army—the same men could fight in line, fire volleys, form attack columns, and skirmish. Integrated infantry tactics were not the result of American stimulus, but a development that occurred throughout. It might be added that rifles were

[6] I have discussed the revolutionary elements on both sides of the conflict in the Vendée in *Internal War and Pacification: The Vendée, 1789–1796*, Center of International Studies, Research Monograph no. 12 (Princeton, 1961).

[7] For analyses of English and continental conditions, see R. Arthur Bowler, *Logistics and the Failure of the British Army in America, 1775–1783* (Princeton, 1975); and *Heeresverpflegung*, vol. 6 of *Studien zur Kriegsgeschichte und Taktik*, ed. Military History Section I of the Great General Staff (Berlin, 1913), 2–73.

[8] The following discussion is based on my essay "Colonial Experience and European Military Reform at the End of the Eighteenth Century," *Bulletin of the Institute of Historical Research* (1964): 47–59.

introduced as military equipment in the middle of the eighteenth century in Europe. Elite light infantry units, *Jäger*, in the Prussian and Hessian services were armed with rifles and acted as tactical models for other light infantry, equipped with the cheaper and in some respects more efficient smoothbore musket. Here too the campaigns in America at most confirmed a trend that was already well under way.

Infantry tactics were only one area of war that saw significant development at the end of the ancien régime. Leaving aside the introduction of universal conscription in some societies, we see at least four other vital changes that occurred to varying extent in the European services. Army structure was recast into divisions or brigades, relatively self-sufficient, standardized operational commands. In 1812, for instance, the reformed Prussian field army consisted of six brigades, each of which permanently combined two infantry regiments, a grenadier battalion, three cavalry regiments, engineer, supply, and reserve units, and a small staff. Restrictions imposed by France and the poverty of the state prevented the organization of artillery and light infantry units in sufficient number to permit their permanent integration in the brigade structure; they were assigned according to operational needs. But basically the former haphazard assemblage of regiments and battalions into ad hoc commands, whose composition was constantly changing, had given way to permanently integrated combat groups, whose components had learned to work together and which, as a whole, could be part of the line of battle one day and perform an independent mission the next. The gain in flexibility and rapidity of operations, as well as in their more securely articulated overall control, is obvious.

Second, the traditional system of fixed supply points was modified in favor of greater logistic flexibility. Third, artillery was made more mobile and powerful, the number of guns was increased, and new tactics were evolved to exploit the army's new potential. Finally, the Napoleonic period witnessed significant changes in strategic doctrine. They were made possible by some of the developments just mentioned—the division organization, for instance, and the development of a more comprehensive and somewhat more authoritative general staff. The essential characteristics of the new strategic style—which, of course, was by no means universally understood or followed—may be summarized as speed, the effectively coordinated action of sometimes widely separated commands, and a greater readiness to risk battle—a belief that destroying an army might bring greater advantages than outmaneuvering it.

The war in America contributed little or nothing to these developments. There is no evidence of standardized divisional organization on either side, though it can be argued that independent commands, which were more significant than in Europe, point in that direction. In logistics, too, the war in America taught the use of improvisation. On the other hand, the scarcity of roads and the great expanse of the theater of war increased the value of depots and forts. So far as artillery goes, overseas influence on its design, manufacture, and tactics did not exist. Finally, operations in America were not distinguished from wars on the continent by greater speed or a more urgent insistence on physical decision. They did, however, include coordinated actions of a kind that had no true parallel in central Europe. An extensive strategic pattern such as that formed by British operations in 1777 was determined by geographic factors and the location of bases to which no equivalents existed in Europe; nevertheless it might be interpreted as a harbinger of the coming cooperation of divisions and army corps. But on the generation of commanders of the Revolution and the Napoleonic conflicts, who were brought up on the campaigns of Maurice de Saxe and Frederick, the American campaigns made little impression. In the military education of Napoleon they appear not to have figured at all. And in general that holds true of every military aspect of the war in America. The war does not figure prominently in the professional literature of the 1780s and 1790s. Even the numerous publications that now deal with the little war, partisan warfare, or the war of detachments rarely draw on American experiences; most of their tactical examples are taken from the Seven Years' War and, after 1792, from the Wars of the French Revolution.

If this still seems surprising, it may be useful to ask what the concept of influence can and cannot mean in relation to our subject. Similarities of doctrine, equipment, actions need not be the result of one society or army learning from another; they may be determined by attitudes general to the times or by its technology. The point might become clearer if we reverse the direction that influence is conventionally assumed to have taken in the Revolutionary War and look at instances of Americans referring to European patterns. I suppose that the adopting of Steuben's simplified drill could be interpreted as exerting a Prussian influence on the Continental army; but really all that is at work here is a commonsense response to fundamental conditions imposed by the basic infantry weapon of the time, the smoothbore musket, which requires volleys—in short, linear formations—to be effective. For Washington to be concerned about precedence in the order of battle, about ceremonial, the correct manner of mounting guard in camp, and other paraphernalia associated with the forces of European absolutism is no more than to think in the common military idiom of his generation—and perhaps also to respond, as leaders of revolutionary forces often do respond, to the attraction of regularization, of demonstrating one's legitimacy by appearing as much like the enemy as possible. Similarly, for Washington to read Bland's *Treatise on Military Discipline* and Guibert's *Essai général*, and to be stimulated by these works to think about organizational and tactical issues in his command and reach his own conclusions, is not to become a link in a chain of influence—especially since these authors had nothing startlingly new to say to him. On the other hand, if Wellington had chosen the Battle of the Cowpens as model for a new defensive doctrine or if Scharnhorst had based the training of Prussian skirmishers on American patterns, we could realistically speak of an American influence on Europe.

To have meaning in our context, "influence" must be a process leading to the adoption of something significantly different from prevailing ideas or methods. It must mean more than similar actions determined by common economic and technological conditions and more than the gradual accretion of professional expertise. Every war, after all, affords lessons; they may be the result of observing one's own forces at work and of recognizing that this or that aspect could be improved—logistic arrangements or promotion policies, for example—or they may be learned from the enemy, which in the Revolutionary War could mean no more than confirmation of matters that were already known. But this process of experience and learning, which certainly occurred on both sides, has no relation to the hypothesis that Americans fighting for their independence necessarily fought in a manner different from that of traditional European societies and that subsequently these societies adopted the more modern style of the patriots. To sum up, European armies acquired very little that was new to them from the American war—in some areas because social and political conditions differed too greatly and remained too dissimilar, even after the French Revolution, to make borrowings possible; in others because every European army already contained significant innovative elements, which enabled each service to adapt—if sometimes with great reluctance—to new military challenges.

Let me now proceed to the second and final part of our analysis: a comparison of numbers of men involved, size of the theater of operations, and the relationship between aim and achievement in the Revolutionary War and the three major European wars of the second half of the eighteenth century. No more than the most fragmentary outline of the opening phases of these conflicts can be given here, but even that may prove enlightening. While I trace events in Europe, the reader may want to keep in mind the first stages of the war in America, beginning with the engagements in April 1775 between four thousand patriots and eighteen hundred British troops at Lexington and Concord during the British return to Charleston. On 10 May, Fort Ticonderoga surrendered. Five weeks later the battle of Bunker Hill was fought between two thousand patriots and twenty-five hundred British soldiers; after this no significant confrontation between land forces occurred until November, when the British surrendered their post at St. Johns in Canada.

When we consider the outbreak of the Seven Years' War, we must first of all dismiss the common half-truth that wars in the eighteenth century were always limited wars. That belief is due in large part to a failure of clearly distinguishing methods of fighting and reasons for fighting and also to the tendency of forgetting that "limited," "unlimited," "total" are relative terms. Total war meant something different in 1812 from what it was to mean in 1917, let alone in 1944. Actually these terms are not very useful as analytic devices unless they are combined with a study of the relationship between effort and aim. It would certainly be difficult to interpret the Seven Years' War as a limited war. The aim of the anti-Prussian alliance was to destroy Prussia as the second major power in Central Europe, which, though not the same as destroying her altogether, is far more than depriving her of some relatively insignificant stretch of territory.[9] Prussia's aim was the maintenance of the status quo, and the method that Frederick employed to achieve it was a preventive attack. Between June and August 1756 he mobilized a field army of 120,000 men. On 29 August he invaded Saxony, the weakest member of the hostile alliance. On 1 October the opening battle of the war was fought between twenty-eight thousand Prussians and thirty-three thousand Austrians, resulting in a Prussian victory at a cost to both sides of some fifty-six hundred casualties. Two weeks later eighteen thousand Saxons surrendered to Prussian forces. The main result of the campaign was that Frederick gained Saxony as an operational base for the war. During the winter he increased his army to 180,000 and the following April opened the new campaign in a theater of operations about the size of Massachusetts.

In contrast to the Seven Years' War, the second conflict in our sample, the War of the Bavarian Succession, was a limited war. Very little fighting took place, most of it small-unit actions in hilly and wooded terrain, raids, ambushes, harassment of marching columns and transport. But while the intensity of violence, in Frederick's words, was insipid, the limited war actually settled a major political issue.

In the last days of 1777 the elector of Bavaria died. He left no direct successor, and Austria used the occasion to claim the country. If the coup succeeded, it would alter the European balance of power by significantly strengthening the Austrian empire. Consequently Frederick objected, mobilized, and, when his threat was dismissed as a bluff, invaded Bohemia and Moravia in July 1778. In effect that spelled the end of Austria's coup, which was predicated on the absence of serious opposition. Austria was not prepared to fight a major war and eventually withdrew from Bavaria.

This brief and uneventful episode provides an illuminating contrast to

---

[9] It is nevertheless notable that such a balanced, critical interpreter of Prussian history as Hajo Holborn defines the aim of the Austro-French alliance as "the total destruction of Prussia" (*A History of Modern Germany* [New York, 1964], ii, 235.)

events taking place at the same time in America. The theater of operations measured about 220 miles by sixty miles. Two Prussian armies of some 160,000 men advanced into this area and were opposed by an equivalent Austrian force, which adopted a fairly passive defense. Prussian strategy was to push both of its armies forward; the one that met major resistance would fix the enemy, permitting the other to maneuver. For a time Frederick hoped to swing his left flank through Moravia and to threaten Vienna. But supply difficulties, epidemics, and the absence of the need to seek a military decision caused the Prussians after some months to withdraw through the Bohemian mountains, retaining only a few bases for operations in the coming year, which turned out to be unnecessary.[10]

Finally, the Wars of the French Revolution opened in April 1792 when France declared war on Austria and Prussia largely for internal political reasons. The Girondins, the party for the moment dominating the revolutionary government, believed that war would unite the nation behind their leadership. The allies, on the other hand, hoped that by invading France they would strengthen the domestic opposition to the Revolution and pressure Paris to modify its policies. To achieve these goals they were prepared to commit only a fraction of their strength—Prussia mobilized no more than one-fourth of her field army—and the 170,000 men that the allies deployed along a three-hundred-mile front proved to be insufficient.

What conclusions can we draw from our survey? It seems apparent that the American Revolutionary War and the three contemporary European conflicts are of entirely different character, different not only in their political features but in the fundamental elements of space and force. In America small armies operated over a very large area that lacked a single center of crucial administrative and social importance, such as Paris or Vienna. In Europe far more powerful forces operated in a fraction of that space. The difference is of a magnitude that has qualitative significance. Staff work, logistics, strategic and operational concepts, even tactics—all functioned in different ways on the two sides of the Atlantic.

That is the basic reason why neither really affected the other. The concentrated battle tactics of Europe lost much of their validity in the territorial expanse and among the political dispersion of the thirteen states. The few thousand soldiers moving back and forth between Canada and Georgia, whose climactic encounters would hardly be considered battles in Europe, could not teach the commander much that would be of value

---

[10] Since the military aspects of this conflict have been largely ignored in the literature, it may be useful to mention the two best brief accounts: Curt Jany, *Geschichte der Preussischen Armee*, rev. ed. (Osnabrück, 1967), iii, 107–29; and far superior analytically, Colmar von der Goltz, *Von Rossbach bis Jena* (Berlin, 1906), 408–17. The chapter dealing with the war in Paul B. Bernard, *Joseph II and Bavaria* (The Hague, 1965), is better on the diplomatic maneuvers than on the course of operations.

in Germany or France. Or so, at least, Europeans thought. And that, obviously, explains what would otherwise be the puzzling absence of thorough treatments of the American war and its lessons in the European literature.

Of all European services, the British was best suited by experience, doctrine, and understanding of naval power to fight overseas. But England was hamstrung by the impact that domestic opposition to the war had on strategic planning and by the political and social character of her army's and navy's command structure and organization. Besides, her efforts and her aims were never fully in accord. No doubt at the beginning it was expected that a show of strength would restore order, but even if the policy of pacification had succeeded, it would not have brought back the political conditions of the 1760s. After the first two years of fighting, England could hope only that a military victory would enable her to treat from strength and to conclude a settlement that would deny the thirteen states total independence, but surely would have granted everything short of it. That was perhaps not a sufficiently compelling motive to help her overcome the obstacles to fighting a war across three thousand miles of ocean.

In this respect, incidentally, the American war is like the others to which we have compared it: in each case, the side whose interests were most profoundly affected emerged as the victor. That holds true for the Seven Years' War, in which Prussia's political autonomy was at stake; for the war of 1778, fought to prevent a shift in the balance of power that would have damaged Prussia more than it would have benefited Austria; and for the campaign of 1792, in which the allies like the British before them, hoped that a show of force would bring the other side to its senses.

And it is crucial to remember that the stronger political motive of the American revolutionaries was held not by a small elite; it expressed attitudes, a sense of what was possible and desirable, that could be found in many individuals throughout society. Furthermore, these feelings and ideas had been shaped by their having developed in a unique environment—the American environment, which was defined by remoteness from Europe and by territorial expansiveness. It was this setting that made American political ideals very different, not only from European concepts of the centralized state, but also from European republican ideologies in the 1770s and 1780s (as well as in the two centuries since then). And it was the same remoteness and openness of the American military environment—so unlike that of the community of European states, smaller, far more densely developed, immediately abutting, pushing against each other—that in the final analysis enabled the patriots to succeed in their political experiment and also to triumph in its defense.

3

NATIONALISM AND THE SENSE OF

MILITARY OBLIGATION

I N 1966 I PUBLISHED a book on the Prussian society and army during the Napoleonic era. Finishing the book did not end my interest in the subject but led me to new questions, among them that of patriotism. What was its character and what was its reach at the time, not as these were defined by political theorists and propagandists but as they existed in the minds of ordinary men and women. The intensification of the war in Vietnam in 1966 and the debate in this country over the draft, the place of ROTC on college campuses, and the limits of the citizen's obligation to his government added contemporary pressures to the historical question. In the fall I wrote the essay that is printed here, which surveys political developments and changes in attitude in European history since the Middle Ages from the perspective of military service. What groups in society were expected to provide men to bear arms as the political system they served evolved from feudal and corporative entities to the centralized state? What arguments were put forward to demand and justify their service as local and regional loyalties slowly expanded into a patriotism attached to the emerging nation? I wanted to clarify these processes in my mind to gain a firmer basis for understanding changing political attitudes in Europe, particularly of groups that were not part of the social and cultural elites.

I presented the paper at the 1966 meetings of the American Historical Association. One of the commentators, a senior professor in a well-known university, criticized me for having ignored an important fact: the paper had not referred to Captain Dreyfus. Since I was tracing developments over several centuries in a thirty-minute talk, it was hardly surprising that I had not mentioned every individual who in one way or another might be linked to the spread of a sense of military obligation in the broad stream of nationalism. Nor did I recognize the relevance of the Dreyfus Affair to my theme, except possibly insofar as Dreyfus was one of a large number of Frenchmen in the 1890s who in spite of racial prejudice and social injustice felt a profound sense of national commitment. My commentator's complaint struck me at the time—and still does today—as an example of the deep-seated inability that has always marked segments of our discipline to look beyond mountains of detail, piled up into "areas of specialization," and see larger forces and tendencies at work. The worst thing about this pedantic fear of leaving out any bit of knowledge one has acquired is that it inhibits historical understanding. But it also plays a part in making historical writing incomprehensible to many nonacademic readers and in limiting its public to other scholars.

ን●

The purpose of this paper is to outline some of the connections that exist between the development of nationalism in France and Germany and the attitudes held by governments and societies toward the question of military obligation—that is, who should bear arms. A discussion of this relationship seems to have a place in the continuing debate over the nature and history of the nation-state, to which the collapse of Europe in 1945 and the delayed beginning of the national era in Asia and Africa have given new impetus. But let me start with a reference to the contemporary American scene. Until opposition to the war in Vietnam became widespread, public opinion in this country agreed on the whole with what might be termed the official opinion that not only national self-preservation but an individual's awareness and appreciation of the qualities of his native land, loyalty to his national community and to its history and ideals, love of his country, are closely and necessarily bound up with the willingness to serve in his country's armed forces.

It is hardly necessary to say that to historians the connection between these two attitudes appears to be more ambiguous. We know that as the modern state emerged, a people's growing consciousness of being different from their neighbors; their love for and loyalty to a particular complex of cultural, geographic, and political factors; the entire body of feelings, aspirations, and fears, which I shall here call nationalism, were by no means always in step with their willingness to serve in the armed forces of the state. We also know that even after nationhood had been achieved, the sense of military obligation was not always generally felt among the adult male population; nor, indeed, would governments always have wished this sense to be universal.

It is true that nation-states and patriotism seem to flourish under the principle that in the eighteenth century Blackstone expressed in these words: "In free states . . . no man should take up arms, but with a view to defend his country and its laws; he puts not off the citizen when he enters the camp; but it is because he is a citizen, and would wish to continue so, that he makes himself for a while a soldier."[1] But the power of

---

[1] William Blackstone, *Commentaries*, chap. 13.

this concept in history, not least in the past of the English-speaking peoples, cannot cause us to overlook the fact that often enough nations and societies have accommodated themselves to a view contrary to that stated by Blackstone. The theorists of absolutism put it plainly: war is the business of the ruler, not of the citizen. It would be ingenuous to claim that the opposing statements reflect only a difference between constitutional and absolutist forms of government. Certainly, nationalism and the sense of military obligation are related; but it is a changing relationship, and one heavily burdened with transient social and political concerns. To explore this point demands a survey that is broad both in space and in time. The limitations of such an approach are apparent; nevertheless a comparative survey has its uses at the present stage of historical debate. And discussing French and Germans together also offers certain advantages. Not only do the two peoples affect one another, and create the friction of differing ideas and conflicting power that underlies a problem that historians too easily see only in the abstract, but they reach political unity and national self-awareness by dissimilar paths and thus afford us very different vantage points from which to observe the part military obligation played in their progress.

I

In the course of the sixteenth and seventeenth centuries, the French kings were able to transform and absorb a sufficient share of the personal, territorial, and religious loyalties that marked French life to give the monarchy cohesion and permanence. Energies that had been diffused or lain dormant were gradually harnessed to the state. In the creation of this new and encompassing structure military force performed the essential task of defeating particularist rivals to the crown, of holding external enemies at bay, and of lending authority to the expanding processes of government. The growth of the monarchy set the soldier his objectives; in turn, the machinery of government was largely a by-product of war. In collecting the moneys needed to maintain a standing army, in reaching deep into local life for equipment and men, in developing central controls over the finances and organization of the military as well as over its employment, the expertise and will of the state were trained and acquired strength. The constantly more elaborate apparatus of regulations and officials helped to define the vague sensation of nationality that existed in French society, until in the eighteenth century the early traces of nationalism had broadened—to employ an image of Carlton Hayes—into the dignity of royal roads.[2] National sentiment had become a fact—if not yet a dominant fact—of French life. But it was unaccompanied by a sense of general military obligation among Frenchmen. They may have been prepared to defend their immediate community when threatened by attack or civil disorder; they resisted this duty toward the greater, abstract whole of the French state. As nearly everywhere in Europe during the ancien régime the military work of the state was carried out by an army of long-term professional soldiers; volunteers from among the adventurous poor of the country (to whom were joined a considerable number of foreigners, who in 1789 still amounted to nearly one quarter of total strength). After the reign of Louis XIV the army was backed up by a militia, conceived of as an economical device to raise home guards and supply regular units that could not fill their ranks in the free market. The system was aimed directly at those groups of the population that were least able to defend themselves against it—the poor. By them it was seen as an unnecessary evil; but even the propertied peasant, the artisan, the village merchant, whom it spared, had doubts about the militia—though its value in times of economic hardship was appreciated. In 1791, by common consent of all regions of the monarchy, the institution was abolished.

By that time the army had progressed a long way from the temporarily mobilized bands of mercenaries and groups of nobles and retainers with which Henry IV fought his battles. It had become permanently embedded in French life through the manifold meshing of the civil and military administration and economy, and in numerous social aspects as well. To be sure, the crown's support of gradations of privilege and duty worked against the truly national army that some reform-minded officers and writers on political and social affairs were beginning to advocate. And yet, when the Revolution came to lower these barriers, popular reaction did not match the newly available opportunities for military service.

In France the tools of centralized government had been developed by the monarchy; in Germany at the same time they were appropriated by the territorial princes, at the price of whatever political unity the empire had once afforded. Except for the Hapsburg dominions even the most powerful of the states into which Germany became fragmented were militarily feeble. Their territories were at once too circumscribed and too exposed, and their armies—mercenaries raised and led by military entrepreneurs—too brittle, particularly when employed by courts with limited finances. Inevitably a search began for sounder military institutions. From the second half of the sixteenth century through the Thirty Years' War, this search led a number of German rulers to experiment with forms of

---

[2] Carlton Hayes, *France: A Nation of Patriots* (New York, 1930), 3.

militia.[3] The so-called Landesdefension sought its legal justification in feudal military obligations, which were now misconstrued to apply to the peasantry. It was visionary to hope—as some did—that the militia could replace professional soldiers entirely; the militia might however add more reliable elements to their ranks, or at least provide a force for home defense and internal policing. But in spite of all efforts, the experiments failed. The factors behind this failure were not unique to the time and place, but were encountered—though increasingly overcome—whenever during the next two-and-a-half centuries attempts were made to turn civilians into part-time soldiers. It was difficult for the militia to achieve professional competence. The implications of arming large numbers of peasants and townspeople were frightening. Nor was it certain that armed civilians were best suited to put down civil disturbances. And finally, there was no great press on the part of the population to join the militia. Peasants evaded enrollment; townspeople, whose opulent and prestigious sharpshooter guilds recalled a more self-reliant past, wanted nothing to do with serious service. It was characteristic of the general mood that when in 1610 the elector of Brandenburg ordered the Berlin militia to conduct practical training exercises, the men refused on the ground that firing muskets with real powder and ball would frighten their pregnant wives.[4] It was not alone the technical difficulties and the political and social risks attendant on militias, nor mercantilist theories, nor their drive towards absolutism that led the German princes to develop long-serving professional armies as their favored military instrument, but also the unwillingness of their subjects to take up arms. By the eighteenth century the militia had become a discredited concept in the German states, leading only the most shadowy of existences beside the mercenaries and the forcibly enrolled peasants who made up the armed power of the state.

On the continent, the views on military organization held by the princes and their advisers pretty well accorded with the forms military institutions actually assumed; in England, however, agreement was not as close. There, after the Restoration, the militia was taken seriously both by crown and country.[5] The royal government wished to use it to help maintain law and order; the country at large valued it as a counterpoise to the standing army; both looked to it to help repel invasion. From the middle of the eighteenth century on, when the government had lost faith

[3] On the German militia during this period, see the excellent edition of documents by Eugen von Frauenholz, *Die Landesdefension in der Zeit des dreissigjährigen Krieges*, vol. 3, part 2, of his *Entwicklungsgeschichte des deutschen Heerwesens* (Munich, 1939).

[4] Hans Delbrück, *Geschichte der Kriegskunst* (Berlin, 1920), 4:275.

[5] Political and social aspects of the English militia are carefully analyzed in J. R. Western's *The English Militia in the Eighteenth Century* (London, 1965).

in citizen soldiers, it sought to convert the militia into a manpower pool from which regulars could be recruited, while to the Whigs the militia remained important as a device for curtailing the size and political influence of the regular forces. The militia, in the words of one patriotic pamphleteer, was the constitutional force: free men heeding "the tocsin of Britannia."[6] But the concept, however interpreted, was only imperfectly realized. Widespread rioting took place when the lists of men eligible to serve were drawn up. The counties found it difficult to fill their small quotas. As late as 1795 militia insurance associations plied their trade; if a member were chosen by ballot to serve in the militia the association would pay a sum sufficient for him to buy a substitute. In short, the great majority of Englishmen saw no difficulty in reconciling national awareness and national pride with a profound distaste for military service, and the constitutional monarchy, though its political controls over the army and navy differed from those on the continent, relied as much on the mercenary soldier and impressed sailor as did absolutist regimes. Everywhere too—whether in the societies of Western Europe in which state and nation were beginning to coincide or in the hundreds of political and administrative units of Germany—men were alike in rejecting the ethical imperative of military service that was held out to them by party propagandists, army reformers, and political theorists.

II

The Revolution, which made the French state more accessible to the people, also expanded its financial and military claims over them. "Preservation of the rights of man and of the citizen," declared the National Assembly in 1789, "requires the existence of a public force. This force is instituted for the advantage of all, and not for the private benefit of those to whom it is entrusted." The army was to be no longer a servant of the executive, but an agent of the national community, and it was the entire French people, according to the Constitution of 1793, that made up the armed might of the republic. The original expectation that the field forces could be formed of volunteers had, however, to be revised under the pressure of counterrevolution and invasion, and recourse was taken to conscription—first as a temporary defensive measure, then as permanent policy. Between 1800 and 1815 Napoleon drafted over 2 million men: during the same period fifty-two thousand men enlisted voluntarily.[7] If

---

[6] The title of an anonymous pamphlet, published toward the end of the century.

[7] Raoul Girardet, *La Société militaire dans la France contemporaine (1815–1939)* (Paris, 1953), 16.

the idea of personal liberty sat ill with conscription, coupling civil and military obligations and rights carried the amalgamation of the interests of the state with the interests of the individual a good distance further. The common experience of millions of Frenchmen serving under the tricolor, first to defend the republic, then in wars of liberation and of conquest, helped build a stronger awareness of national community. No doubt the illiterate majority in the army and in civilian life remained less affected than the bourgeoisie, the artisans, and small shopkeepers; but to a growing number of the poor and the uneducated, too, the Grande Nation, its leaders and symbols, took on meaning as the center of their thoughts and feelings on public affairs. Political ideals and cultural achievements had made the nation great; in the eyes of some it was made even greater by defeating and subjugating its neighbors, a conclusion that succeeding generations were to find increasingly appealing.

And yet, the groups that benefited most from the destruction of provincial particularism and that were most receptive to the message of the nation-state were the ones that could best avoid the attendant military consequences. Throughout republic and empire, except during crises in the early revolutionary wars, the principle of universal military service was alleviated by the possibility of substitution. Under the law of 8 March 1800, which remained in effect until the fall of Napoleon and was the basis for the country's manpower policies until the 1870s, those young men who were held to contribute more to the state by continuing their work or their studies than by becoming soldiers could fulfill their obligations by providing a substitute or paying a sum that was well within the means of most middle-class families. Consequently the army's rank and file continued to be drawn largely from the poor. Against the dangers to social stability that might result from an army of underprivileged men excited by revolutionary ideas, the bourgeoisie sought to protect itself through the National Guard, a body organized to maintain internal order, whose members had to meet certain economic and residence qualifications. The only defense against the military demands of the state available to the poor was to evade the draft or desert; the incidence of both was high from the early 1790s on, and it grew to the dimensions of a public scandal in the later years of the empire. As a close observer, Carl von Clausewitz, commented at the time, though the French state was "marked by extreme militarism . . . no trace of this tendency could be found in the character of the nation."[8] While a prisoner of war in France, Clausewitz had watched policemen lead shackled conscripts by a rope to the prefecture; the spectacle shocked him, but he did not fall in with the

---

[8] "Travel Journal of 1807," in Carl von Clausewitz, *Politische Schriften und Briefe*, ed. Hans Rothfels (Munich, 1922), 33.

conservative argument that open resistance to military service proved the instability of the regime. On the contrary, he and other Prussian reformers were fascinated by the dynamics of a system that triumphantly survived irregularities that would have crippled their own army and state.[9]

Whatever their differences on specific reforms, the officers who set about modernizing the Prussian army after 1806 agreed that broadening the obligations of military service to all sections of society and increasing middle-class participation in military leadership were necessary for the survival of the state. This required the breakup of the Frederician class structure, with its enclaves of duties and privileges. Considered in purely mechanistic terms, the state needed unobstructed access to the citizen; in turn, to gain his willingness to work and fight for the state, the individual had to be offered political power, or—if that was impossible—new psychological inducements and social opportunities to enable him to reach his full potential. But not everyone shared the reformers' concern for the survival of Prussia, at least as a major power. Few dangers more discomfited Frederick William III than the thought that enlarging the subject's dynastic loyalties to include the more abstract values of community and fatherland might compromise absolute royal control over the army. The nobility feared conscription as an egalitarian force, especially if it was coupled with a limitation of their privileged access to officer rank. Nor did the middle classes evince general eagerness to serve the state in uniform; on this point, many who worked for innovation elsewhere turned against the military reformers. Typical in its range of concerns was the denunciation by Ludwig von Vincke, Stein's adviser on constitutional questions, who attacked conscription as placing the heaviest burden on the propertied classes, as being "the grave of all culture, of science and industry, of political freedom and all human happiness." Under it men would no longer be "respected as valuable in themselves . . . [but] degraded to simple means to an end."[10]

If the patriotism of the educated continued to be attached more strongly to German civilization than to one of its numerous political subdivisions, the inert mass of the population was scarcely beginning to be an object of political argument and education. The concept of the nation penetrated only slowly into German society; but to the extent that it took on form it provided a new note of idealistic justification to the broadening

[9] A comprehensive and reliable analysis of political and social attitudes, morale, and desertion rates in the Napoleonic armies is still lacking, though some good studies on particular units have appeared. See, for instance, Max Tacel, "Notes sur la composition et l'esprit d'un régiment pièmontais de l'armée Napoléonienne le IIIᵉ d'infanterie de ligne (1802–1814)," *Revue Internationale d'Histoire Militaire*, no. 16 (1955).

[10] Letter of 30 September 1808 to Stein, cited in my *Yorck and the Era of Prussian Reform* (Princeton, 1966), 135.

demands of the state. Not that the executive was eager to make these demands. What finally compelled Frederick William to adopt conscription was the dynamic of the reform movement and foreign policy considerations. Henceforth the ranks of the Prussian army were filled by volunteers and conscripts; others joined a militia—the Landwehr—whose officer corps gave some scope to the middle class; together the two institutions incorporated nearly all ablebodied men in the kingdom.

The Napoleonic era ended with Prussia and other German states, as well as France, having laid down the principle that universal military service was a duty society owed to its government and to itself. But the state still lacked the means, and in ordinary times the necessity, to pursue this claim to the limit. The rights for exemption of the educated and wealthy continued to be respected, as in France, or, where they had to serve, as they were compelled to do in Prussia, received social and professional advantages in return. The needs of the state, as it entered the industrial age, for more resilient, reliable, and far larger armies than absolutism had been able to provide were met through a compromise with the interest of the properties and educated classes.

III

Throughout the nineteenth century the relationship between nationalism and military obligation was largely determined by the struggle of class against class. Population growth, industrialization, the rise of the bourgeoisie, and the emergence of a vast and increasingly literate proletariat created a new environment for the ideas of the democratic revolution. As the national idea spread throughout French and German society, civic rights were also extended. But repeatedly the reciprocal process of nationalization and the acquisition of rights by the majority was disturbed by the bourgeoisie's reluctance to share its new power. Middle-class opposition gave the workers, in the formulation of Werner Conze, the choice either of claiming that social justice formed part of the national ideal, or of turning—in solidarity with foreign comrades—against the nation as a bourgeois invention.[11] The decision they made affected the military institutions of the state, whose increasing demands for manpower could be met only by the working classes and the peasants. The traditional elites and the new middle classes were equally in conflict over the manner in which the power that the state deemed necessary for its external relations

[11] Werner Conze, "Nation and Gesellschaft," *Historische Zeitschrift* 198, no. 1 (February 1964): 12.

and internal policing could best be accommodated to the hierarchic arrangements of society.

Both in France and in the German states the struggle was marked by repeated changes in front. During the Bourbon restoration the legitimist aristocracy and the greater part of the bourgeoisie suspected the army as the child of the revolution and of the Corsican usurper. "Military merit is no longer in fashion," Julien Sorel observed in Stendhal's *The Red and the Black*. Only among the liberal opposition was the military upheld—in honor of the glorious traditions it incorporated, and because a strong army would one day be needed to achieve the triumph of freedom and of universal democracy. In his brilliant study of the army in French society, Raoul Girardet writes that the liberals were driven by "a great dream, made up of confused humanitarianism and of passionate nationalism; of the liberation of oppressed nationalities and the reconquest of France's natural frontiers; of peace established among peoples, and war made on kings; of Poland liberated and Italy unified; but also of the left bank of the Rhine reoccupied, and the tricolor borne victoriously through all the capitals of Europe."[12] As the century progressed, however, the army's work in putting down social unrest estranged it from republicans, while moderates and men of the right began to appreciate the soldier as guardian of internal peace. The events of 1848 did nothing to weaken these tendencies. Henceforth the propertied classes never lost their trust in the army as a defense against anarchy, nor the workers their suspicion of it as one of the weapons by which the bourgeoisie maintained its rule. Even the flowering of the Napoleonic legend and the colonial campaigns that brought new glory to the nation were unable to prevent the fact that until 1870 military service was not only unpopular but held in low repute by most Frenchmen, and that consequently the French army was made up largely of apolitical, long-serving professionals.

Apart from the socially mixed background of its officers, it was a force looked on with envy by Prussian conservatives, who had never been able to accustom themselves to a royal army consisting of the people in arms. As late as the constitutional crisis of 1862, some of William I's more hardbitten supporters wished to encourage long-term professional service and water down the potentially subversive institution of conscription by borrowing from the French their practice of substitution and exemption for cash payment. Such proposals struck at the very core of the liberals' belief that the Prussian state could attain the physical and moral strength to achieve German unity only by granting the citizen continued participation in military service and a greater share in public affairs. The citizen in uniform and the rise of middle-class officers to positions of influence,

[12] Girardet, *Société militaire*, 23.

would, it was hoped, modernize the dynastic army into a force inspired by broader ideals and loyalties. In the end the liberals gained a formal victory; universal conscription was retained, and it continued to introduce a cross section of Prussian society to military service; but this did nothing to make the army more liberal. On the contrary, the conservatives learned that if due precautions were taken, such as bringing the militia completely under the control of regulars and weeding out socialist agitators, the people in arms could be an asset. Since the men who championed Prussian particularism and the officers who were in command of the conscripts more often than not came from the same families, this experience gradually affected the conservative position on the question of unification. To the history of German nationalism the conscript army is important not only because it created the military conditions that made unification possible, but because it helped make the national idea acceptable to Prussian conservatives.

With the establishment of the empire, nationalism did not cease to be a party matter. The former enemies of the national idea now tried to appropriate it, while accusing socialists, social democrats, and at times Catholics of being antinational. In propagating their ideology of disciplined loyalty to monarch and fatherland, the army took on new significance as an institution of popular education; in turn, its position in the country benefited from the intensified patriotism that it fostered. Once more the interaction between France and Germany becomes apparent. After the defeat of 1870, the French adopted from Prussia not only true conscription—though the last inequities based on social status were not removed until 1889—and the modern general-staff structure, but also the collaboration of the elementary schools and the conscript army to teach nationalism to the masses. The French army, in the words of one of its most gifted members, was charged not alone with a military but also with a social role: to protect the thousands of young men entrusted to it every year against the anarchic mood of the age, to help keep alive the longing for *revanche*, to promote social stability, and to render Frenchmen worthy of their country.[13] But more than in Germany the army and military service remained in political contention; the memory of the Commune and the use of troops against striking workers accentuated the left's dislike of the army. Though the old Jacobinism remained alive, antimilitarism became a part of every program of the left, until the threatening atmosphere in the last years before 1914 led to a patriotic reawakening even among the trade unions.

In the age of imperialism, of aggressive nationalism, when each country

[13] Louis Hubert Lyautey, "Du Rôle social de l'officier dans le service militaire universel," *Revue des Deux Mondes*, 105 (15 March 1891).

saw itself hedged in by historic enemies, the army had come to symbolize cohesion and will of the national community. As agent of the state the soldier had helped create the nation, now he personified it and guaranteed its continuing existence. In the summer of 1914, when Frenchmen and Germans rushed to the colors to defend their countries and the highest values of civilization against aggression, nationalism and the sense of military obligation finally had become one. The kaiser spoke with his usual irritating grandiloquence when he said that henceforth he knew no parties, he knew only Germans; but for once his pathos captured the truth of the moment.

IV

The First World War forms the appropriate end for this survey. Our discussion sought out the connections of military service with the growth of nationalism, not its relationship with nationalism's nihilistic exaltation and decline. At most, in conclusion, some general remarks suggested by this decline may be in order.

In both France and Germany—indeed, throughout the West—the sense of military obligation as a dominant phenomenon was a late product of nationalism. By the beginning of the twentieth century the two rising curves of national self-awareness and the sense of military obligation had met. They coincided briefly; then they lost their clear contours, obstructed each other's progress, and finally laid insupportable burdens on each other. Two generations of Frenchmen and Germans have now experienced doubts—at times of the greatest severity—over the part military service plays in the allegiance that men feel to their cultural and political communities. At the latest since the Second World War, the political persuasiveness of nationalism has lost most of its force in Western Europe—as has its aggressiveness, which for some decades was its most striking trait. Today large segments of French and German society appear unconvinced that the state is wholly identified with the nation and that its demands on the citizen for military service must always be morally right. The reluctant development of the state's claim, its frequent subordination to class interest, and its relative newness invest these doubts with a certain historical justification.

That is not to minimize the achievements of the citizen soldier. The willingness of men to fight for their beliefs has created nations and kept them alive. It is in revolutions—the overturning of intolerable conditions—and in the defense of his home that the citizen soldier has scored his most convincing achievements. To be effective, self-defense and rebellion must be not only highly motivated but also well organized and led, and throughout history the concept of the people in arms has been derived from a presumed identity of interests between the political leadership and the community. In France and Germany the institution of the citizen soldier from the militia and Landesdefension on was linked to the purpose of defense. But as national power and national aims expanded, as the state exploited its real and its ideological strengths, it became more difficult to demonstrate the defensive character of government policy. Nationalism implies a measure of sacrifice of men's immediate concerns for the greater good; but on occasion the common cause may appear to be imperfectly represented. A few years before 1914, Jean Jaurès wrote that if war broke out the proletariat must fight to defend France; but if France should be the aggressor, the people, although continuing to defend their country, would have the right to overthrow the government and the social system that engendered the conflict.[14] The impracticability of Jaurès solution should not obscure the reality of the problem, and not only socialists have been concerned about its implications.

Man must subject himself to authority if the community of which he is a part is to survive. The possible bases for this authority are many. After 1789 it became increasingly common for French and German governments to see in their people's national self-awareness at least one justification for their authority. No one will deny that the validity of these claims has varied. It is one of the major characteristics of nationalism—and probably one of its significant weaknesses—that while claiming to derive its power from the feelings of the people, these feelings in fact support the totality of its demands only intermittently and often with reluctance. And it is a weakness of historical interpretations of nationalism in its many forms that scholars have not yet adequately studied this disparity.

In piecing together the history of the armed nation-state, historians have paid far greater attention to the thoughts and actions of politicians, soldiers, and writers than to the feelings of the mass of the people, without whom nationalism would be nothing more than theory. Despite obvious methodological difficulties, a great deal of research is possible in this field, from comprehensive analyses of desertion during the first Napoleonic empire to studies on the way attitudes toward military service have been altered by the transformation in this century of the soldier from a hunter to a mechanic, or on the way peoples' feelings about military service have been affected by the totality of modern war, in which civil-

---

[14] See his response in L'Humanité, 18 September 1905, to Clemenceau's accusation of lack of patriotism. Similar arguments, which tried to reconcile the national and international loyalties of the European working classes, form a major theme in Jaurès's writings during these years, culminating in the section "Internationalisme et patriotisme" of his book L'Armée nouvelle, 2d ed. (Paris, 1915), 435–64.

ians may have to be as heroic as the men in uniform. No doubt one fact will again and again emerge from these inquiries: however men have felt about fighting for their country—ecstatic, resentful, resigned—whatever their attitude, it has rarely been in perfect harmony with the principles and expectations of their governments. We should see in this repeated disparity a challenge to penetrate more deeply a central problem of history: the relationship between public and private man.

4

CONSCRIPTION AND THE END OF THE ANCIEN RÉGIME IN FRANCE AND PRUSSIA

FIFTEEN YEARS after I had written the short essay on "National-ism and the Sense of Military Obligation," I returned to the subject, or more correctly to one of its component parts: manpower policies in France and Prussia at the end of the eighteenth century and how they changed during the French Revolution and the Napoleonic era. In the intervening years I had written a book on Clausewitz, in whose life the introduction of conscription in some European armies, with all its mili-tary and political consequences, had played a large role. But I believed there might still be value in a study of conscription at the beginning of its modern history. As in many of the essays in this volume, I formulated my analysis in comparative terms. Tracing and interpreting the process in one country against the background of the related process in its neighbor might create a clearer, more precise picture of each than would emerge from a study limited to one society or the other. Analyzing the two to-gether might also contribute to our understanding of the phenomenon of conscription in general, as it spread beyond the geographic and chrono-logical limitations of France and Prussia between 1789 and 1815 and grew into a force that shaped politics and war and helped change Western society in the nineteenth and twentieth centuries.

અ

The military institutions and manpower policies of the ancien régime re-flected and expressed the claims of sovereignty of the centralizing state, while satisfying the privileged character of its society, and, in general, the operational requirements of its army. By the end of the seventeenth cen-tury, the standing army—controlled by the crown, commanded by elites, its rank and file made up of men who enlisted for increasingly long peri-ods of service—had become established throughout most of Europe. But although identical in its main features from Madrid to Vienna and War-saw, the newly dominant type accommodated important regional differ-ences in organization and recruitment, a variety of home-defense forces, and, often, remnants of an earlier international entrepreneurial system. It is the purpose of this discussion to outline the conditions of military service as they had evolved in two states—the French monarchy and the new kingdom of Prussia—and to trace the development of the manpower policies that replaced them during the upheavals that destroyed the ancien régime in both societies.

As late as 1789, the French army included twenty-three Swiss, German, and Irish regiments, in addition to the Swiss of the Maison du roi and of the guards of the royal princes. Even if not all officers and men in these units were, in fact, foreigners, the foreign component was significant—more than 10 percent of total strength. In this, as in some other respects, the army remained closer to an imperial rather than to a national force: the army of a unifying and centralizing state still on the way to nationhood. The great majority of the army's rank and file nevertheless consisted of Frenchmen who had voluntarily enlisted. The system of recruitment functioned reasonably well until the last years before the Revolution, and was sufficiently flexible to provide more men in times of greater need, since to the poor military service offered a livelihood and the opportunity for some social betterment. If the government thought it necessary, the militia, chosen by lot and intended primarily for fortress and garrison duties, was drawn on to replenish the losses of the regular army.

In Prussia, smaller, poorer, with a more primitive society, the same institution of the standing army was based on very different manpower policies. Between the beginning of the century and the early 1730s, these changed markedly. Under Frederick I the rank and file was recruited largely within the country. Two types of recruitment existed: voluntary recruitment, under which regimental recruiting officers enrolled men by persuasion, trickery, and even force; and compulsory recruitment, occasionally employed in times of war. The crown assigned quotas to towns and counties, which were filled by agents of the municipal authorities or the estates. The men selected received a small bounty—a link with the older method of voluntary recruitment—and served for an indeterminate period, generally for as long as they were physically able, in contrast to the six (later eight) years of service in France. As in France, militia forces supplemented the standing army, but since they proved to have little military value except in East Prussia and since their members were immune from army service, they were abolished in 1713.

Although providing the needed number of men, both voluntary and compulsory recruitment were difficult to administer and socially and economically disruptive. The system was adjusted repeatedly until Frederick William I recast it in 1733 in a form that it retained until the collapse of the state in 1807.

Foreign recruitment was considerably expanded, so that by Frederick the Great's accession, foreigners constituted one-third of the rank-and-file, a proportion that rose slightly over the next six decades to 37 percent at the beginning of the War of 1806. For native recruitment, a grid of permanent recruiting districts, the so-called cantons, was established, which limited each regiment but the guards to its own recruiting pool. The former arbitrary, often illegal hunt after men was replaced by the harsh but predictable imposition of long-term military service on a minority of young men of the poorest groups of the population, almost without exception serfs, journeymen, and the urban unemployed. Exempt were urban inhabitants who had some property, free peasants, most craftsmen, the sons of noblemen and officers, as well as all inhabitants of certain regions and towns. Both in the long-term, indeed lifelong, obligations it imposed and in its exclusions, the canton system suited corporative society. Its institutional roots were the previous quotas that had been intermittently leveled on towns and counties in the 1690s and the later years of the War of the Spanish Succession. An emergency measure had taken on permanence.

The ideological justification for forcing men to serve in the army derived from more ancient sources. Its origin lay in the individual's instinct for self-defense, institutionalized into an obligation to defend the immediate and the larger community and further expanded by the claim that men had the duty to defend not only their community but also its interests. The laws of the Carolingian and medieval German empires declared that the protection of the country was everyone's duty; and although the application of this principle was increasingly narrowed by feudalism, it persisted in theory, and even in practice, in such parts of Europe as the Swiss cantons. Since Machiavelli's advocacy of general conscription, coupled with the moral and political regeneration of the people, the idea of armies of native conscripts or volunteers did not disappear from the literature. A few princes actually tried to turn their home-defense forces into effective replacements for mercenary armies, but they failed because they were still too weak to overcome the resistance of the estates and other corporative entities. When the standing army with its heavy reliance on native manpower developed in Prussia, the concept of the subject's military obligation, already imperfectly institutionalized in the militias, lay ready to hand. "By birth and Almighty God's order and command," Frederick William declared soon after his accession, men were obliged to serve their sovereign "with their possessions and their blood." Three generations later, a Prussian commentator defined the principle of the canton system of 1733 with the phrase, "All inhabitants of the country are born to bear arms."[1]

[1] "Edict wegen Auffhebung gewaltsamer Werbung . . . vom 9. Mai 1714," in Eugen von

In practice, we have noted, the totality of this assertion was limited very largely to the rural poor. It should be regarded as an expression of Prussian absolutism, which claimed the right to draw on the human resources of the state as it saw fit, rather than as defining the moral obligation of society as a whole to defend the country. And certainly the political results of the new system were significant increases in the state's external and internal power. The army now disposed of a dependable supply of men, the size of which the crown determined by balancing policy concerns and military needs against economic constraints and political interests. Long-range planning became possible, and further weight was added to the state's foreign policy. At home, the canton system began to intervene between the squire and his serfs. Even if the landowners ran the system, they did so to fulfill demands of the king, not for themselves; while to greater or lesser extent the men placed on the muster rolls, and the smaller number that were actually inducted, were removed from their former subjection to the squire and brought under a higher, more general authority. The individual remained helpless, but the power of the monarch, standing for the state, began to replace privilege.

To summarize, France employed a pure system of voluntary enlistments, barely diluted by the moribund militia; Prussia, a mixed system: voluntary recruitment beyond her borders, compulsory service for a percentage of precisely defined segments of the population within. In both countries theorists discussed the military obligation that all men owed the state, but proposed no practical implementation of the principle. The idea gained broader currency in the late Enlightenment, without yet affecting the methods by which armies were raised. Finally the French Revolution and the Reform era in Prussia dismantled these by-now-traditional policies. Their place was taken by systems that applied a far more encompassing degree of coercion to serve and combined it with ideologies, emphasizing the political idealism of the autonomous individual, as a justification of the new demands. The changes are well known, yet they interacted so closely with major political and social concerns of the two societies that it is difficult to see them clearly. Nor have they been investigated sufficiently. In particular, a comprehensive study of the development of conscription in France does not yet exist. The ambiguities of conscription during the Revolution seem to have deterred scholars from systematically analyzing the proceedings of such bodies as the *comité militaire* of the Constituent and Legislative Assemblies. But although research in the subject is incomplete, the great lines of development are known and can be traced in some detail in the published documents and

---

Frauenholz, *Das Heerwesen in der Zeit des Absolutismus*, vol. 4 of *Entwicklungsgeschichte des Deutschen Heerwesens* (Munich, 1940), 225; Curt Jany, *Geschichte der Preussischen Armee*, new ed. (Osnabrück, 1967), 3:698.

the secondary literature. For Prussia, important sources, for instance Scharnhorst's official correspondence, were destroyed during the Second World War or are lost. But here, too, we know the general outline of the conflict over military manpower policies. A comparative enquiry into the manner in which universal conscription was established first in France, then in Prussia may reveal more of the essential features of the two related processes.

I

In November 1789 the Constituent Assembly opened its first debate on the changes needed to restore the army's discipline, which had suffered from the country's turmoil during the past six months, improve the army's efficiency, and turn it into a force appropriate to the new constitutional monarchy.[2] Among the first issues raised by the Assembly's military committee was the manner of recruiting, which despite numerous other pressing questions was—and for the next three years remained—the basic problem. The committee's spokesman, the Marquis de Bouthillier, began his report by declaring that every citizen must serve the army either with his person or his wealth. Two different systems of recruiting could implement this principle: obligatory enrollment, which, however, gave men chosen to serve the option of providing a replacement; or voluntary enlistment, financed by taxes, the payment of which would satisfy the service obligation of those citizens who did not enter the army.

The report weighed the advantages and disadvantages of the two. Obligatory service would bring a superior class of men into the army and thus raise the status of the rank and file. It would be cheaper than voluntary recruitment, could provide all the men needed, and would benefit the nation's morale since the obligation would fall equally on everyone. If the period of service were reduced from eight to four years, the soldier would be less tempted to desert. The drawbacks were, first, the difficulty of assigning quotas to the various parts of the monarchy. Not all provinces had the same military spirit and aptitude; in the Midi men were shorter and less healthy than in the North. At most 20 percent of the population lived in towns, yet towns currently supplied nearly two-thirds of all recruits. Obligatory service would deprive agriculture of needed workers. Finally, conscription would be unpopular. It could be made to work only if minds, attitudes, and prejudices were changed.

Voluntary recruitment, on the other hand, would not force men to serve against their will, deprive the economy of productive workers, or

---

[2] Session of 19 November 1789, *Archives parlementaires*, 1t series (Paris 1878), 10:118–22.

bear too heavily on any part of the country, since only the surplus of the population would volunteer. Current recruiting practices were flawed; they were expensive, often cruel, and even criminal. But the abuses could be corrected. Better treatment, new conditions of service, and increased possibilities for advancement would raise the quality of the recruits. Consequently the committee recommended that recruitment, rid of abuses, continue in peacetime and as long as possible during war. Universal conscription, which could be interpreted as an attack on the personal liberty of the citizen, should be imposed only when necessary and then only to raise a militia to ensure internal security and provide a reserve in times of crisis. But even this force should, if at all possible, consist of volunteers.

These proposals are characteristic of enlightened military opinion toward the end of the ancien régime. The need for change was recognized, even stressed; but what was envisaged was reform of the customary policies, not their replacement. Bouthillier's concern for the particularity of the regions of France rejected any universalizing tendency that might have resulted from the principle with which he introduced his report. He admitted that a measure as radical as universal conscription would demand new attitudes; but far from being a call to arms, his acknowledgment was merely another reason for dismissing conscription. His report breathed the spirit of the "Discours preliminaire" of Guibert's *Essai général de tactique* two decades earlier, a work whose occasional revolutionary insights into the potential of modern war had also been stifled by conventional realism.

It was shortly after this debate, and with reference to it, that Guibert published what was to be his last book, *De la force publique*, in which he presented himself as a precursor of the Revolution of 1789. In its frank discussion of the political power and implications of military institutions, the little work reflects the time in which it was written. But like Bouthillier, Guibert feared conscription as the tyranny of liberty: "Today a citizen army is an impossibility; the duties and qualities of the soldier and the citizen are opposed." He was the readier to reject conscription since he was satisfied with the army-strengths of his day—a blindness typical, as Clausewitz was to note subsequently, of eighteenth-century theorists. His dismissal of the "gigantic armies of Louis XIV" may seem to contradict his demand that all citizens should enroll in a national militia; but to Guibert the militia was merely a local defense force, its training limited to a few meetings a year, and, more important, a beneficent factor in domestic politics: "The militia is the guardian of liberty against the throne."[3]

[3] Jacques Antoine Hippolyte de Guibert, *De la force publique, considérée dans tous ses rapports* (Paris, 1790), v–vi, 12, 28, 56, 68, 138.

After Bouthillier had ended, another member of the committee, Dubois de Crancé, the future Montagnard, objected that the report gave the views of at most half of the committee—an exaggeration since the committee approved of voluntary enlistment by a vote of nine to two—and was promised time to speak at a later session. On 12 December, he presented the committee's minority report. He defended the popular revolution and stated as axiomatic that every citizen should be a soldier, without the possibility of providing a substitute, and every soldier a citizen. But once again this encompassing principle did not lead to conscription. Instead Dubois de Crancé envisaged a volunteer regular army, over which the crown had limited control in peacetime, backed by a provincial militia, incorporating all healthy, unmarried men between the ages of eighteen and forty, and a third-line reserve, a national militia, which included all able-bodied men who "have the right to vote, married or unmarried, young or old . . . , what I call a national guard, the true seal of the constitution."[4]

He was supported by another member of the committee, Baron de Menou, who did call for conscription, without, however, explaining on what basis he would select the percentage of men needed for the small army of 120,000 he envisaged.

Dubois de Crancé and Menou rather ambiguously called for the people in arms; the subsequent debate made it apparent that the assembly would neither impose the obligation for long-term service on all able-bodied men, nor arm the people without regard to social distinctions, nor accept an effective national militia that was controlled locally rather than by the executive. Obligatory enrollment in the militia was acceptable as long as the militia was little more than an untrained manpower pool for the army. That merely expressed the view held throughout the chamber that all men had the duty to defend their homes and to serve in a national crisis—which was close to actual practice before 1789. Objections to extending this obligation to service under more normal conditions in the regular army ranged from noting the strong opposition conscription would encounter in all parts of society, and the technical difficulties of implementation—requiring a speaker warned prophetically, constant supervision and spying—to denouncing its unjust, tyrannical nature, which Bouthillier had stressed. One speaker termed it a despotic method, another was astonished to hear the spirit of liberty invoked to support the most obvious and cruel slavery. In the end, the assembly unanimously

---

[4] Session of 12 December 1789, *Archives parlementaires*, 10:520–23. French historians, even those specializing in military affairs, tend to regard Dubois de Crancé's speech as more radical than it actually was; see, for instance, Gustave Vallée, *La Conscription dans le département de la Charente* (Paris, 1935), 4–5.

voted that the army, other than the militia, would continue to rely on voluntary engagements.[5]

The debate already hinted at the future development of military policy. In the next year and a half, the assembly, besides trying to raise the army's effectiveness, worked to detach it from royal control. It limited the soldier's mission to the country's defense against foreign enemies—internal security was to be the task of others—assumed budgetary power over the army, introduced more non-nobles into the officer corps, issued a new oath. These ideologically motivated steps—often characterized with some exaggeration as democratizing the army—had greater impact than the reforms in manpower policies, organization, and other institutional changes the assembly decreed. In more stable times, the reforms might have taken hold; but they were rendered inadequate by the political currents of 1790 and 1791, which reflected the assembly's own ambivalence toward the army: a force to be strengthened and to be feared. Inevitably the army declined. It was weakened by insubordination, a confusion of loyalties in the rank and file, desertion, the emigration of some two thousand officers, while, contrary to the wishes of a majority in the assembly, a new force, the National Guard, was emerging as a significant factor in internal affairs and to some extent as the army's rival. From improvised beginnings in the summer of 1789, the Guard two years later had taken the place of the royal militia and coalesced into a nationwide force, made up largely of volunteers who paid for their own equipment and of former regular soldiers, the units controlled not by a central authority but by the localities in which they were raised. It became a force of the bourgeoisie and petite bourgeoisie, although in disregard of the law many poor men who had been armed in 1789 remained in the ranks. All able-bodied active citizens between the ages of eighteen and sixty were obliged to register for its service, which did not, of course, mean that all put on uniforms. But the assertion of a universal obligation constituted a significant step in the mobilization—political even more than military—of the population. The Guard was intended to act as a civilian militia or police, to lend weight to the new policies, and as a force for social control, although its political position varied according to local circumstances. But it also served as a reserve for the national defense and eventually even as a manpower pool for the line army.

In the early summer of 1791, when the attempted escape of the king caused a war scare, the assembly called for volunteers from the National Guard to help defend the eastern frontiers. Over a hundred thousand men responded. They were organized into regional battalions, received higher

[5] Sessions of 15 and 16 December 1789, *Archives parlementaires*, 10:579–88, 10:615–20, and annexes 10:591–614.

pay than the regulars, and elected their officers. In the fall they were given the right to return to civilian life after 1 December, 1792. The rank and file consisted primarily of shopkeepers and craftsmen; peasants and members of the bourgeoisie made up perhaps another quarter of the total. The officers were mainly former soldiers, wealthier bourgeois, even lesser nobles.[6] It was a force controlled by the bourgeoisie, in which the more radical members of the assembly placed greater confidence than in the line army. As a military force it left much to be desired, but proposals to incorporate the volunteers into regular units were rejected by the left. When war did break out in April 1792, a second call for 83,600 volunteers was issued; the goal was met, this time primarily by peasants, although in parts of the country recourse had to be taken to bounties and even to forced enlistments.

By November the French armies had overrun much of the Austrian Netherlands and west bank of the Rhine and had occupied Nice and Savoy—successes owed largely to the government's exceptional efforts to increase the strength of the army with volunteers, while Austria and Prussia were waging a limited war with a fraction of their forces. The territory of France seemingly secure, and the end of their service obligation at hand, tens of thousands of volunteers ignored appeals by the convention and returned home. The convention nevertheless continued its aggressive foreign policy. War was declared on the United Kingdom, the United Provinces, and Spain; and a new appeal for volunteers became necessary. In February 1793 the convention issued a call for three hundred thousand men, in order to raise total effectives of 502,900, a force larger than the standing armies of Austria and Prussia combined.

This third call for men comprised both voluntary enlistments and conscription. All unmarried men and childless widowers between the ages of eighteen and forty were liable for service; on the other hand, quotas were set for each department and commune, which everywhere fell below the number of men available. It was hoped the quotas would be filled by volunteers. Only if their number proved insufficient were municipal authorities obliged to enroll the rest, either by choosing the recruits themselves or by a lottery. Any man selected could provide a substitute if he found someone willing to take his place and could afford the price.

The new appeal was, at best, a partial failure. It encountered broad opposition—a sign of the increasing differences between the government and large groups of the population—helped bring about the uprising in the Vendée, and fed other revolts. By June possibly 150,000 men had volunteered or been drafted; the great majority, in contrast to the earlier volunteers, coming from the rural and urban poor. It was the relative

[6] Jean-Paul Bertaud, *Valmy: La démocratie en armes* (Paris, 1970), 199.

failures of the *levée* of three hundred thousand men that prepared the way for the *levée en masse* and made it politically possible, although historians have usually presented the decision to resort to it in very different terms.

Is it the extraordinary hold the French Revolution continues to exert on our political imagination that leads historians to contradict themselves or to blur clear distinctions when they discuss the first war of the Revolution and the *levée en masse*? If such a knowledgeable and balanced interpreter of the Revolution as Jacques Godechot declares that in 1792 France was compelled to defend her frontiers against the attack of nearly all of Europe, it is not the historian of the Revolution who is speaking, but the man who has been brought up on its ideals and legends.[7] More precisely, the historian for the moment enters the minds of the men he analyzes, and his own better knowledge to the contrary gives voice to their emotions and to their rhetoric. That the main impetus for war in 1792 came from Royalists and Girondins is as certain as that the war began with a French offensive in the Austrian Netherlands and that it was the left in the Assembly that expanded the war in the early months of 1793. It was the convention that created the military crisis it now had to resolve. The solution it chose was to raise the largest army the world had seen.

This was an effective solution, but not the only possible one. While the French government could not predict how Austria and Prussia would conduct the war, it soon became evident that the two powers would not mobilize fully. In the campaign of summer and fall 1792, no more than 81,000 Austrians and Prussians, together with six thousand Hessians and a few thousand French emigres, opposed the republican armies. They operated on a front stretching from the channel to Switzerland, and numerous units were detached to secure the lines of communication. From later summer on, the incidence of disease was high, so that at Valmy the main Prussian army amounted to thirty-five thousand men at most.

Forces of that magnitude scarcely posed an insuperable challenge to a country that already had between 350,000 and four hundred thousand men under arms, even if many line units were in a state of partial dissolution and the volunteer battalions not yet adequately trained and disciplined.[8] The convention took measures to correct these weaknesses, but

[7] Jacques Godechot, *Les Institutions de la France sous la révolution et l'empire* (Paris, 1968), 353. It would not be difficult to cite similar contradictions or blind spots in the writings of many modern historians of the revolution, from Georges Lefebvre to Albert Soboul and Jean-Paul Bertaud. On this question, see also the recent monograph by T. C. W. Blanning, *The Origins of the French Revolutionary Wars* (London and New York), 1986.

[8] I recognize that this is merely a supposition. The strictly military need for increasing the strength of the French armed forces to over a million men, as had happened by 1795, has

in the framework of an increase in army strength that imposed enormous demands on the economic and administrative as well as human resources of the country. A military problem was dealt with in essentially political and ideological terms. General conscription meant the mobilization of the people for the Revolution as much as for war. It extended and deepened the government's control over the country, and like the war itself contributed to the further radicalization of the Revolution. The army's transition from a royal to a republican force while fighting a major war had created a vacuum, which was filled by egalitarianism and the expanding power of the centralized state.

In the first half of 1793 conscription still remained in contention, not least among the Jacobin leadership. It was advocated primarily by soldiers with Jacobin views and by sans-culottes and their radical spokesmen and allies. Their preference for thinking and speaking in absolute terms—*all* men should be drafted—expressed not only their rigorous view of equality but also an understanding of mass psychology. As a spokesman of the forty-eight Parisian sections advised the convention: "It is easier to rouse the whole nation than a segment of the citizenry."[9] That such a policy owed more to rhetoric than to reality was disregarded by its supporters. Until the *levée en masse* was finally decreed, they were reluctant to acknowledge that to arm and send to the fronts every able-bodied man was neither desirable nor possible. Nor, ideally, should compulsion have been needed to bring about total mobilization. That the third *levée* had been a relative failure was blamed on political ignorance or corruption, and on the ability of segments of the population—especially wealthier groups—to escape from some of the consequences of the revolutionary experiment. Radicals would have favored conscription in any case; that not enough volunteers had come forward gave their arguments special weight.

This again raises the issue of popular attitudes. Even during a revolution it is unlikely that more than a minority would volunteer to fight, even for a cause enjoying widespread support. Nevertheless, the historical legend of the *levée en masse* interprets the *levée* as expressing the people's enthusiastic defense of the Revolution and the nation. It was, however, less a measure of popular enthusiasm than of the political acumen of the Montagnard leaders, who came to recognize that on the issue of conscription radical pressures could not be resisted, and who then implemented an essentially ideological measure, whose appropriateness they doubted, with energy and common sense.

---

never been adequately investigated, if, indeed, the question has ever been raised in a scholarly rather that in a political context.

[9] Session of 16 August 1793, *Archives parlementaires* (Paris, 1907), 72:251.

The *levée* was a product of the military, economic, and political crises of July and August 1793, a stage in the evolution of the Committee of Public Safety as the executive power of the government. But it also logically resulted from one of the major trends of the Revolution, the claim that the revolutionary government gave expression to the *volonté générale*, and it had been advocated here and there in the course of the preceding six months.

At the beginning of the year, Carnot proposed that "all citizens between the ages of twenty and twenty-five [should] leave for the frontiers," a measure the Convention rejected.[10] During the summer, as the military situation worsened, the *levée* was called for in some communities, and by radical journalists and speakers at the Jacobin Club. It was interpreted as an implementation of the new constitution of June 1793, which gave all French males the vote while imposing on all the obligation of military service. Men began to talk of the army as "the school of the Nation." On 19 July the Paris sections petitioned the Convention to abolish the practice of replacement as favoring the wealthy, one among many expressions of the widespread desire in radical and populist groups for an all-encompassing leveling manpower policy.[11] On 5 August the Commune demanded the immediate mobilization of all men between the ages of sixteen and twenty-five. Some days later a speaker complained at the Jacobin Club that the convention appeared reluctant to support such a law, while others either raised doubts about the practicality of a general *levée* or suggested drafting only a fraction of the available men.[12] On the fourteenth the Committee of Public Safety through its spokesman Barère issued a general call to arms in the Convention.[13] This seems to have been meant as a sop to radical pressure, for that same evening at the Jacobin Club Robespierre once more tried to stem the tide: "That magnanimous but perhaps overly enthusiastic scheme of a *levée en masse* is useless [inutile]; it is not men that we lack, but rather virtuous, able, and patriotic generals." Other speakers, however, declared in favor of the *levée*; and when on the sixteenth the Paris sections sent a call for the *levée en masse* to the Committee of Public Safety, the committee gave way.[14] That same evening, Barère announced the committee's recommendation of the *levée* to the Convention. He contrasted the tournament-like war of monarchs to the war of liberty, which by means of the *levée en masse* would sweep

[10] Session of 18 February 1793, *Archives parlementaires* (Paris, 1901), 59:24.

[11] Session of 19 July 1793, *Archives parlementaires* (Paris, 1906), 69:191.

[12] Meetings of 12 and 13 August 1793, *La Société des Jacobins*, ed. F. V. A. Aulard (Paris, 1895), 5:345, 348.

[13] Session of 14 August 1793, *Archives parlementaires*, 72:160.

[14] Meeting of 14 August 1793, *La Société des Jacobins*, 5:350–51. See also the meetings of 15, 16, and August 20, *ibid.*, 5:354, 355, 359, 364.

away its enemies in "a seething flood of courage and patriotism." The statement was prepared so hurriedly that there had been no time to draft specific steps of implementation, which were not issued until the twenty-third.[15]

The intense wish of the Enragés and sans-culottes to draw everyone into the war for the Revolution and to eliminate the immunity from military service of the wealthy and influential, a wish that some experienced soldiers like Carnot and Dubois-Crancé believed could be turned to good use for the national defense, had overcome the committee's resistance. Under the circumstances, the committee and its supporters could only seek to reduce the application of the *levée* to practical proportions, and hint at the political bad faith of those who insisted on taking the *levée en masse* literally: it was only common sense that not all men would serve, what was intended was the "levée d'une force suffisante"—perhaps 10 or 20 percent of the men available. Danton declared that obviously not all Frenchmen could become soldiers, "but let us not stop the momentum of national energy."[16] In the Jacobin Club, Hébert began to have second thoughts: the *levée*, by emptying Paris of all Republicans, would open the gates to the counterrevolution. The law of suspects, legalizing the imprisonment of anyone whose loyalty to the Revolution was doubted, helped solve the problem; and although this law, too, had long been demanded by the Commune, its passage now exemplifies the close link between the *levée* and other radical policies. Barère further calmed both the fears of the radicals and the practical concerns of administrators and soldiers by stating in the Convention on the twenty-third that while the government needed the authority to call up all men, it would be sufficient to employ them gradually.[17] But on the same evening at the Jacobin Club, Robespierre continued to minimize the significance of the new policy.[18]

The *levée en masse* of 23 August 1793 declared that until the enemies of the republic had been expelled from its territory, all Frenchmen and women were on call to serve the war effort. So far as actual military service was concerned, all unmarried men and childless widowers between the ages of eighteen and twenty-five could be inducted. If necessary, additional age groups would be called up. Replacements were no longer permitted. The *levée* was not yet universal military service—married men were excluded—but it went far to translate the principle into practice. Supplementary laws under the Directory added exemptions and restored the conscript's right to furnish a substitute; nevertheless the decree of 23

[15] Session of 16 August 1793, *Archives parlementaires*, 72:261–62.
[16] Session of 20 August 1793, *ibid.*, 72:488–89.
[17] Session of 23 August 1793, ibid., 72:677.
[18] In an exchange with Chaumette, *Procureur* of the Commune, meeting of 23 August 1793, *La Société des Jacobins*, 5:371.

August 1793 opened a new phase in the relations between the French government and its citizens and set the pattern for the military manpower policies of subsequent French regimes and eventually of the Western world.

II

The debate over conscription—which in France took place in the open, stormy atmosphere of the National Assembly and the political clubs, and was swayed by public opinion—was in Prussia conducted mainly between the king and his senior officers and officials. Their deliberations took note of memoranda or petitions submitted to them; but except in one respect, these did not significantly affect the outcome. The decisive impetus for replacing the canton system, and with it the corporative character of the army, undoubtedly came from the defeats of 1806 and 1807. Even before the French Revolution, however, the manpower policies on which the monarchy had relied since the 1730s were seen to need adjustment, a need that became urgent after the Revolutionary Wars began to reshape the political map of Central Europe.

Soon after his accession to the throne, Frederick William II appointed a commission to revise the canton regulations, in particular to improve the coordination between civil and military authorities in selecting recruits, and to reduce the categories of exemption. The commission completed its task after four years by issuing the canton law of 12 February 1792, which in most essentials remained in effect until 1814. The law opened with a refined version of the traditional claim that all men owed military service to the crown: "The obligation of military service is incumbent upon our loyal subjects . . . It is the crown's desire that to the greatest extent possible this obligation is borne equally by all." A restatement of this general principle, "no-one who enjoys the protection of the state can evade the duty to defend the state," introduced the list of exemptions, which, nevertheless, had grown longer. The nobility being "personally free," conscription did not apply to it. Subject to the conscription law but permanently exempt by government fiat were such individuals as untitled owners of manorial estates of more than twelve thousand Taler in value, officials above the lowest ranks, Mennonites, Moravian Brethren, and Jews, all foreign immigrants, and the sons of senior officials and university teachers. Qualified exemptions were granted to groups ranging from sons of subaltern officials and parsons— provided they pursued academic studies—to a wide variety of artisans, craftsmen, and free peasants, as well as to the residents of most cities and larger towns.[19] In 1799 it was estimated that 1.7 million adult males out of a total population of 8.7 million remained exempt. Concern for the country's economy and social considerations nullified the effort to simplify the law and reduce exemptions: the duty to serve in the army continued to fall almost exclusively on serfs and other poor groups of population.

The war with France led to the loss, in southern Germany and on the left bank of the Rhine, of the army's most desirable sources of foreign mercenaries. Within the foreseeable future, most of its recruits would have to come from Prussia herself. The importance of native manpower further increased because the native soldier was held to be more loyal, a factor of new significance in view of the ideological character that the French were giving to the fighting. The canton districts could have provided twice or even three times as many men as previously, but budgetary constraints and the government's unwillingness to deprive agriculture of more workers limited the increase. Consequently a few officers and officials, from the middle of the 1790s on, proposed to solve the army's manpower problems by reinstituting the militia.

Common to most of these schemes, which reverted to organizations that were abolished at the beginning of the century and had briefly resurfaced during the crisis of the Seven Years' War, was their limited, defensive purpose. Drawn from the canton registers, the rank and file were to be trained only for a few weeks, so as not to disrupt the economy; in wartime they were to provide replacements for the line army or serve in rear areas to release regular units for field duty. In the extreme case of an enemy invasion, they might operate as a homeguard or Landwehr.

Although even before 1806 army reform was a major field of conflict between conservatives and progressives, it should be noted that several of these proposals were the work of relatively conservative officers. Men like Rüchel, who in 1798 vainly argued for the elimination of geographic exemptions, or Knesebeck—whose plan for a "patriotic reserve" of 1803 proclaimed that "in case of need every native-born [*Eingeborene*] is a soldier, and must contribute to the defense of the state"—were sufficiently worried about Prussia's military weakness to suggest changes that while strengthening the armed forces would have broken down some of the barriers of corporative society.[20] Their only success was the establishment on paper of a home reserve, drawn in part from the exempt towns, to garri-

---

[19] "Kantonreglement vom 12. Februar 1792," in Frauenholz, *Das Heerwesen in der Zeit des Absolutismus*, 309–36. Note also the supplementary regulations, ibid., 338–39, 340, 349–52.

[20] On Rüchel's proposals see Colmar v. d. Goltz, *Von Rossbach bis Jena* (Berlin, 1906), 255–56, 269–71. Knesebeck's memorandum is extensively excerpted, ibid., 280–94, and in Reinhold Höhn, *Revolution—Heer—Kriegsbild* (Darmstadt, 1944), 449–56.

son fortresses in wartime; but no more than a few units were actually raised. In the narrower sense, manpower policies could not be changed significantly before 1806 because distrust of the militia concept was ingrained in the army since the days of Frederick William I. Some officers also feared that even a moderately effective militia would call into question the need for the intense discipline and drill of the regular army, thus compromising the army's prestige and conceivably even forcing it to alter its methods. The civil administration was unwilling to renounce the exemptions that protected its clients in the cities and towns, and the economy in general. In the larger sense, as Otto Hintze has noted, before Jena all internal reforms lacked an essential propulsive force—"the vital connection with the great issues of political existence and power"—which after 1807 was provided by the determination to liberate the state of foreign rule.[21]

The defeated Prussian army was far larger than the country could now afford and the French would tolerate. The Convention of Paris of 1808 limited the army to forty-two thousand men for the next ten years and prohibited all militias, home guards, and other auxiliaries. By maintaining records of retired soldiers and by the so-called Krümper system, in which trained soldiers were periodically sent on indefinite leave and replaced by recruits, the French restrictions were circumvented and the basis laid for the force of 125,000 combat troops with which the war against France was renewed in March 1813. If Scharnhorst and his closest associates at the core of the reform movement determined early on to fight for universal conscription, it was not to solve a shortage of trained men but for the sake of their conception of reform as such. They believed that Prussia could reestablish herself, which required defeating the French, only by breaking down the former isolation of the army in society and by making war the business of everyone.[22] Beyond that, they wanted corporative society and autocratic government replaced by a more open system of mutual obligations between monarch, administration, army, and citizen in the service of the twin ideals of the nation and the ethically autonomous individual. A comprehensive program of reform followed from these wishes: an army of conscripts of all classes could not be treated in the traditional manner. Discipline, military justice, access to officer rank, to some extent even tactical doctrine would have to be modernized, and length of service would have to be considerably shortened—

[21] Otto Hintze, "Prussian Reform Movements before 1806," in *The Historical Essays of Otto Hintze,* ed. Felix Gilbert (New York, 1975), 86.

[22] Twenty years later, Clausewitz recalled his beliefs of that period, and generalized them: "A people and nation can hope for a strong position in the world only if national character and familiarity with war fortify each other by continual interaction." *On War,* ed. Michael Howard and Peter Paret, rev. ed. (Princeton, 1984), 192 (Book III, chap. 6).

because those changes, desirable in themselves, became essential if the sons of the educated and well-to-do were to serve in the ranks. As in France, the army would become the school of the nation. By fulfilling a duty common to all in a supra-local and -regional institution, men would learn to be patriots. Such an army, the reformers hoped, would change from an inert instrument in the hand of its commander to a vital force that might even put pressure on the leadership if it was overly cautious or relapsed into purely dynastic policies. It is not accidental that every member of Scharnhorst's group, from Gneisenau and Boyen to Grolman and Clausewitz, was preoccupied during these years with the possibilities of insurrection.

Until the Convention of Paris prohibited auxiliary forces, the reformers approached conscription by way of the militia, which they regarded as a useful halfway house since it incorporated the universal obligation to defend the country and in its earlier existence, at the beginning of the eighteenth century, had included men from wealthier groups. Immediately after the armistice Scharnhorst repeated a proposal for a militia drawn from the exempt groups, that he had first made shortly before the outbreak of war.[23] In August 1807 the new Military Reorganization Commission under his chairmanship based its plans for the new army on the principle that "all men are obliged to defend their fatherland."[24] The following March the commission sent the king a detailed proposal for the establishment of a "Provincial Army"—a name chosen to avoid the still unpopular "militia." The plan, derived from "the simple, straightforward concept of Prussia's military constitution, that every inhabitant of the country is its natural defender," envisaged a standing army of volunteers and of conscripts from the cantons, supported by *Provinzialtruppen*, made up of a percentage of all able-bodied men between the ages of sixteen and thirty-one who could afford to equip themselves. Since in case of need this group could also be drafted, all exemptions would be eliminated. The proposal stressed the relative cheapness of such a force, declared that it would serve to unite government and nation, and sought to allay conservative anxieties by claiming that as long as the militia included the well-to-do, it posed no threat to the crown and to internal order.[25] Frederick William III was not wholly won over; nevertheless he approved publication of a general and rather indirect statement in the

---

[23] Gerhard von Scharnhorst, *Memoire*, April 1806, in Goltz, *Von Rossbach bis Jena*, 543–59; *Denkschrift*, 31 July 1807, in *Das Preussische Heer vom Tilsiter Frieden bis zur Befreiung, 1807–1814*, part 2 of *Die Reorganisation des Preussischen Staates unter Stein und Hardenberg*, ed. Rudolf Vaupel (Leipzig, 1938), 1:19–23.

[24] Minutes of meetings of the commission, 20 August–7 September 1807, ibid., 1:63.

[25] "Immediatbericht der Militär-Reorganisationskommission," 15 March 1808, ibid., 1:320–32, see especially 321, 323.

new articles of war: "In future, every subject of the state is to be obliged to perform military service . . . under yet to be determined conditions."[26]

After the Convention of Paris made it necessary to shelve the militia proposals, the reformers pressed for approval of conscription in principle, even though its implementation would have to await changes in the political situation. They could point to the organization during these years of a Landwehr in Austria and the adoption of conscription in Westphalia, Bavaria, and Württemberg, which, however, followed their French model by allowing a variety of exemptions and the possibility of replacement. Scharnhorst and his associates, on the contrary, rejected any provision that would detract from their ideal of uniting all segments of society in service to the nation.

Negative reactions to the news that the government was considering imposing conscription in the future came not only from traditional interest groups but also from some of the most liberal civilian reformers. Theodor von Schön, Ludwig von Vincke, and Barthold Georg Niebuhr denounced the universal obligation of military service as senseless since the state would not again need a strong army, as an unfair burden on young men of the propertied and educated classes, whose careers would be interrupted, and, in Vincke's encompassing condemnation, as "the grave of all culture, of science and industry, of political freedom and of all human happiness." Conscription, he warned, would turn Prussia into another imperial France.[27] They thought it inconsistent to create a free society while its young men were to be subjected to new constraints. Of a different order were the protests of formerly exempt towns, of employers wanting to protect their workers, of the wealthier Silesian merchants, and of nobles, a group of whom petitioned the king that "this universal conscription . . . which first saw the light of day as the creature of a revolution that shattered all existing order and conditions in France, this conscription, which by its very nature can be based only on the concept of universal equality, would, we dare suggest, lead to the complete destruction of the nobility."[28] As late as 1818, after conscription had been in effect for some years, a significant minority of the country's regional governments still doubted the wisdom and justice of the new policy of universal military service.

The opposition of many of the educated and well-to-do helped bring about favored treatment of these groups when conscription was at last

[26] "Krieges-Artikel für die Unter-Officiere und gemeinen Soldaten," 3 August 1808, in Frauenholz, *Das Heerwesen des XIX. Jahrhunderts*, vol. 5 of *Entwicklungsgeschichte* (Munich, 1941), 101.

[27] Vincke to Karl vom Stein, 30 September 1808, in Vaupel, ed., *Die Reorganisation*, 598.

[28] Petition of Counts Dohna-Schlobitten and Dohna-Schlodien and of other nobles of *Kreis* Mohrungen, 17 November 1808, ibid., 748–49.

introduced after the first Peace of Paris. The process was already set in motion in the weeks preceding the outbreak of war in 1813. In February a decree called on young men with some schooling and the financial means to equip themselves to volunteer for service in new elite units, which would qualify them for promotion in the expanding army. A threat was joined to the inducement: men between the ages of seventeen and twenty-four who did not serve for at least one year in the line army or in the new Freiwillige Jäger detachments would be ineligible for employment in the civil administration or in any other state agency.[29] After the war the legend spread that the educated classes had been the main carriers of patriotic enthusiasm in the population and had contributed the greatest number of volunteers. If in France the myth of the defensive and voluntary character of the *levée en masse* was propagated mainly by republican and, more recently, by Marxist writers, in Germany it was primarily liberal historians who emphasized the middle-class character of the volunteers of 1813. The political message this assertion sought to dignify with the authority of history was that the Prussian middle classes had by their self-sacrifice shown themselves worthy of being accepted as full partners in governing the country. Actually no more than 12 percent, about three thousand out of a total of some twenty-seven thousand volunteers, came from these groups. The great majority of volunteers consisted of craftsmen, shopkeepers, and peasants, who entered the line army rather than the new elite units.[30]

The conscription law of 3 September 1814 made permanent the favored treatment of the better classes. Young men who met certain educational qualifications and could pay for their uniforms and weapons needed to serve only one year instead of the three years of the ordinary conscript. A good record gave them first call on officer positions in the reserves. The institution of the one-year volunteer, a significant feature of

---

[29] "Bekanntmachung in Betreff der zu errichtenden Jägerdetaschements," 3 February 1813, Frauenholz, *Das Heerwensen des XIX. Jahrhunderts*, 141–43.

[30] See the detailed statistical analysis by Rudolf Ibbeken in *Preussen 1807–1813* (Berlin, 1970), 393–450. Ibbeken also takes note of the middle-class legend, ibid., 411–18, which entrapped even such conscientious scholars as Friedrich Meinecke and Franz Schnabel. Meinecke and Schnabel must have known the facts in general, though not the specific figures; but they were blind to the importance of explicitly stating the preponderance of volunteers from the lower classes.

As the glorification of the *levée en masse* was questioned in French scholarship by conservative writers—for example, by Camille Rousset in his frequently reprinted book *Les Volontaires 1791–1794*—so in Germany before the First World War the liberal emphasis on the patriotic volunteer, especially if he belonged to the propertied and educated, was firmly rejected by conservatives and official army historians. A representative example is the discussion of the inferiority of the Landwehr in *Das Preussische Heer der Befreiungskriege*, edited by the Historical Section of the Great General Staff (Berlin, 1914), 2:199–306.

the Prussian army and of German society until the First World War, was the equivalent of the French army's exemptions and the right of replacement, which remained in effect until the laws of 1872 and 1889. The German system, however, kept the middle classes in stricter dependence on the state and on its military ethos by compelling them to serve as soldiers, if on advantageous and prestigious terms.

The Prussian conscription law of 1814 once again declared that defense of the fatherland was a universal obligation, but now the rhetoric was meant literally. The institutional expression of this common duty took three forms: the line army, made up of volunteers and of as many conscripts as were needed, drafted for three years from men between the ages of twenty and twenty-five. Secondly, the Landwehr or National Guard, in peacetime limited to a few weeks' annual training, consisting of men up to the age of thirty-nine who had not been drafted or who had completed their three-year service in the line army. Army and Landwehr were backed by the Landsturm, in peacetime a paper organization, which incorporated all able-bodied men between the ages of seventeen and twenty, and again between thirty-nine and fifty.[31] Military service became an experience shared by all social groups.

In Prussia even more clearly than in France, no pressing military need had led to conscription. As the new manpower policy was introduced, the reduction of the army and its partial demobilization was under way. Conscription in the summer of 1814 seemed primarily desirable as lending weight to the Prussian negotiations at the Congress of Vienna. But the whole thrust of military reform since 1807 had been toward conscription, and with the break-up of corporative society and the freeing of the serfs, the old canton system rooted in the social distinction between the exempt and nonexempt male population could not be retained. Conscription realized the reformers' ideal of uniting all segments of society in service to the nation; but did so in highly authoritarian form. In particular, the reformers had hoped to give the Landwehr the characteristic of a people in arms; instead it was placed firmly under control of the line army, and increased rather than diminished the power of the crown and of the old elites.

III

Can a policy as coercive as conscription result from, or express, the enthusiasm of those to whom it is applied? When they first imposed the

[31] "Gesetz über die Verpflichtung zum Kriegsdienste," 3 September 1814, Frauenholz, *Das Heerwesen des XIX. Jahrhunderts*, 180–84.

obligation of universal military service on their peoples, the French and Prussian governments associated conscription with popular enthusiasm. Men who were drafted, it was claimed, not only had the moral and legal duty to bear arms, but actually wanted to do so.

These claims should not be dismissed altogether. The imposition of conscription may suggest a certain readiness for it in society, at least among some groups. Conscription may also be a necessary method to systematize the undisciplined enthusiasm and good will of the population, to harness energies that otherwise would dissipate. But without doubt the coercive and didactic features of conscription are more impressive. Rather than reflecting attitudes already widely held in 1793 or 1814—loyalty to a cause, hatred of the foreigner, patriotism—conscription helped create and diffuse these attitudes. It constitutes one of several channels through which ideas, feelings, and energies flow to give substance to the new concept of the state and eventually to nationalism.

Essential to the success of this process are the obedience the state can exact and the asserted identity of values of the state and the individual. To a great extent the credibility of this assertion rests on the universality of the obligation. The canton system had declared that some men owed a service obligation to authority; conscription proclaimed from the outset that everyone owed this obligation to the greater community and to himself as a member of the community. At the same time, the nature of the community was changing. Once the militia had stood for the determination to defend one's home; now conscription expanded the horizon of loyalties from the farm, the town, the province, to what people must have seen as an abstract entity, the nation. By drawing on all segments of society, armies became one of the institutions by which men were taught the reality and worth of the national concept.

The development by which local and regional loyalties were attached to a larger whole was paralleled by the change from corporative to a more open society. Again the obligation to bear arms played a part. The theory of universal military service could never become reality in corporative society. Like the imposition of taxes applicable to all, the imposition of conscription is part of the process that abolished legally defined privilege. As the legal and institutional forms of society changed, so did men's rights, duties, and—often—attitudes. Though acting in very dissimilar conditions, French revolutionaries and Prussian reformers after them put forward similar arguments: the new universality of obligations helped turn passive subjects of the ancien régime into citizens of a commonwealth that was shedding absolutism, or had already destroyed it. Some historians could interpret even the earliest phase of the process in this light: Shortly before the unification of Germany, Droysen characterized the canton system of Frederick William I as "the first step toward citizenship."[32] He wrote before it became evident that in Germany the process would be stunted; but in France, too, conscription did not inevitably bring political rights to those who served.

Nor, if examined closely, could conscription be equated with duties equally shared, as its advocates always claimed. In its final form in France and Prussia, conscription with its preferred treatment of the educated and well-to-do proved a victory for the bourgeoisie, which in France was soon followed by the acquisition of genuine political power. That those remnants of privilege have accompanied conscription in other societies and at other times as well is shown by the deferments American college students enjoyed during the Vietnam War.

The circumstances under which conscription was introduced differed in France and Prussia, but in both countries the new system was brought about as much by politics as by war. If we look beyond the immediate factors to the long-term forces involved, we see that conscription is a phenomenon of the growth of the centralized state. The ability to draft soldiers from all social groups constituted a significant expansion of the power of government, whatever its ideology, in its relations with its people as well as with other states.

Conscription also soon led to an expansion of war. It made possible the raising and maintenance of large armies, even when their operations were very costly, and eventually became an essential part in the efficient exploitation of the military potential of society. When conscription first became law, the administrative machinery of the state was not yet capable of implementing it fully. Hébert might cry that all able-bodied young men would rush to the frontiers, but that was unrealistic if prophetic rhetoric. What occurred in 1793 and 1814 were merely the first inefficient revolutions of a crude machine, which required generations to refine and perfect. In our century the comprehensive mobilization of the people for fighting or for economic support of the war has become commonplace. Here, too, as in so much else, the French Revolution and the emerging nation-state lie near the source of ideas, attitudes, and techniques that for good and ill have retained their power to the present.

[32] Johann Gustav Droysen, *Geschichte der preussischen Politik*, vol. 4, part 3 (Leipzig, 1869), 417.

5

NAPOLEON AS ENEMY

IN THEIR EARLY PHASES political revolutions are often defined by a program, a list of issues, recommendations, or even demands that helps direct events and propels them forward, even if eventually it is superceded. By contrast, the revolution in war that occurred at the end of the eighteenth century was not consciously structured. Reformers and innovators were engaged in all areas of tactics, technology, and organization; but they worked in isolation and often at cross-purposes. Eventually it was the political explosion in France that brought their work together and gave it reason and scope to develop further. Political change and the social changes associated with it—for instance, conscription and broader access to officer rank—infused technical and tactical innovation with a revolutionary impulse.

A critical element in the revolution in war was the ability of soldiers and governments to come to recognize the changes that were now possible, and then to act upon their recognition. This was true first for the French and soon also for their opponents, who found themselves at a disadvantage if they failed to analyze the nature of the innovations used against them and to develop effective responses. Analysis and reaction would have presented fewer problems had they taken place in a military vacuum. But even minor organizational or tactical changes could have implications throughout society. To become effective, technical objectivity had to interact with economic, social, and political considerations. It could accept or oppose them, but they could not be ignored.

These issues—which, of course, are not unique to the eighteenth century—had interested me almost as long as I had studied the history of war. My dissertation on Hans David von Yorck dealt with a Prussian soldier of the Napoleonic era whom historians have usually categorized as an arch-conservative, but who as a soldier and in some respects politically championed many of the changes of the military revolution. At about the time the revised dissertation was published, I gave a lecture at the Air Force Academy, in which I attempted to generalize the problems of innovation and change in war and to apply a historical perspective to issues of modernization and of understanding potential opponents that were then occupying the American services. Subsequently—at a conference dedicated to the memory of Bernard Brodie, whose analyses of modern conflict possessed the kind of intellectual daring that may justly be called revolutionary—I drew a parallel between the generation of the French Revolution and analysts after 1945 who tried to come to terms with war in the nuclear age. Some years later, an invitation to address the Consortium on Revolutionary Europe gave me a further opportunity to explore the problem of understanding and exploiting new forces in war and to suggest that it held an explanation for Napoleon's successes and for his eventual failure.

Few subjects have been as extensively discussed in the literature on war as Napoleon's battles and campaigns, and his qualities as military leader. And yet much remains to be learned about them; both about specifics—especially the institutional and economic features of Napoleonic war, and even its tactics—and about such fundamental questions as the reasons for the emperor's successes and failures, or, to take the longer view, his place in the general development of war from the ancien régime to our own day.

In the following discussion I address the issue that seems to me to link the specific and the general, that connects the organizational and tactical with the expansion and collapse of the French empire: How did Napoleon's opponents appraise him? How did they see him as enemy? That they were slow to fathom his military style certainly contributed to his success, the more so since this problem of perception increased their already great difficulties in adjusting their institutions, their strategy and tactics, to the new realities. I shall limit my comments to one group of analysts, Prussian officers, and among these primarily to two men: Heinrich Dietrich von Bülow, and Carl von Clausewitz. I do not mean to put Bülow and Clausewitz forward as representative of general views—they were too self-willed and intelligent for that; but their ways of evaluating the emperor do indicate larger developments in the intellectual responses to Napoleon on the part of German soldiers and, indeed, of many soldiers throughout Europe; a response, that, in turn, constitutes a significant element in the continuing historical problem of Napoleonic war.

ॐ

It would not be difficult, and could be quite amusing, to enumerate contemporary judgments of Napoleon that were badly off the mark: for instance, that notorious assertion by a senior Prussian officer during the last year of the old monarchy: "His Prussian Majesty is served by any number of generals the equal of the Emperor Napoleon"—a statement that may strike us as redolent of the arrogance and blindness of the old order. But I shall follow the less entertaining tack of asking what might cause an experienced soldier to make such a grotesque statement. And a provisional answer might be that at least before 1805, before Ulm and Austerlitz, it was not unreasonable for qualified, if perhaps unimaginative, observers to regard Napoleon as merely one among a number of competent and lucky French commanders. However impressive the outcome of his campaigns, none of the elements that made them up seemed particularly novel. His tactics were those of the later revolutionary armies, which the Prussians had checked in the Rhineland and Alsace. His practice of enveloping the opposing front, or breaking through it, belonged to the staple of generalship the world over. Finally, the strategy of operating on interior lines (according to Jomini, the key to the understanding of the emperor's victories) was in Berlin considered almost a Prussian specialty ever since Frederick the Great during the Seven Years' War had demonstrated what might be made of Prussia's central position. As Jean Colin wrote seventy-five years ago, in what remains one of the most searching analyses of Napoleonic warfare in the literature: "If we take any of the most brilliant of Napoleon's projects, and compare with them the corresponding plans of his adversaries, we shall hardly perceive any difference. What decided victory was the manner of execution, the promptitude in [decisions] and movement."[1] But the speed with which decisions were made and carried out, as well as other essentials of the emperor's system—mutual support among the larger subordinate commands, the holding back of strong reserves for the decisive attack or counterattack—had not yet been sufficiently documented and analyzed to have become generally recognized.

The ultimate reason, however, for the interpretive fuzziness that characterized much of professional opinion was the fact that Napoleon had not made his appearance in a stable military environment. His was not the case of a victorious commander who after a brilliantly innovative campaign suddenly towers above the familiar military landscape. Rather he was one of many generals swept along on a flood of change that engulfed Europe. It is preferable not to attach grandiose labels to historical processes, but the upheaval in war that occurred in the 1790s—both in its techniques and in its goals—was sufficiently severe and far-reaching to deserve the name revolution. The military world was challenged to query its assumptions and institutions, to rethink its methods. From our own experience with the development of the atom bomb we know how difficult it is to master such a basic transformation intellectually. After 1945 many people in this country at first claimed that conventional war was a thing of the past. For a time the doctrine of massive retaliation dominated American strategic thought, to be succeeded by the concept of flexible response and the tragically illusory fashion of unconventional, politico-

---

[1] Jean Colin, *The Transformations of War* (London, 1912), 253–54, 290.

military operations, until more realistic syntheses of the old and the new were at last developed. The task of understanding the new forces of war was at least as difficult in the 1790s as it proved to be in the 1950s and 1960s. It might be useful to devote a few words to this general issue before returning to Napoleon.

I

The most powerful impetus that the revolution in war received from the French Revolution came through the break-up of corporative society. The elimination of privilege enabled the French government to impose conscription in the service of a national ideal. Conscription created the large armies that became the mainstay of the new warfare. These numbers necessitated, or made possible on a large scale, changes in organization, in methods of supply, in discipline and training—all of which increased the tempo and range of operations; and further, changes in tactics and in the function and frequency of battle in the strategic design. The result was not an entirely new kind of war, but war became more complex and less predictable than it had been since the beginning of the century. It became more destructive, and political goals of unheard-of magnitude were now within its reach. Clausewitz, looking back on these developments, commented that "it cannot be expected that the great changes that occurred were immediately understood, and at once led to new policies." But, he added, in reference to Prussian overconfidence, by 1806 people "might have come to realize that a war with the new France would be a war not only against a government, but also against a people, and therefore a struggle of life and death."[2]

How men reacted to these great changes depended, of course, not only on their intellectual and psychological readiness to perceive and understand.[3] Between 1792 and 1815, Europe experienced scarcely four years of relative peace, and the student of war rarely enjoyed the luxury of standing at a distance from his subject. If he was French, he tried to make the new methods work; if he was a foreigner he tried to defend himself against them, or could expect to become their next target. Because analysts were motivated less by the wish to understand in the abstract than by the need to perfect innovation, or to counter it, their particular social

[2] Carl von Clausewitz, *Nachrichten über Preussen in seiner grossen Katastrophe; Kriegsgeschichtliche Einzelschriften* (Berlin, 1888), 10:469.

[3] For this and the following, compare the fuller discussion in my essay, "Revolutions in Warfare: An Earlier Generation of Interpreters," in *National Security and International Stability*, ed. Bernard Brodie, Michael D. Intriligator, and Roman Kolkowicz (Cambridge, Mass., 1983).

and political environment often warped their interpretations. Without descending into the technical minutiae of military history it is possible to outline one example of the impact the environment might have: the foreign reaction to skirmishing, which during the second half of the 1790s became an integral part of French infantry tactics.[4]

Skirmishing demanded a degree of independence and initiative on the part of the soldier that could not easily be accommodated by the discipline and tactics of such services as the Russian, British, or Prussian. Not surprisingly, it was difficult for observers to reach an accurate appraisal of skirmishing, if its adoption by their own forces would require fundamental changes in their system of recruiting, in the relationship between officers and men, and in a recasting of tactical doctrine—to say nothing of its impact on society. Many officers, therefore, were tempted to dismiss skirmishing as the unwanted result of the French having to fight with half-trained men—which had, indeed, been a factor in its early history.

The picture presented by innovation was further blurred by the fact that the changes did not emerge full-blown, but were gradual and ongoing. For example, the new French supply system, which relied heavily on living off the country, could be misinterpreted as the outcome of unsettled conditions, which eventually would be replaced by a return to more traditional ways.

Even more important, the continued success of old methods impeded understanding of the new. It was not the case, after all, that innovation triumphed everywhere and triumphed easily. For example, to mention an obvious instance of the persistent vigor of the old system, the British army, throughout the Napoleonic wars, remained an eighteenth century force, faithfully reflecting the stable class structure of its society. At the time it could easily be overlooked that the British fought only limited campaigns and never attempted to create an army on the continental scale. Had they done so, Michael Howard suggests, they would have had to take the French model more seriously, which, in turn, would have had far-reaching implications for their own society.[5] As it was, the spectacle of the British line defeating French skirmishers and attack columns called the validity of the new into question.

To sum up, the changes of the 1790s were so diverse that they affected most areas of war. But the value of each innovation was difficult to appraise since the observer received confusing, incomplete, contradictory messages. Often he had to tailor his evaluation to meet crises that were approaching or already upon him. Political and social constraints might

---

[4] I have analyzed this issue in detail in my *Yorck and the Era of Prussian Reform* (Princeton, 1966).

[5] Michael Howard, *War in European History* (Oxford, 1976), 88–89.

further cloud his view. It may be the case that soldiers who favored or were prepared to accept political and social change on the whole reached a clearer understanding of the new warfare, and reached it sooner, than did defenders of the status quo. Certainly the politics of the more radical military reformers in Prussia enhanced their ability to recognize, interpret, and counter the new forces in war.

II

Where did Napoleon figure in this mass of phenomena? Today we know that early on he understood the energies for war that the revolution had generated in France. He was among the first systematically to employ these resources and the new techniques that gave them form against opponents who still lacked them. Once these methods or their practical equivalents were acquired by his adversaries, the Napoleonic system sputtered and failed, which suggests the relative significance of the man and the new forces. But in the 1790s it was still difficult to isolate him from the many political and military elements that provided the dynamic of French expansion into Italy and Central Europe. Only gradually could Napoleon be seen more clearly, and then, for many, he came to personify the tremendous changes that were taking place.

Bülow was among those writers who took Napoleon as the measure of modern war, a correlation he developed in several widely read books that appeared from the late 1790s on. Even the emperor's early career struck him as exemplary. He himself had failed to make his way in the Prussian service, and he now delighted in scaring his former comrades with the specter of the Jacobin who would smash the sham perfection of the Prussian system. Professional German soldiers, he declared, regarded Napoleon as an irritating embarrassment, a general who waged unmannerly wars. Instead they should recognize him for the giant he was, "the emperor of emperors."[6] At times Bülow felt that he himself could defeat Napoleon; but since his talents were ignored, he thought the best prospect for Europe lay in accepting what he called—perhaps sarcastically—the enlightened and gentle domination of France.

It would be difficult to find a more admiring student of Napoleon anywhere; but how accurate were Bülow's perceptions of his generalship? Two explanatory principles inform his writings: one, that Napoleon was

---

[6] Heinrich Dietrich von Bülow, "Der Feldzug von 1805," (1806), reprinted in *Militärische und vermischte Schriften von . . . Bülow*, ed. Eduard Bülow and Wilhelm Rüstow (Leipzig, 1853), 90, 491.

a genius; the other, that the reasons for his opponents' failures should be sought in themselves—an explanation that in this context rather contradicts the first. According to Bülow, the institutions and methods of the Prussian army failed to meet the demands of modern war; its soldiers had all initiative drilled out of them; its tactics remained in a linear straight jacket; a strategy of rapid movement was neither desired nor possible. This critique had much to commend it, but Bülow pushed it to fantastic conclusions. The sweep of French armies through Europe so impressed him that he believed strategy now counted for more than battle, and in his later books he went so far as to claim that battles had become outdated: "Battles are no longer decisive," he wrote in 1805; "battles will no longer be fought. Instead the enemy will be outmaneuvered."[7]

It was in the same spirit of eighteenth century methodical warfare that Bülow argued that the success of an offensive depended largely on the angle formed by two lines running from the outer limits of the base of operations to its objective. If the base was suitably placed and sufficiently extended for the lines to converge on the objective at an angle of ninety degrees or more, victory was as certain as could reasonably be assured. Bülow went to extremes to demonstrate that Napoleon's campaigns did, in fact, follow this principle. We might say that he interpreted the emperor as the supreme military geometrician. At the same time he praised him as a genius who disregarded the rules of ordinary men. What Bülow meant by genius was precisely this triumphant disregard. In language reminiscent of the German dramatists of the Sturm und Drang, he proclaimed that genius smashed all rules. It was a boundless, violent force shattering every law, sufficient unto itself. While this was not a bad appraisal of some of Napoleon's traits, it completely ignored his professionalism, his concern for detail, his careful calculation of time and space— let alone his understanding of, rather than disdain for, the mundane facts of power.

Bülow was probably the best-known German writer on military affairs in the decade before Jena. The mix of insight and error in his books, the superstructure of avant-garde rhetoric rising from what fundamentally were old-fashioned views, suggest how difficult it must have been for Napoleon's contemporaries to progress from a recognition of some of the new features of war to an understanding of all, and to a sense of their interdependence and interaction.

[7] Wilhelm Rüstow, "Einleitung," ibid., 124, 131. See also Heinrich Dietrich von Bülow, "Geist des neuern Kriegssystems" (1799 and 1805), reprinted ibid., 255–57; and "Der Feldzug von 1805," ibid., 502. Compare further Bülow, *Lehrsätze des neuern Krieges* (Berlin, 1805), xii: "Schlachten werden heutigen Tages nicht mehr geliefert," as well as 303, 306–7, 657; and *Neue Taktik der Neuern wie sie seyn sollten* (Leipzig, 1805), 2:166–68.

III

Bülow's very controversial writings evoked many responses, among them, in 1805, a long, critical essay by the twenty-five-year-old Carl von Clausewitz—his first publication.[8] Clausewitz dismissed most of Bülow's theories as illogical or developed from inaccurate evidence. Especially interesting for our purpose was his rejection of Bülow's use of the concept of genius. By itself, Clausewitz said, the term explained nothing. For Bülow to hold that genius was above all rules meant either that Bülow had got the rules wrong or that he was abdicating before a phenomenon he could not understand. To make sense of war, not only quantifiable factors had to be analyzed, but also such less easily measured phenomena as political intentions, morale of the army, the psychology of the commander. The analyst should neither seek to eliminate the irrational from war, as many eighteenth century theorists had tried to do, nor throw up his hands and surrender to it.[9] Twenty-five years later, in *On War*, Clausewitz repeated his attack on Bülow and like-minded theorists: "Anything that could not be reached by [their] meager wisdom . . . was held to be beyond scientific control: it lay in the realm of genius which rises above all rules." On the contrary, he added, "what genius does is the best rule, and theory can do no better than show how and why this should be the case."[10]

Clausewitz's own interpretation of Napoleon went several steps beyond Bülow's. Today we might not find it entirely persuasive. He neither had enough information, nor was sufficiently detached from his subject. However much he sought understanding for its own sake, first, above all, he wanted to learn how to defeat the emperor. But on this immediate practical level his analysis made sense—we might even say it worked.

The main reason for the strength of his interpretation—which owed much to Scharnhorst and other members of the reform party—was that it took its origin in the study not of the man but of his environment: the French Revolution. What impressed the reformers above all was that it was the revolution that had given Napoleon the weapons with which he defeated the old monarchies—the same weapons the reformers now wanted to introduce to Prussia.

To his admiration of the revolutionary achievement, Clausewitz added two further interpretive components: an extremely positive analysis of

---

[8] [Carl von Clausewitz], "Bemerkungen über die reine und angewandte Strategie des Herrn von Bülow," *Neue Bellona* 9, no. 3 (1805).

[9] Ibid., 98. For a fuller discussion of Clausewitz's critique of Bülow, see my *Clausewitz and the State*, rev. ed. (Princeton, 1985), 91–94.

[10] *On War*, trans. and ed. Michael Howard and Peter Paret, rev. ed. (Princeton, 1984), Book II, chap. 2, p. 136.

Napoleon as military commander; and a skeptical, even harsh analysis of his personality. In 1805 he described him as a latter-day Roman, but more tyrannical, and therefore in the end less successful.[11] The emperor's need to dominate, he thought, was accompanied by a willingness to gamble, which eventually would betray him. He suspected that Napoleon fought not merely to implement his policies, but that he liked war for its own sake. With Gneisenau he agreed that peace with such a man could never be more than an armistice. Coexistence was impossible; he would have to be defeated.

A long, very favorable evaluation of the technical and intellectual elements of Napoleon's generalship could be assembled from Clausewitz's writings, and since interest in these two men continues unabated, it is surprising that such a compilation does not yet exist. But although the emperor's greatness was beyond question for Clausewitz, he also pointed to some weaknesses, which he associated with flaws in his personality: Napoleon's unwillingness to moderate his policies; his reluctance to delegate authority; his failure to train subordinates who could act on their own within his grand design. The difficulties he experienced in coordinating the large armies of the later empire gave his enemies the opportunity to oppose the autocratic but increasingly handicapped emperor not with a leader of similar stature, but with a network of commanders and staff officers not yet acting according to a generally held doctrine but each directing his particular force in the pursuit of an agreed-on plan.

It is interesting to trace the gradual spread of the belief that while Napoleon was undoubtedly the most dangerous soldier of the age, his system of command was severely flawed. We find this idea expressed in any number of Prussian and Russian memoranda before and during the invasion of Russia, and of course it served as the basis of Allied practice in the fall of 1813: to retreat before any army the emperor himself led, while advancing against armies commanded by his marshals, a policy that resulted in the battle of Leipzig and the final collapse of French power east of the Rhine.

These remarks have mainly addressed the issue of weaker men trying to understand a stronger one. I might have said: men of lesser ability analyzing someone far abler than they; but that would not have been quite the point. Napoleonic war, after all, was not an evenly matched contest, with one side favored by a superlative commander; rather this supremely gifted commander, until late in the day, led the stronger battalions. Just as Hitler—had he been a citizen of, say, Albania—could never have become more than a local nuisance, so Napoleon's glory was dependent on

[11] Carl von Clausewitz, "Aufzeichnungen aus den Jahren 1803 bis 1809," in Hans Rothfels, *Carl von Clausewitz: Politik und Krieg,* 2d ed. (Bonn, 1980), 202.

the human and economic resources of the most powerful country in Europe. His ability to regularize, make permanent, the revolutionary exploitation of French energies, which enabled him almost always to begin a conflict from strength, was as much a part of his system as maneuvering on interior lines or concentrating his reserves for the decisive breakthrough.

In theory, weakness may not inhibit understanding. But if to understand the enemy's capabilities means to recognize the hopelessness of one's own situation—which was the Prussian case in 1806—then most men will probably shrink from realistic conclusions. His victim's psychological as well as intellectual and political barriers to perception made Napoleon even more dangerous than he would have been in any case. But as he squandered his resources reaching for unattainable goals, as he found himself unable to prevent potential adversaries from drawing together, the balance of strength shifted. With adequate resources, the Allies began to master the new realities of war; and this pragmatic mastery—though still encumbered with false theories and human inadequacy—is itself perception of a kind. At the end, Napoleon remains a genius—either Bülow's giant towering above all rules, or, as Clausewitz saw him more accurately, a man who harmoniously combines universal human qualities raised to exceptional power. But now that he faces opponents whose resources exceed his, we can almost believe that—not in his fantasies but in his actions—he has become what ten years' earlier the reactionary or obtuse Prussian officer said he was: merely one among a number of competent generals.

6

JENA AND AUERSTEDT

AS A BOY, when I began to explore my parents' books, two kinds of reading interested and puzzled me equally. One was the description of paintings by art historians. I checked text against image, speculated on reasons for a description to begin in one place in the picture rather than another, and tried to understand why some aspects of the work were emphasized while others were merely mentioned or even left out altogether. When I attempted to write a description myself I found that to include everything led to nothing but muddle. But even the texts of the art historians were very different from the paintings they described. It was an early object lesson in the scholar's need to delete and an even more compelling lesson in the limitation of all descriptions and interpretations, of all scholarship.

The other kind of text that fascinated and mystified me was the description of battles. This seemed still more demanding than art history because the reality of the object under study was not present even in the distorting form of photographic reproduction. Maps were not an adequate substitute. The rectangles and squares that were superimposed on outlines of terrain features seemed not only maddeningly abstract, they never fully conformed to the written accounts; and yet map and text claimed to address the same event.

Some years later, in the southwest Pacific during the Second World War, I traced the stages of an engagement after it had run its course but found that even as a participant I could never fully reconstruct so much as a skirmish. In the larger perspective, certainly, most details of an engagement were unimportant. What really mattered was known: the outcome and how and at what cost it had been achieved. But if a skirmish in all its confusion stood for reality in general, the obscurity that enveloped an event as soon as it occurred could not be simply dismissed.

Ever since, I have been skeptical of accounts of battle. I recall the offense I caused many years ago when in reviewing a book on Napoleonic war I recommended that all passages dealing with combat be printed in a different color so that readers would know at once that they were entering treacherous territory. Before I wrote the review I already had my own experience with the genre. Cyril Falls, the recently retired Chichele Professor of the History of War at Oxford, asked me to write an essay for a volume he was editing. The subject was the campaign in which Napoleon crushed the Prussian army in 1806. The literature was somewhat conflict-ing—Clausewitz, himself a participant, wrote two rather differing analy-ses two decades apart—but in the brief space I was given I could not at-tempt a reinterpretation. But an account of the campaign that balanced opposing claims might be linked with brief discussions of its causes and implications. In the book, my essay was accompanied by two maps. These are missing here. In their place I have added a few words to help the reader see the relations between politics and the geography of the cam-paign more clearly. In particular, it was a political fact—that after the war of 1805 French troops remained in southern Germany—that enabled Na-poleon the following year to launch his offensive not from France but almost due north, passing the Prussian army and turning west against it. The result was an envelopment on the grandest scale, pushing the Prus-sian army away from Berlin and possible Russian help and ending with the opposing armies facing each other with fronts reversed.

∂⬤

The Jena campaign, which led to the total defeat of the Prussian monar-chy, is generally viewed as an encounter between two epochs, in which the old order collapsed before the drive and energy of the new. In the Napoleonic era the state of Frederick the Great was found wanting; but the events of 1806 are misunderstood unless it is recognized that, even as she fell, Prussia evinced great tenacity, while her conquerors were not as surefooted as the grandeur of their triumph might suggest. That the two powers were of unequal strength should also be noted, but it was the way in which Napoleon coordinated the political and military means at hand that proved decisive. The Grande Armée had more than half won the battles of Jena and Auerstedt before the opening shot was fired, and the climactic 14 October proved of smaller significance than its aftermath.

In 1805 Prussia had remained aloof from the Third Coalition until the chance for successful common action was past, and by her indecision had made the Austerlitz campaign possible. The rearrangement of Germany's political map that now followed worked increasingly to her disadvantage. Austria was temporarily enfeebled; Napoleon's south-German allies gained in strength; Prussia herself was induced to cede her possessions in the South and West, and given leave in return to occupy Hanover, which predictably led to war with Great Britain. Her isolation would have been complete but for her alliance with Saxony and the covert support ex-tended by Russia; but Alexander's armies were still refitting, and in the meantime Napoleon's domination of Germany posed a growing threat to the independence of the state. By the summer of 1806 French pressure had become extreme and, though it would have been wiser to postpone an open break until the Russians could again operate in central Europe, Frederick William mobilized. Fear of the consequence of further passivity and a remnant of faith in the heritage of the Great Frederick pushed the monarchy into disaster. Until the very end there was no formal declaration of war; during August and September Prussian columns gradually moved south, the king and his commander-in-chief, the duke of Brunswick, hoping to the last that Napoleon would negotiate.

After the campaign of 1805 the Grande Armée had not returned to France, but taken up quarters along the Rhine and in southern Germany. Only the Guards had accompanied the emperor to Paris. When it became apparent that Prussian military preparations were in earnest, the thirty-seven hundred men of the Guards Grenadiers and Chasseurs were hurriedly loaded on wagons and transported in relays to the Rhine, where they arrived on 28 September. The regiments had already begun to leave their garrisons; the emperor now accelerated their concentration toward the northeast. By the first week of October the corps were assembled in lower Bavaria and began to penetrate the wooded hills that barred the approaches to Saxony and Prussia. The positions and intentions of the enemy could not be estimated with assurance, but lack of information was not permitted to hinder the troops' rapid deployment.

Napoleon's plan of campaign hinged on mobilizing the greatest force possible and then creating an opportunity for its exploitation by advancing on Berlin. Any Prussian move would be interrupted by the need to defend the capital, and once the armies met, French numerical superiority should decide the issue. Under the circumstances, an offensive from any quarter promised success; but an advance from the west would have pushed the Prussians back on Berlin and toward possible Russian assistance, while an offensive from the south could be launched more rapidly and stood the chance of separating the enemy from his capital and the Russian border.

The Grande Armée advanced in three columns on parallel roads separated by one to two days' march. In the center, on the Bamberg-Leipzig highway, moved Bernadotte's I Corps, Murat's cavalry, III Corps under Davout, Imperial headquarters and the Guards—together seventy thousand men. On the road from Bayreuth to Plauen to their right marched the fifty thousand men of IV and VI Corps, commanded by Soult and Ney; to their left, on the Bamberg-Coburg-Saalfeld road, marched the somewhat weaker V and VII Corps under Lannes and Augereau. Together these 160,000 troops formed what Napoleon termed a gigantic battalion square, able to deploy either to the front or flank, each division ready to engage the enemy until others could come to its support. The advance was not without its dangers. During the first stage, until the river

Saale was reached, the units were dispersed over an area thirty miles across and fifty miles deep, in terrain that was difficult for cavalry and transport. Few lateral connections between the three roads made it uncertain that a corps, if attacked, could be supported in time. Particularly the left column, weakest of the three and closest to the Prussians, afforded opportunities to an energetic opponent. But the potential advantages of the flank march outweighed its risks, which an overall superiority in numbers made it the easier to accept.

The Prussians had decided to forestall the expected attack by rapidly moving south against the Main, with the hope of defeating the French divisions piecemeal before they could combine. This scheme soon proved to be inoperable. Limited manpower and a fatal tendency to cover every exposed point resulted in scarcely 120,000 troops being available for offensive operations, a total that included eighteen thousand Saxons. The mobilization of this inferior force proceeded too slowly. When the army reached the northern slopes of the Thuringian Hills at the end of September, the enemy was already massed in Bavaria, and the opportunity for surprise was lost. The following week was given over to councils of war. By 8 October the main army of fifty-three thousand men, which the king accompanied, and Rüchel's corps still occupied the districts between Eisenach and Erfurth. Twenty-five miles away, along the Saale, stood Prince Hohenlohe's forty-three thousand men, and smaller detachments were scattered from Meiningen in the South to Magdeburg in the North. Both Brunswick and Hohenlohe remained well to the west of Napoleon's line of advance; only a weak detachment under Tauenzien observed the French approach on the right bank of the Saale, where on the morning of the ninth it was attacked by Bernadotte's forward units and severely mauled.

The king, his commanding generals and their staffs could not decide whether Napoleon should be met head-on, whether the army should take up a flanking position on the left bank of the Saale, or whether it should retreat north to join its reserves and make a stand on the Elbe. At last they determined to concentrate all forces left of the river near Jena and there await further developments. Few officers, even those who still held to the military ways of the ancien régime, felt confident with this temporizing; some were certain that it spelled the end of the army. But even the most progressive among them had not been in combat for over a decade—unlike their opponents, they knew Napoleonic warfare only from study. Not that modern concepts wholly dominated on the French side: in particular there was frequent failure in reconnaissance and communication, and occasionally inadequate staff work, for which the emperor himself was to blame since he attempted to do too much himself. But such flaws were made good by a pervasive energy, by the instinctive understanding of thousands of veteran soldiers led by a man who recognized the essentials of the problem he faced and who would allow no side issue to distract either himself or his subordinates from its solution.

On the morning of the tenth, while Tauenzien withdrew toward Jena after his skirmish with Bernadotte, Lannes reached the Saale and immediately attacked Hohenlohe's advance guard on the left bank of the river near Saalfeld. The Prussian commander, Prince Louis Ferdinand, a nephew of Frederick the Great, delayed his retreat too long; his positions were enveloped, and he was killed. The news of his defeat and death further lowered Prussian morale, which was already affected by fatigue and loss of confidence. Everywhere the lack of a strong hand was apparent. Commanders and staff officers went without sleep attending to trifles, while needless marches and countermarches exhausted the men, some of whom had not drawn rations for days. On the eleventh a panic broke out among the troops stationed in Jena; the next day the Saxon contingent threatened to leave unless it was assured of a daily issue of bread. Little of this became known to the French. Napoleon remained in doubt over Prussian positions and plans, though he imagined Brunswick to be withdrawing north to the Elbe, and he continued his march northeast to head him off. Not until the twelfth did he realize that significant Prussian forces still stood between Erfurth and Weimar. He was outflanking what appeared to be a large part of the main Prussian army. By turning against it he might maneuver or push it away from its lines of communication to Magdeburg and Berlin. He had succeeded in concentrating an enormous amount of military power in an area from which it endangered the very existence of the Prussian state. The opportunity he sought had come. He swung his right column and the cavalry reserve west toward Jena, which was already being approached from the south by Lannes and Augereau. Meanwhile, he ordered Davout north to Naumburg, barely 115 miles southwest of Berlin, where he would threaten the Prussian flank and rear. He also directed Bernadotte to a central position at Dornburg, from which he could support either Davout or the main force. The Prussians finally recognized their peril and decided to march north. Brunswick quit Weimar for Auerstedt, while Hohenlohe remained opposite Jena on the left bank of the Saale with orders not to be drawn into serious fighting until the Royal Army had passed the Unstrut. When Napoleon entered the town on the thirteenth he believed he was about to attack the assembled Prussian forces. Hohenlohe, in turn, arguing that Napoleon would be at Naumburg to interject himself between the Prussians and Berlin, thought until well after the battle of Jena had begun that he was engaged only by a detached corps.

Opposite Jena the left bank of the Saale rises steeply to a plateau dotted with villages and woods and cut by valleys to the north and south. On the morning of the fourteenth Hohenlohe's main body consisting of Grawert's division and the Saxons still faced south along the Weimar-Jena road over which Rüchel's corps of some fifteen thousand men was slowly approaching. An outcropping of the plateau toward Jena—the Landgrafenberg—had been occupied by Lannes against slight opposition; access to the open ground beyond was barred by the thin line of Tauenzien's battalions, their left flank and rear covered by a detachment of five thousand men under Holtzendorff. A personal reconnaissance on the afternoon of the thirteenth convinced Napoleon that his first task must be to gain sufficient space on the plateau to permit deployment of large forces. During the night of the thirteenth to fourteenth he hurried the remainder of Lannes's corps up the Landgrafenberg, and before sunrise the following morning, with the fog still thick on the ground, he gave the order to attack. In coordinated moves, Augereau in the south and Soult in the north penetrated the valleys that flanked the forward part of the plateau. By 9 A.M. the villages of Lützeroda and Closewitz had been taken and room was made for the deployment of the regiments that were starting to arrive from the other side of the river. The next French objective was Vierzehnheiligen, a village one and a half miles west of Closewitz. Skirmishers advanced over the rolling ground and were engaged by Prussian light troops, while to their right the retreating Tauenzien was slowly followed by Saint-Hilaire's division, itself for a time heavily engaged by Holtzendorff, who had come down on its flank. By 10:30 he too was forced to withdraw. It was an indication of the gradual breakdown of Prussian operational control that instead of turning behind Vierzehnheiligen where intense fighting was now in progress, Holtzendorff continued to Stobra and Apolda, removing his command from further participation in the battle.

Hohenlohe and his chief of staff, Massenbach, had only reluctantly realized that they were involved in an all-out fight. When soon after daybreak Grawert wheeled his division left to face the sound of the guns, he had to convince his superior of the need for this change. By eight, however, Hohenlohe had come to sense some of the gravity of his position and sent the first of a series of messages to Rüchel, urging him to hurry. He seems never to have entertained seriously the possibility of withdrawing toward Brunswick's army in accordance with his mission to act as flank and rear guard. Instead he busied himself like a regimental officer arranging Grawert's battalions for an attack on Vierzehnheiligen, now occupied by units of V Corps and light infantry of Ney's advance guard, which had reached the plateau. The fog had lifted by ten, and the attack started under a bright autumn sky. As the Prussians moved forward they received scattered musket fire. Soon they could hear the cries of the tirailleurs pointing out officers to each other, but casualties did not slow the advance. The French were wavering and the moment to fell bayonets was at hand, when the lines were halted, possibly to give Rüchel's men time to arrive. The charge could not have won the day, but possession of Vier-zehnheiligen would at least have given the Prussians a more favourable defensive position; as it was the battalions stood on open ground for the next two hours, firing volley after volley at an all but invisible enemy and slowly being reduced to cinders. In the meantime the build-up of French strength continued. Shortly past noon the emperor had at his disposal more than eighty thousand men; Hohenlohe retained less than thirty thousand, and Rüchel still had not arrived. The sky had clouded again from the intense gunfire when Soult began to envelop the Prussians from the north, while in the south Desjardin's division forced a wedge between them and the Saxons. By 1 P.M. the French advanced everywhere, and the Prussian and Saxon formations were breaking when Rüchel finally appeared. Instead of deploying defensively behind the Werlitz ditch to give Hohenlohe a chance to reform, Rüchel advanced in battalion eche-lons against the oncoming French tide. In half an hour the attack had been smashed, Rüchel himself was shot through the chest, and his deci-mated battalions joined the thousands of fugitives streaming back to Wei-mar in almost total dissolution. A battle that could not be won was lost more fully than need be because Hohenlohe fragmented his strength and wasted it in unrelated attacks against an opponent who not only had ac-cumulated greatly superior force but knew how to coordinate its use. Nevertheless the victory had not been easy—one French division lost nearly a quarter of its strength, and other units also suffered badly.

At about the time Grawert's battalions were beginning to give way, the main Prussian army fifteen miles to the north was turned back in its at-tempt to regain its lines of communication. During the night Napoleon had ordered Davout at Naumburg to return south by way of Apolda and operate against the left flank of the Prussians behind Jena. Bernadotte was given the option of joining Davout or continuing to Dornburg; he chose the latter and thus took no part in the battle that followed. His motives have been questioned, but at the time neither he nor Davout realized that the enemy columns moving north were anything more than an advance guard.

The Royal Army had bivouacked near Auerstedt during the night of the thirteenth to the fourteenth and continued its march northeast by day-break. The commanding officers had failed to secure the defiles towards Naumburg where French troops were known to be, and proved incapable of bringing tactical cohesion to the units that were strung out for miles along a single road. At 7 A.M., in dense fog, the leading squadron of the Prussian advance guard encountered fire near the village of Hassen-hausen. Both sides hurried troops forward and a pitched battle developed, with the front soon extending hundreds of yards north and south of the village as Davout and Brunswick attempted to envelop each other's position. Scharnhorst, the duke's chief of staff, took charge of the left flank; soon afterwards Brunswick was shot through both eyes, and with the king hesitating to assume command operations quickly degenerated into a mass of uncoordinated local engagements. Davout, though hard-pressed, was able to retain control of the battle. The climax came at 10:30. The French left had been partly surrounded and Hassenhausen was evacuated when the First Division under Morand reached the front in double time, stopped the enemy's forward movement, and in turn advanced beyond the village. This committed Davout's entire corps while the two Prussian reserve divisions had not yet seen action. A counterattack would at least have stabilized the situation; but Frederick William had lost heart and decided to break off the battle. The Prussians withdrew in fair order, followed by French cavalry but not by the exhausted infantry—in ten hours of fighting Davout's corps had lost over 25 percent killed and wounded. But now the Prussian cause suffered a final disaster. Instead of swinging north by way of Buttstädt to gain the Elbe, the king panicked and turned southwest to rejoin Hohenlohe. He was still unaware of the catastrophe at Jena, but under the best of circumstances this move was fatal since it took the army away from Berlin and deep into the French embrace. When news arrived of Hohenlohe's defeat during the night the direction of the retreat was changed first to Erfurth, then to Sommerda. By morning the Royal Army had ceased to exist as a fighting force.

Nothing is more characteristic of Napoleonic warfare—its inadequate reconnaissance, the occasional lack of cooperation and even of competence among subordinates, and at the same time its almost universal energy and the magnificent sense of purpose in the center—than the pursuit now launched by the emperor. After his twin defeats the enemy was not allowed to recover. With Blücher's surrender on the Baltic coast three weeks later Prussian resistance west of the Oder and Neisse ceased. To be sure, the war continued through the spring of 1807 in Silesia and East Prussia, but Napoleon's triumph appeared complete. And yet the true victors of the Jena campaign were not the French. As the destruction of the Holy Roman Empire proved to be a long step forward toward the unification of Germany, so the destruction of the old Prussian army was the necessary condition for the reforms that now began, and that after a few years turned the lessons against the master from whom they had been learned.

PART TWO

CLAUSEWITZ

7

CLAUSEWITZ: LIFE AND THOUGHT

T HE MOST IMPORTANT ESSAY on Clausewitz published in this country was written during the Second World War by Hans Roth-fels for a collection of essays by different authors, *Makers of Modern Strategy*, a book that soon became famous. As a young man Rothfels studied history at the University of Freiburg, where his principal teacher was the historian of ideas Friedrich Meinecke. His studies were interrupted by the First World War, in which he served in the German army and was severely wounded, suffering the loss of a leg. In 1920 an expanded version of his dissertation on the development of Clausewitz's thought until 1815 appeared; two years later he published a selection of Clausewitz's political writings and letters, which for the first time firmly placed Clausewitz in the ranks of significant political thinkers in the German past. Between 1926 and 1934 Rothfels taught at the University of Königsberg, until a student mob closed down his lectures because he was Jewish. He emigrated to England and then to this country, where he taught first at Brown and then at Chicago. In 1951 he returned to Germany as professor of modern history at the University of Tübingen.

The interpretation of Clausewitz's theories by this knowledgeable and sophisticated scholar raised Clausewitz studies to a new level in this country and established a standard for all subsequent work in the field. Rothfels's essay in *Makers of Modern Strategy* was among those that helped make the volume a classic in the literature on the history of war. When some forty years later I was asked to bring out a revised and expanded edition that would take account of events and research since the early 1940s, I hoped to be able to retain Rothfels's essay. But like most of the volume, it proved to be too strongly oriented on concerns of its time. Clausewitz's ideas are measured against the unfolding events of the Second World War, and Rothfels never had completely shed the romantic and nationalistic view of Clausewitz that had informed his dissertation—a view that reflected widespread attitudes and anxieties in Germany's academic elite in the first years after 1918, when the disastrous war had fatally weakened German society. Because the original *Makers of Modern Strategy*, unlike the new version, lacked a chapter on Napoleon, Rothfels had also found it necessary to expand his essay with an outline of Napoleonic warfare. His essay still repays reading, but for the new *Makers of Modern Strategy*, which appeared in 1986, I replaced it with the essay that follows, which combines an account of Clausewitz's life with analyses of the structure and content of his theories and of the methods by which he arrived at them.

ᏒᎠ

The questions that Clausewitz ultimately sought to answer in his writings—How can we analyze war? What is war?—have come to assume greater importance in the nuclear age than they possessed for his generation. From 1792 to 1815 waves of violence swept across Europe, brought death or suffering to millions, shifted frontiers, but also changed and opened societies. But when the flood receded, no urgent desire to study and explain the cataclysm was left behind. As after every war, men wrote about their experiences and drew what they took to be the lessons for the future; but there was little interest in delving beneath the surface of tactics and strategy to explore the phenomenon of war itself, to study its structure, its internal dynamic, its links with other elements of social existence that might be its causes and that were altered or destroyed under its impact. War continued to be accepted as a permanent force in human existence, whose technical aspects might change over time, but could always be mastered. Clausewitz, too, proceeded on his unusually innovative course of inquiry without a sense of cultural or historical crisis. Today, in the shadow of nuclear proliferation, we cannot escape that sense, and the awareness of the crisis in which we live affects not only our thinking about war in the future but also about war in history. It intensifies our interest in early attempts to understand the nature of violence between states. Clausewitz's most important theoretical work, *On War*, is read more widely today than at any time since it was first published in the 1830s. Probably that is so not only because the book has gradually acquired the aura of a classic, a unique achievement that combines intellectual and aesthetic attributes of the age of Goethe with an uncompromising realism that might be termed modern (if such realism were not rare even now); the book is also read because we hope to find its ideas useful.

Whether war can be understood and, by implication, intellectually mastered and controlled is merely one of several related questions we might ask. Others are: Is war an ethical instrument of foreign policy? Can war be limited, even eliminated? Or, on the other hand, how can war be waged most effectively? In *On War* Clausewitz scarcely addresses the first two of these questions. He was conscious of the ethical problem but dealt with it differently than we would. He regarded war as an extreme but natural expression of policy and never regretted that he himself had fought in seven campaigns. His first war, against the French Republic, he thought a justified if politically and strategically inept defense of Prussian and German interests. The others, against Napoleon, he believed passionately to have been not merely justified but ethically imperative. On the third question—how to fight effectively—he had a great deal to say, much of it no longer relevant, at least not directly so. But after the Napoleonic threat receded, he regarded prescription as secondary to analysis. To devise effective strategic schemes and tactical measures mattered far less to him than to identify the permanent elements of war and come to understand how they function. It is for this reason that *On War* may still be relevant to issues of war and peace facing readers who are separated from the author by the industrial revolution and the military cataclysms of the twentieth century.

The work's relevance is, however, of a particular kind, to be expected of theories that were formulated under conditions very different from our own. Clausewitz liked to compare the study of war with the study of painting; both concern activities that demand specific technical expertise, but whose processes and outcome are not predictable and cannot be mechanically pursued if we strive for important results. Few artists today would read an early nineteenth-century treatise on painting to help them practice their art, or even to gain a theoretical understanding of it. An artist interested in the history and theory of painting may nevertheless read the treatise for its observations and concepts, some perhaps of permanent validity, which he can use to construct his own theories and which might even influence the application of his ideas.

A further example may clarify the point. Some years after the Napoleonic wars had ended, Clausewitz began work on a manuscript on strategy. "My original intention," he commented later, "was to set down my conclusions on the principal elements of this topic in short, precise, compact statements, without concern for system or formal connection. The manner in which Montesquieu dealt with his subject was vaguely in my mind."[1] When he realized that this approach did not suit his tendency of systematic and expansive analysis, he revised the manuscript; when it still left him dissatisfied he abandoned it and used parts as building blocks for a new, longer work, *On War*. But his choice of Montesquieu as a model tells us something of his intentions and also raises a question about the intentions and expectations of his readers. Is it not the case that today we read *The Spirit of the Laws* not with the hope of encountering a comprehensive theory of government that we can make our own, but for different, less immediately utilitarian reasons? On the one hand, we want to become acquainted with a work that has held the interest of readers for

---

[1] Carl von Clausewitz, "Author's Comment" [1818?], *On War*, trans. and ed. Michael Howard and Peter Paret, rev. ed. (Princeton, 1984), 63.

more than two centuries; on the other, we read it to advance our thinking on basic issues of politics, to be stimulated by Montesquieu's ideas and arguments. In the sphere of war, *On War* calls for a similar approach.

Like *The Spirit of the Laws*, Clausewitz's work is a highly personal, in some respects almost autobiographical document, a characteristic that removes it even further from modern varieties of theory. The two books reflect their author's antecedents, their position in society, their professions, such turning points in their lives as Montesquieu's sojourn in England and Clausewitz's in France, their views of history, their political beliefs. Both men develop the generalizations, the high levels of abstraction that give their works lasting value, by pondering and reacting to the specifics of their condition and experience, specifics that are clearly apparent in their work. It will help our understanding of Clausewitz's ideas if we remain alert to his historical environment and to his personal fate.

I

Carl von Clausewitz was born in 1780 in the small town of Burg, seventy miles southwest of Berlin, the fourth and youngest son of bourgeois parents, who claimed nobility on the strength of family tradition. His father, a retired lieutenant who served in the local tax office, was the son of a professor of theology, himself son and grandson of Lutheran pastors; his mother's father managed a royal farm. It was only after the death of Frederick the Great, who in his later years took great pains to keep his officer corps free of commoners, that the army accepted Clausewitz and two of his brothers as officer cadets. All became generals, and in 1827 their noble status was at last attested to by royal order. Together with many other families during this period, the Clausewitzes entered the nobility by way of the church and service in the army or bureaucracy of the expanding Prussian state.

Clausewitz first saw combat as a twelve-year-old, in the campaign that drove the French out of the Rhineland in the winter and spring of 1793. After Mainz had been recaptured in July, his regiment marched south to the Vosges Mountains, where it fought a war primarily of detachments, raids, and ambushes. When the army was demobilized in 1795, Clausewitz returned to Prussia with some understanding of skirmishing and small-unit tactics, in contrast to the majority of infantry officers whose main, almost sole duty in combat was to maintain the close alignment and rapid volleys of their men. Imperceptibly at first, his career began to take a somewhat atypical course. For the next few years he was stationed in a small garrison, a post that nevertheless provided some unusual advantages. His regimental commander was a pioneer of military education in Prussia who organized schools for the children of the rank and file and for the noncommissioned officers and ensigns of his regiment, and who encouraged his junior officers to study professional subjects, literature, and history. In this supportive if provincial environment, Clausewitz progressed sufficiently to apply for admission to the military school in Berlin, and in the summer of 1801, soon after his twenty-first birthday, was accepted to the three-year course.

The school had been recently reorganized by a newcomer to the army, Gerhard von Scharnhorst, who was to play a major role in the history of Prussia and in Clausewitz's life. Scharnhorst, the son of a retired cavalry sergeant, had been a soldier since his sixteenth year, first in a small German principality, then in the Hanoverian army, where he made a name for himself as a gunnery officer and writer on military affairs. After Hanover entered the war against France in 1793, Scharnhorst revealed himself to be an exceptionally enterprising fighting soldier as well. His reputation led to an offer from Prussia of a colonelcy and a patent of nobility, and he transferred to the Prussian service in 1801. Among numerous other duties, he assumed the directorship of the military school in Berlin, soon turning it into one of several channels through which he hoped to introduce modern ideas on war to the Prussian army. Scharnhorst was among the first anywhere to recognize and analyze objectively the interdependence of military innovation and social and political change in the Revolutionary Wars. As he saw it, the problem facing the Central European powers, far weaker than France, was how to appropriate essential components of modernization in time to prevent being overrun by the republic, and he had the self-confidence to believe that he could make the difference in Prussia. No one could have been a better teacher for Clausewitz than this scholarly soldier, who encouraged the young man's theoretical interests while reinforcing his dissatisfaction with the traditionalism of the Prussian army.

In 1804 Clausewitz graduated at the top of his class and was appointed adjutant to Prince August of Prussia. His social and professional horizons expanded. He was frequently at court, where he met Countess Marie Brühl, lady-in-waiting to the queen mother, whom he was to marry some years later. Scharnhorst recommended him to the editor of the most important military journal in Germany, which in 1805 published his first article, a lengthy refutation of the strategic theories of Heinrich Dietrich von Bülow, in those years the most widely read German interpreter of Napoleonic warfare.

Bülow had the great merit of recognizing that the recent changes in war constituted a revolution. But he failed to understand the nature of this revolution; in particular, he could not grasp the new importance of battle. He refused to dismiss the new ways as temporary expedients or anarchy, as some other writers did; instead he searched for mathematical principles that would reveal the rational structure beneath the seemingly chaotic surface. Typical of this effort was his assertion that the appropriateness of a military operation was largely determined by the geometric relationship between its geographic objective and its base. Clausewitz saw war very differently. His article raised three main criticisms, which are worth noting for the light they throw on the distance that separates even the work of an unusually gifted late-Enlightenment theorist like Bülow, who wanted to turn war into a kind of applied mathematics, from the realistic, yet methodologically rigorous approach that Clausewitz was trying to develop.

Above all, Clausewitz objected, Bülow's method was flawed. For example, Bülow defined strategy as "all military movements out of the enemy's cannon range or range of vision," and tactics as "all movements within this range." Clausewitz rejected this distinction as superficial, timebound—because it would be affected by technological change—and irrelevant, because the purpose of the two concepts was left unstated. Instead he proposed definitions that were functional and applied to every war, past, present, and future: "Tactics constitute the theory of the use of armed forces in battle; strategy forms the theory of using battle for the purposes of the war."[2] It hardly needs adding that for Clausewitz the term *use* also meant *threat of use*.

Second, Clausewitz considered Bülow's view of war unrealistic. By basing his analysis on geography and mathematics, Bülow ignored the actions of the enemy and the physical and psychological effects of the fighting. "Strategy, however, is nothing without battle, for battle is the raw material with which it works, the means it employs."[3]

Finally, Clausewitz insisted that any meaningful theory should be able to accommodate—as Bülow's does not—all elements pertaining to its subject. In his urge to understand the use of violence, turn it into a science, and make it predictable, Bülow excluded essential parts of war. A theory of war must address not only elements "that are susceptible to mathematical analysis," distances and angles of approach, for instance, but also such imponderables as the soldiers' morale and the commanders' psychology.[4]

Although Clausewitz, eager to make a name for himself, was not reluctant to show up Bülow's confusions and errors, his major concern was to construct a reliable method with which to test Bülow's and other men's theories, and with which he himself could develop an analysis of war that was intellectually defensible. Underlying his arguments even at this early

---

[2] [Carl von Clausewitz], "Bemerkungen über die reine und angewandte Strategie des Herrn von Bülow," *Neue Bellona* 9, no. 3 (1805): 271.

[3] Ibid.

[4] Ibid., 276.

stage is the interplay between the observable present and hypotheses concerning timeless phenomena of war, which are discovered by historical study, common sense, and logic. He agreed that Bülow's idea of the significance of the geometric relationship between the base of operations and its objective was interesting and might even help explain this or that Napoleonic campaign. But if history demonstrated that campaigns had been won from bases that Bülow thought inadequate and lost with bases that met his requirements, and if logic and common sense as well as history and contemporary reality suggested that an objective need not be stationary, but might be the enemy army, then Bülow's idea could not stand.

Clausewitz welcomed war in 1806 as the only means to check Napoleon's drive to dominate Europe; but he was not confident of victory. The Prussian army was outnumbered, its leadership too divided for Scharnhorst—now chief of staff of the main force—to impose his views; and its organization, administration, and supply, as well as its tactical doctrine, precluded rapid operations. At the battle of Auerstedt, Prince August, in command of a grenadier battalion, and Clausewitz tried to oppose the flexibility of the French with similar tactics, Clausewitz turning one-third of the rank and file into skirmishers. After the battle was lost, the battalion formed part of the rear guard of the retreating army, until it ran out of ammunition and surrendered. As a nephew of the king, Prince August was of some value to Napoleon. The prince and his adjutant were ordered to France, where they were given relative freedom of movement; but it was not until the fall of 1807 that they received permission to return to Prussia.

Apart from his stay in Russia in 1812, these ten months were the only long period in his life that Clausewitz spent outside Germany. It gave him some direct knowledge of French society and culture and the opportunity to see conditions in Prussia from a new intellectual and emotional perspective. His criticism of the attitudes and policies that he blamed for the defeat was harsh: the government had not used war as an instrument of foreign policy but allowed itself to be isolated from prospective allies and then gave its soldiers an impossible task. The army, although antiquated and inefficient, might have achieved more if its leaders had sought battle instead of relying far too long on the efficacy of maneuvering into and out of strong positions. Above all, Prussian society had been inert; the country regarded the war as a matter for the army alone. Because the government had kept society in a condition of passivity and total obedience, it could not tap the population's potential energy and idealism when the crisis came. Only revolutionary changes could now save the state.[5]

[5] See especially Clausewitz's letters to his fiancée between December 1806 and October 1807, in *Karl und Marie von Clausewitz: Ein Lebensbild in Briefen und Tagebuchblättern,*

During the later phases of the war, Scharnhorst had again demonstrated his worth as a fighting soldier and strategic planner, and he became an obvious choice to head a commission to draft plans for the reorganization of the army when the fighting ended. Scharnhorst soon made the commission the center of a new campaign to modernize the country's military institutions, from its manpower policies to the design of muskets and the development of up-to-date operational and tactical doctrines. Opposition was immediate and powerful. Reforms as far-reaching as those Scharnhorst proposed would not only transform the army but affect the country's society and economy, break the nobility's near monopoly on officer positions, and release the rank and file from the bondage of the old, often inhumane system of drill and discipline. The conflict over reform, which really was a struggle over the character of the Prussian state, raged for the next five years. When in the spring of 1808 Clausewitz left occupied Berlin for Königsberg, the temporary seat of the Prussian government, he was soon drawn into the inner circle of reformers, and among conservatives acquired a reputation of possibly dangerous radicalism, which he was to retain for the rest of his life.

At first Scharnhorst employed Clausewitz as a personal assistant. He helped organize secret rearmament measures and wrote articles to explain and defend such socially sensitive innovations as competitive examinations in the selection and promotion of junior officers. When the government returned to Berlin, Clausewitz became the head of Scharnhorst's office, a position that placed him at the center of the reform movement. Through Scharnhorst's influence he was appointed to the general staff and to the faculty of the new war college, where he lectured on strategy and on partisan warfare. In October 1810 he became military tutor to the crown prince, and a few months later joined the commission that drafted new operational and tactical regulations for the infantry and cavalry. The range of his duties over these years gave Clausewitz a rare opportunity to come to know the intellectual, technical, organizational, and political problems of rebuilding an army almost from the ground up.

These new responsibilities did not lessen his earlier interest in the scientific analysis of war. In essays and notes during these years he clarified his ideas on the appropriate goals and procedures of a theory that deals with a complex activity such as war. He distinguished between the cognitive, pedagogic, and utilitarian potential of theory. In the first instance, the function of theory is to structure past and present reality intellectually, to show "how one thing is related to another, and keep the impor-

---

ed. Karl Linnebach (Berlin, 1917), 67–149, and his later history of Prussia during this period, "Observations on Prussia in her great Catastrophe," in Carl von Clausewitz, *Historical and Political Writings*, ed. Peter Paret and Daniel Moran (Princeton, 1992), 30–84.

tant and unimportant separate"; to reach the irreducible elements of the phenomenon of war, and to discover the logical and dynamic links that bind them into comprehensible structures. A theory that is logically and historically defensible, and that reflects present reality, has the pedagogic function of helping the student organize and develop his ideas on war, which he draws from experience, study, and from history—the exploration of the past extends the reality that any one individual can experience. Theory can never lead to complete understanding, which is an impossibility, but it can strengthen and refine judgment. It is not the primary task of theory to generate doctrine, rules, or laws of action. Knowledge and performance are different; but utilitarian benefits may flow from valid theories.

Theory must be comprehensive, that is, it must be able to accommodate all aspects of its subject, whether of the present or of other times. It must be based on the constants or absolutes of its subject, not on phenomena that may be temporary, even if currently these phenomena seem to dominate war. Napoleonic warfare is a temporary phenomenon. Examples of absolutes are the social and political nature of war, and the psychology of the commander. Absolutes serve as the organizing principles of theory. All other phenomena depend on them, and are linked—often indirectly—to each other, links that theory must reveal. Clausewitz noted in 1808 that the opposite of such an intellectual structure, in which a logical place is left for every current or subsequent observation and insight, is the practice of writers like Bülow or Jomini of constructing definitive doctrines around thoughts and recognitions haphazardly arrived at—of generalizing from ideas that have only limited or temporary validity.

Theory must constantly pass the test of reality. In the name of logic it cannot insist on something that is disproved by reality. At any given moment, reality appears narrower than theory; eighteenth-century warfare, for example, does not exhaust all possibilities of war, nor do the campaigns of Napoleon. On the other hand, since reality constantly changes and is marked by imponderables and the unforeseen, no theory can ever completely reflect, let alone explain it. Theory must be sufficiently flexible and open to take account of imponderables, and it must have the potential for further development.[6]

[6] This summary is drawn from such writings during the Reform era as Clausewitz's additions of 1808 and 1809 to an essay on strategy originally written in 1804, published by Eberhard Kessel under the title *Strategie* (Hamburg, 1937); and the essay "Über den Zustand der Theorie der Kriegskunst," published by Walter Schering in his collection of Clausewitz's writings *Geist und Tat* (Stuttgart, 1941). Subsequent restatements and developments of these ideas can be found throughout *On War*, particularly in Books 1, 2, and 8. Note also such passages as: "Our aim is not to provide new principles and methods of conducting war; rather we are concerned with examining the essential content of what has

Many of these ideas were borrowed from the philosophy of German idealism and from the scientific thought of the time, which is not to say that Clausewitz was deeply versed in philosophy. As a young officer he attended introductory lectures on logic and ethics by Johann Gottfried Kiesewetter, a popularizer of Kant. Then and later he read books and articles on mathematics, philosophy, and aesthetic theory, which he came to believe had some relevance to the analysis of war—for instance in its treatment of talent and genius. Above all he drew ideas at second and third hand from his cultural environment: his use of the concept of polarity, for instance—the separation and connection of active and passive, positive and negative, which he employed to analyze the relationship of attack and defense—and his dialectical development of ideas through thesis and antithesis were the common property of educated Germans at the time. But if the components of the theoretical system he formulated during the years of reform were derivative, he was unique in systematically applying these ideas to phenomena that transcendental philosophy would not have regarded as "real," or real only in a naive sense. The reality that Clausewitz wanted to understand was not the abstract reality of pure reason but the actual physical, intellectual, and psychological components of political and military existence.[7]

The outbreak of war between France and Austria in 1809 raised Clausewitz's hopes that Napoleon had at last overreached himself. He applied for an Austrian commission, and only the sudden armistice after the French victory at Wagram kept him in Prussia. Throughout the next years he never entirely renounced the possibility of armed insurrection in Germany. When at the end of 1811 Napoleon forced Prussia to make her territory available to him as a staging area for the invasion of Russia, and to contribute twenty thousand men to the Grande Armée, Clausewitz was among the most outspoken opponents of what he called a surrender that was both unheroic and politically unwise, and with some thirty other officers resigned his commission, a step that confirmed his reputation as a man who put his own values above the policies of the king.

During the war of 1812 he served as a Russian colonel in various staff positions, little more than an observer because he hardly spoke the language. Toward the end of the campaign, however, he grasped the opportunity to strike a blow against the French by helping to persuade the commander of the Prussian auxiliary corps, General von Yorck, to defect

---

long existed, and to trace it back to its basic elements" (Book 6, chap. 8, p. 562); or "We cannot formulate principles, rules, or methods. . . . [Nevertheless] while history may yield no formulae, it does provide an *exercise for judgment*, here as everywhere else" (Book 6, chap. 30, p. 756).

[7] The relationship between Clausewitz's ideas and German philosophy is discussed in my *Clausewitz and the State*, rev. ed. (Princeton, 1985), see particularly 147–208.

from the Grande Armée and neutralize his force. The so-called Convention of Tauroggen that Yorck concluded with the Russian Count Wittgenstein, on whose staff Clausewitz served, not only prevented the French from regrouping at the Russian border but carried the revolutionary message that under certain conditions a Prussian officer's conscience or political judgment took precedence over his oath of obedience.

Clausewitz returned with Yorck to East Prussia, where he drew up a plan for raising the provincial militia—a further act of potential revolutionary import, because twenty thousand men were armed without the king's permission. When Prussia at last joined the war against France in March 1813, Frederick William III repaid Clausewitz for his independence by turning down his request to reenter the Prussian service. Still in Russian uniform, he acted unofficially as Scharnhorst's assistant until Scharnhorst was fatally wounded in the battle of Grossgörschen. In the fall of 1813 he served as chief of staff of a small international force that cleared the French from the Baltic coast. After being at last readmitted to the Prussian army, he was appointed chief of staff of the third corps during the Hundred Days, which by tying down Grouchy's corps at the battle of Wavre prevented it from reinforcing Napoleon at Waterloo.

The suspicion in which Clausewitz was held by conservatives at court and in the army undoubtedly kept him from the more important assignments in which his friends wanted to place him; nevertheless, as the Napoleonic wars drew to a close, few officers his age could look back on experiences as varied as his, ranging from combat and staff duties to strategic planning and participation in politico-military decisions of the highest significance. The reform movement of which he had been an active though not leading member had succeeded in a few years in revitalizing the Prussian army from one of the more cumbersome military organizations of the ancien régime to a force that in many respects now was superior to that of the French. Social change was linked to the innovations, but it did not go as far as the reformers had hoped. As Prussia returned to an increasingly rigid conservatism, Clausewitz reacted to his personal and political disappointments by renouncing the excessive expectations he had once placed in the idealized reformed state. The intense if often critical patriotism of his twenties and early thirties gave way to a more balanced view of his country—as early as 1814 he disagreed with a friend who called for a vindictive peace. France, he argued, should not be weakened beyond a certain measure because it was needed to maintain the balance of power in Europe. In politics, too, he was becoming more of a theorist than a partisan.

During the first years of peace, Clausewitz served as chief of staff of the Prussian forces in the Rhineland. In 1818, at the age of thirty-eight, he was offered the directorship of the war college in Berlin, an administrative position he accepted without enthusiasm, and was promoted to the rank of major general. For a time he sought the appointment of minister to the Court of St. James, but once again his reputation for independence and political unreliability ruined his chances. In 1816 he had returned to the intensive study of military history and theory, which the climatic struggle against Napoleon had interrupted. In the remaining fifteen years of his life he wrote numerous histories of wars and campaigns, but also a biographical study of Scharnhorst, subsequently published by Ranke, some political essays of exceptional originality, and a history of Prussia before and during the defeat of 1806, which remains one of the notable interpretations of these years. In 1819 he began the writing of *On War*, and in the next eight years completed the first six of eight planned parts, as well as drafts of Books VII and VIII. But by 1827 he had come to realize that the manuscript did not bring out with sufficient clarity two constants that he had first identified in his early twenties and that were key elements in his theory: the political nature of war and the two basic forms that war assumes. In a note explaining the need for extensive revisions, he wrote:

> I regard the first six books, which are already in a clean copy, merely as a rather formless mass that must be thoroughly reworked once more. The revision will bring out the two types of war with greater clarity at every point. . . .
>
> War can be of two kinds, in the sense that either the objective is to *overthrow the enemy*—to render him politically helpless or militarily impotent, thus forcing him to sign whatever peace we please; or *merely to occupy some of his frontier-districts* so that we can annex them or use them for bargaining at the peace negotiations. Transitions from one type to the other will of course recur in my treatment; but the fact that the aims of the two types are quite different must be clear at all times, and their points of irreconcilability brought out.
>
> This distinction between the two kinds of war is an actual fact. But no less practical is the importance of another point that must be made absolutely clear, namely that *war is nothing but the continuation of policy with other means*. If this is firmly kept in mind throughout, it will greatly facilitate the study of the subject and the whole will be easier to analyze.[8]

Before beginning the changes, Clausewitz wrote histories of Napoleon's Italian and Waterloo campaigns to understand more clearly how his ideas of the dual form of war and of the political character of war worked in reality. Consequently he could revise only a few chapters before he received a new assignment in the artillery inspectorate in 1830

---

[8] Clausewitz, "Note of 10 July 1827," *On War*, 69. Emphasis in the original.

and was forced to put the manuscript of *On War* aside. Later that year, when the French Revolution and the Polish revolt against Russia raised the possibility of a European war, Prussia mobilized part of its army, and Clausewitz was appointed its chief of staff. The great cholera epidemic of 1831, which spread from Russia to Poland and then to Central and Western Europe, caused his death at the age of fifty-one in November 1831.

II

On War is divided into 128 chapters and sections, grouped into eight books.[9] The first, "On the Nature of War," defines the general characteristics of war in the social and political world and identifies elements that are always present in the conduct of war: danger, physical and mental effort, psychological factors, and the many impediments to carrying out one's intentions, which Clausewitz collected under the concept of "friction." Book II, "On the Theory of War," outlines the possibilities and limitations of theory. Book III, "On Strategy in General," includes not only chapters on force, time, and space, but also a more detailed treatment of psychological elements—all, according to Clausewitz, "the operative elements in war."[10] Book IV, "The Engagement," discusses "the essential military activity, fighting, which by its material and psychological effect comprises in simple or compound form the overall object of the war."[11] Book V, "Military Forces"; Book VI, "Defense"; and Book VII, "The Attack"—the three most conventionally military parts of the work—illustrate and elaborate earlier arguments. Finally, Book VIII, "War Plans," again takes up the most important themes of the first book, explores the relationship between "absolute" war in theory and real war, and in a sweep of theoretical and historical essays of great originality analyzes the political character of war and the interaction of politics and strategy.

Except perhaps for Book V, "Military Forces," for which no completely satisfactory place exists in the sequence, the material is arranged logically, beginning with a survey of the whole in the opening chapter, proceeding to the nature of war and to the purpose and difficulties of theory. Books III through VII discuss strategy and the conduct of military operations. The work ends with an analysis of the most important functions of political and military leadership in war, and more fully integrates war into social and political intercourse.

[9] The following analysis relies in part on my discussion of *On War* in *Clausewitz and the State*, especially 356–81.
[10] Clausewitz, *On War*, Book 4, chap. 1, p. 225.
[11] Ibid.

Even this brief outline will indicate that Clausewitz set himself two primary goals: one, to penetrate by means of logical analysis to the essence of absolute war, "ideal" war in the language of the philosophy of the time; the other, to understand war in the various forms it actually takes, as a social and political phenomenon, and in its strategic, operational, and tactical aspects. But the philosophic, scholarly aim meant far more to him than an intellectual exercise, a play with abstractions that had little bearing on reality. Theoretical analysis alone, Clausewitz was convinced, could provide the means by which actual war in its incredible variety might be understood. In turn, the analysis of real war continually tests the validity of theory. According to Clausewitz's simile: "Just as some plants bear fruit only if they don't shoot up too high, so . . . the leaves and flowers of theory must be pruned and the plant kept close to its proper soil—experience."[12]

The organization of the work into eight main parts does not, however, constitute a sure guide for the reader. The distinctions between the parts are less important than is the network of themes and arguments that links them. An idea is defined with extreme, one-sided clarity, to be varied, sometimes chapters later, and given a new dimension as it blends with other propositions and observations. Thesis is followed by antithesis; the characteristics of one phenomenon are ultimately fixed by analyzing its opposite. Discussions of the nature of war in the abstract alternate with the application to real war of such analytic devices as the theory of purpose and means, of the major concepts of friction and genius, of propositions of lesser magnitude such as those concerning the relationship of attack to defense, and with detailed operational and tactical observations—all embedded in historical evidence.[13] The text is characterized by movement, cross-references, and allusions, not only to other parts of the book, but also to the experiences of the author and of his generation. Through the entire work, creating an internal unity surpassing that of its external design, run two dialectical relationships, both introduced in the opening chapter: the relationship between war in theory and real war; and the relationship between the three factors that together make up war—violence, the play of chance and probability, and reason.

Organized mass violence is the only feature that distinguishes war from all other human activities. War is "an act of force, and there is no logical

---

[12] Clausewitz, "Author's Preface," *On War*, 61.

[13] Clausewitz defines the four theoretical functions of historical examples: "A historical example may simply be used as an *explanation* of an idea. . . . Second, it may serve to show the *application* of an idea. . . . Third, one can appeal to historical fact to support a statement . . . to prove the *possibility* of some phenomenon or effect." Finally, a tenet or proposition may be derived from the detailed, circumstantial treatment of a historical event (*On War*, Book 2, chap. 6, p. 171).

limit to the application of that force." It is not "the action of a living force upon a lifeless mass (total nonresistance would be no war at all), but always the collision of two living forces." Neither side is wholly in control of its action, and each opponent dictates to the other; consequently as they seek to outdo each other, their efforts escalate. "A clash of forces freely operating and obedient to no law but their own" eventually reaches the extreme—absolute war, that is, absolute violence ending in the total destruction of one side by the other.[14]

The thesis of total war as the ideal war is followed by the antithesis that war, even in theory, is always influenced by forces external to it. War is affected by the specific characteristics of the states in conflict and by the general characteristics of the time—its political, economic, technological, and social elements. These may inhibit the escalation to total violence. Furthermore, if a particular war does not seek the enemy's total defeat but a lesser goal, then even theory does not demand escalation toward extremes. Violence continues to be the essence, the regulative idea, even of limited wars fought for limited ends, but in such cases the essences does not require its fullest expression. The concept of absolute war and the concept of limited war together form the dual nature of war.

In the real world, the absolute is always modified, although sometimes it is closely approached, as in certain Napoleonic campaigns or in the attempt of one primitive tribe to exterminate another. War is never an isolated act, but the result of other forces, which affect it and may modify its violence. Nor does it consist of a single, decisive act, or of a set of simultaneous acts. If war were one short, uninterrupted blow, preparations for it would tend toward totality, because "no omission could ever be rectified." But in reality war is always a longer or shorter succession of violent acts, interrupted by pauses for planning, the concentration of effort, the recovery of energy—all on the part of two or more antagonists, who interact. A variety of elements within the opposing societies, the "free will" of the leadership, which may or may not conform to the objective realities, and the political motives of the war, will determine the military objective and the amount of effort to be expended. "War is merely the continuation of policy by other means."[15]

Clausewitz's thesis of the dual nature of war creates a basis for the analysis of all acts of organized mass violence, from wars of annihilation to armed demonstrations that differ from other diplomatic maneuvers solely by their direct threat of violence. The thesis makes it impossible to consider any one type of war as the norm that should determine policy, the standard by which all wars are measured.

[14] Ibid., Book 1, chap. 1, pp. 77–78. See also Book 1, chap. 2.
[15] Ibid., Book 1, chap. 1, 87.

Clausewitz's recognition of the political character of war reinforces the point expressed in the dual nature of war that war is not an autonomous or isolated act. The defeat of the enemy's armed power and of his will to use it is not an end in itself but a means to achieve political goals. Violence should express the political purpose, and express it in a rational, utilitarian manner; it should not take the place of the political purpose, nor obliterate it.

Consequently the political leadership should ultimately control and direct the conduct of war. That is not to say that it should displace soldiers in the planning and conduct of operations. It should take care not to ask the impossible and should collaborate with the senior commanders in developing overall policy; but the armed forces do not exist for their own sake. They are an instrument to be used. In demanding the subordination of the military to the political leadership, Clausewitz was far from expressing an ideological preference; he merely drew the logical conclusion from his analysis of the political nature and purpose of war.

Because war is the continuation of policy, "there can be no question of a *purely military* evaluation of a great strategic issue, nor of a purely military scheme to solve it."[16] If the political purpose demands it, the armed forces must be content with the partial mobilization of resources, and with limited achievements; or, on the other hand, they must be prepared to sacrifice themselves, and neither society nor government should regard this sacrifice, if it is an expression of rational policy, as beyond their mission.

These are some of the more significant implications of Clausewitz's theory of the dual nature of war and of the political nature of war for war in reality. The second major dialectical relationship that runs through the eight books of *On War* is encompassed in the assertion that real war is a composite of three elements. Its dominant tendencies, Clausewitz declared, "always make war a remarkable trinity," composed of violence and passion; uncertainty, chance, and probability; and political purpose and effect.[17]

To analyze war in general or to understand a particular war, but also to plan and conduct a war, requires the study or the exploitation of all three of these elements. A theory or policy would be flawed if it ignored any one of them or paid attention only to some of their component parts—for instance, only to the military aspect of the second element: how planning, leadership, and effort might succeed in the uncertain process of defeating the enemy. Equally inadequate would be a view that

---

[16] Carl von Clausewitz, "Two Letters on Strategy," below p. 127. Emphasis in the original. Compare also *On War*, Book 8, chap. 6B, p. 607.

[17] Clausewitz, *On War*, Book 1, chap. 1, p. 89.

primarily considered the political aspects of the war or the emotions that were expressed in the war or caused by it.

Theory and leadership must remain suspended, to use Clausewitz's metaphor, between the three magnets of violence, chance, and politics, which interact in every war.

Having identified the three areas that together make up war, Clausewitz assigned each as the main field for action to a different segment of society. On the whole, he thought, the first element, violence and passion, concerns mainly the people. The second, uncertainty and chance, provides scope primarily to the courage, determination, and talent of the commander and his forces. The third, politics, "is the business of government alone."[18]

These assumptions—probably made in the interest of theoretical neatness—are, of course, highly subjective. They reveal the author of *On War* in his historical posture, a soldier who regards himself as the servant of the Prussian state and the protector of a society whose raw emotions must be exploited but also controlled. In his view it was the task of the political leadership to abstract the energies of society without succumbing to their irrational power: a government channels psychic energy into rational policy, which the army helps carry out.

Even in Clausewitz's somewhat tentative formulations, these affinities—hatred and violence mainly identified with the people, chance and probability with the army and its commander, rational policy with the government—are of questionable validity. In the Napoleonic wars, to draw on Clausewitz's favorite pool of examples, the passion and violence of the emperor certainly carried more weight than whatever hatred the French population might have felt toward the rest of Europe; and at least in the final years of the empire, common sense, that particularly impressive form of rationality, rested more with the war-weary people than it did with Napoleon. But the affinities Clausewitz suggests—obviously the product of personal experience acting on his psychology and his intellectual and political outlook—do not diminish the validity and analytic power of the tripartite definition: war is composed of, and exists in, the realms of violence, chance, and politics.

III

The trinity of violence, chance, and politics encompasses the progression of violence between states, from the preparation and beginning of hostilities to the conclusion of a peace and beyond. Within each of the three

[18] Ibid.

parameters, and often in all of them, the actions and occurrences that make up war find their place. But to render them susceptible to analysis, recognize their links, and prevent them from overwhelming the analytic framework, the mass of practical detail must be grouped and abstracted. For this purpose Clausewitz developed concepts ranging in magnitude from general significance to specific operational characteristics. Of these the most comprehensive are the concepts of friction and of genius.

Friction refers to uncertainties, errors, accidents, technical difficulties, the unforeseen, and to their effect on decisions, morale, and actions:

> Friction is the only concept that more or less corresponds to the factors that distinguish real war from war on paper. The military machine . . . is basically very simple and therefore easy to manage. But we should bear in mind that none of its components is of one piece: each part is composed of individuals, every one of whom retains his potential of friction. . . . A battalion is made up of individuals, the least important of whom may chance to delay things or somehow make them go wrong. The dangers inseparable from war and the physical exertions [that] war demands . . . aggravate the problem. . . .
>
> This tremendous friction, which cannot, as in mechanics, be reduced to a few points, is everywhere in contact with chance, and brings about effects that cannot be measured. . . . One, for example, is the weather. Fog can prevent the enemy from being seen in time, a gun from firing when it should, a report from reaching the commanding officer. Rain can prevent a battalion from arriving, make another late by keeping it not three but eight hours on the march, ruin a cavalry charge by bogging the horses down in mud, etc.
>
> Action in war is like movement in a resistant element. Just as the simplest and most natural of movements, walking, cannot easily be performed in water, so in war it is difficult for normal efforts to achieve even moderate results. Friction, as we choose to call it, is the force that makes the apparently easy so difficult.[19]

This passage, which in its shuttling between the abstract and the specific is characteristic of Clausewitz's manner of thinking and expression, outlines some of the many psychological as well as impersonal possibilities of friction. In one form or another, friction is always present. Friction would dominate war if it were not countered by the creative employment of intellectual and emotional energy. To a degree at least, intelligence and determination can overcome friction, and beyond that they can exploit chance and transform the unpredictable into an asset. In turn, these forces should be subject to analysis. Just as theory must not ignore imponderables and the singularity of events, "which distinguish real war from war on paper," so theory must address the often unquantifiable forces that

---

[19] Ibid., Book 1, chap. 7, pp. 119–21.

combat friction: the intellectual and psychological strengths of the commander and of his subordinates; the morale, spirit, and self-confidence of the army; and certain temporary and permanent traits of society as reflected in its soldiers—enthusiasm for the war, political loyalty, energy.

On War examines these qualities directly, as "moral or psychological elements," and indirectly through the medium of "genius." The use of genius in this context would make little sense unless we recognize that for Clausewitz the term applies not only to the exceptional individual but also to abilities and feelings on which the behavior of ordinary men is based: "We cannot restrict our discussion to genius proper, as a superlative degree of talent. . . . What we must do is to survey all those gifts of mind and temperament that in combination bear on military activity. These, taken together, constitute the essence of military genius."[20] Originality and creativity raised to the highest power—which is how the late Enlightenment and idealist philosophy defined genius—were thus used by Clausewitz to identify and interpret general intellectual and psychological qualities, just as they represented and helped explain the freedom of will and action that was potentially present in every human being. The psychological configuration of the great man, "genius," is meant to clarify the emotions of all men, much as the concept of absolute war illuminates all wars.

This manner of conceptualizing and discussing psychological qualities may appear needlessly complex. Clausewitz was driven to it by the primitive state of the discipline of psychology in his day. In the chapter "On Military Genius" in *On War* he refers to psychology as an "obscure field," and in a subsequent chapter regrets that psychological elements will not yield to academic wisdom. They cannot be classified or counted. They have to be seen or felt.[21] But although good reasons exist for his approach, in some respects it is bound to be unsatisfactory. His enumeration of psychological traits remains conventional; his speculations on their relevance to war, although full of common sense and marked by flashes of brilliance, suffer, as he himself admits, from the same impressionistic defect that he condemns in the writings of other theorists.[22] The psychological characteristics of the great leader are the prism through which Clausewitz interprets the feelings and abilities of the average man; but in his fascination with a Napoleon or Frederick, who alone are capable of supreme achievements, his analysis usually limits itself to exploring their exceptional talents.

This one-sidedness, however, does not diminish the significance of the

[20] Ibid., Book 1, chap. 3, p. 100.
[21] Ibid., 106; ibid., Book 3, chap. 3, p. 184.
[22] Ibid., Book 3, chap. 3, p. 185.

fact that Clausewitz incorporated psychology as a major component in his theory. Since antiquity writers had stressed the importance of emotion in war; but beyond listing desirable and undesirable characteristics, they had done little with the subject. More recently, in the train of the Revolutionary Wars, some authors had emphasized the importance of the irrational, linked it with the power of chance, and concluded either that the psychology of the soldier was too obscure or that war was too anarchic to be subject to scientific analysis. Clausewitz took the decisive step of placing the analysis of psychological forces at the very center of the study of war. In accord with Kantian philosophy he acknowledged that some things could not be fully understood; but that did not mean that they should be ignored. *On War* made the psychology of the soldier, his commander, and the society they served an essential part of the theory of war. As more comprehensive and dynamic theories of human behavior were developed at the beginning of the twentieth century, the psychological context of Clausewitz's theoretical structure could be strengthened without doing damage to his tripartite definition of war or to the dialectical relationship that he posited between "genius"—the psychological roots of initiative and other kinds of military creativity—on the one hand, and "friction" on the other.

Their interaction defines every clash between the antagonists, every incident of fighting, large or small, that occurs in the course of the war. Clausewitz categorized and conceptualized these constituent parts in a series of propositions, which despite their importance are of more limited relevance than are the concepts of friction and genius. The two theses, already mentioned, of the reciprocal relationship of the antagonists and of the tendency of their efforts to escalate, give rise to the thesis of the interdependence of attack and defense in strategy and tactics. Another proposition holds that for reasons of time, space, and energy the offensive gradually weakens until a "culminating point" is reached—the stage beyond which the attacker can no longer easily defend himself against a counterattack. A third argues that the defensive consists of counterattacks as well as of resistance, just as the offensive is made up of attack, pause, and resistance.

From analyzing the nature of war as a whole, Clausewitz has moved to the study of the various forms in which a conflict is waged. This secondary class of propositions continues to apply to all wars in history—the culminating point of an attack may be present in a fight between two tribes just as it was in the German advance on the Marne in September 1914 or in the North Korean invasion of the South in June 1950. But Clausewitz's discussion of these principles reflects the specific experiences of his generation far more directly than do his thoughts on the basic nature of war. Because it concerns the action of forces in the field, his analysis is couched largely in terms of the Revolutionary and Napoleonic era—the most recent significant incidents of large-scale warfare—while to illustrate the character of raids and of other small-unit operations, Clausewitz often refers to his first years as a soldier, in the Allied campaigns against France in the 1790s.

These propositions and the discussion of detailed topics that grows from them constitute the immediate reality that provided much of the raw material for Clausewitz's theories. They also had another function that went to the core of his entire theoretical effort. They demonstrated that although the higher reaches of war, where reason, emotion, and the play of imponderables resolve the fate of states and societies, posed tremendous difficulties for theory, large if relatively subordinate areas of war were readily susceptible to analysis, and thus proved that a theory of war was in fact possible. As he wrote toward the end of his life:

> It is a very difficult task to construct a scientific theory for the art of war, and so many attempts have failed that most people say it is impossible, since it deals with matters that no permanent law can provide for. One would agree and abandon the attempt, were it not for the obvious fact that a whole range of propositions can be demonstrated without difficulty: that defense is the stronger form of fighting with the negative purpose, attack the weaker form with the positive purpose; that major successes help bring about minor ones, so that strategic results can be traced back to certain turning-points; that a demonstration is a weaker use of force than a real attack, and that it must therefore be clearly justified; that victory consists not only in the occupation of the battlefield but in the destruction of the enemy's physical and psychic forces . . . that success is always greatest at the point where the victory is gained . . . that a turning movement can only be justified by general superiority or by having better lines of communication or retreat than the enemy's; that flank positions are governed by the same considerations; that every attack loses impetus as it progresses.[23]

Many of these propositions were not, in fact, as self-evident as Clausewitz hoped his readers would find them. For instance, his statement that defense was the stronger form of fighting was misunderstood and rejected by several generations of German soldiers, whose analytic capacities were dimmed by their country's geopolitical situation. But for Clausewitz the dialectical logic of action and reaction, which no ideological preconception prevented him from following to its necessary conclusion, provided the assurance that his pronounced pragmatic outlook craved: violence on the tactical and operation level, and therefore violence on all levels, could be analyzed and mastered intellectually.

[23] Ibid., "Unfinished Note, Presumably Written in 1830," 71.

To conclude this summary of the principal themes of *On War*, we must revert to Clausewitz's ideas on the function and relationship of purpose, objective, and means, which run through the entire work. The political purpose for which a war is fought should determine the means that are employed and the kind and degree of effort required. The political purpose should also determine the military objective. Sometimes the two are identical—Clausewitz gives the example of a war fought to conquer a particular territory. In other cases, "the political objective will not provide a suitable military objective. In that event, another military objective must be adopted that will serve the political purpose."[24] To destroy the political system of an antagonist, it may become necessary to destroy his armed forces, or to occupy his political and economic centers, or both. To defend oneself against attack, it may be sufficient to ward off the attacking force. Or it is possible that its bases will have to be destroyed, or it may become necessary in other ways to raise the price of further hostilities to such an extent that the opponent will desist.

The military objective is dependent on the political purpose, but also on the enemy's political and military policies and on the conditions and resources of the two antagonists. It should be proportionate to these factors.[25] The means of war consist in the application of force, or the threat of force. Force, too, should be suitable and proportionate to the military objective and the political purpose.

The relationship between purpose, objective, and means exists in tactics and operations no less than it does in strategy and the overall conduct of the war.

> If a battalion is ordered to drive the enemy from a hill, a bridge, etc., the true purpose is normally to occupy that point. Destruction of the enemy's force is only a means to an end, a secondary matter. If a mere demonstration is enough to cause the enemy to abandon his position, the objective has been achieved; but as a rule the hill or bridge is captured only so that even more damage can be inflicted on the enemy. If this is the case on the battlefield, it will be even more so in the theater of operations, where it is not merely two armies that are facing each other, but two states, two peoples, two nations. . . . The gradation of objects at various levels of command will further separate the first means from the ultimate objective.[26]

On the tactical and operational levels, the political element is usually remote, but it will always be potentially present. Furthermore, any particular military act may have immediate or indirect political implications.

[24] Ibid., Book 1, chap. 1, p. 81.
[25] Ibid., Book 8, chap. 3B, pp. 585–86.
[26] Ibid., Book 1, chap. 2, p. 96.

From the struggle of a few soldiers to the clash of armies and the intellectual and emotional battlefields of grand strategy and ultimate political decisions, the network of purpose, objective, and means determines events, and should guide the thinking and behavior of the antagonists.

IV

Much of *On War* may on closer reading appear to be mere common sense. Even highly abstract passages, when dissected, generally point to self-evident facts or reveal implications that almost necessarily follow from them. The close focus on the familiar was, of course, in accord with Clausewitz's purpose in writing the book. The problems he studied were not new, and he was not interested in suggesting new solutions for them. What he wanted was to clarify well-known phenomena and restate them in such a way that theory could deal with them, while in turn the conceptualized phenomena contributed to the overall theoretical structure. The invention of *friction* is an example. Everyone knows that unexpected changes in weather, misunderstood orders, and accidents may affect events. By grouping such occurrences under the concept of friction, Clausewitz turned them from ideas of haphazard familiarity into a firm component of an analytic description that seeks to explain its subject.

His description, it should be noted, is incomplete, and not only because the manuscript is unfinished. *On War* contains a comprehensive analysis of the strategy, operations, and tactics of Napoleonic war and of their eighteenth-century background. Left out of account are most technological, administrative, and organizational factors; characteristically, even the institution of conscription, the major lever in the new machinery for generating military energy, is not thoroughly studied, even though it is often referred to and its share in making war more dynamic and destructive is emphasized. *On War* deals almost entirely with the ultimate issues as Clausewitz saw them: political and strategic planning, and the conduct of hostilities.

The theory of war that emerges from, and accompanies, this partial view may seem equally incomplete. Not only does it not directly address the roles of administrative and institutional elements in war, technological change, or the fundamental significance of economics; barring a reference or two to amphibious operations, *On War* ignores naval warfare. Clausewitz has often been criticized for his inability to transcend his experiences as a soldier of a landlocked monarchy and to recognize the other half of war of his time. But this criticism confuses his theory with the experiences from which it sprang. It is possible to develop and analyze a concept without illustrating it exhaustively. Friction, escalation, the interaction of attack and defense exist in war on and under the sea—and in the air—as much as they do on land. It is fallacious to consider the theoretical structure of *On War* incomplete on the ground that its illustrations are drawn only from the types of conflict that Clausewitz knew best and that interested him most.

Much the same may be said about the absence of systematic treatments of the role of technology and of economics in war. Clausewitz took it as a matter of course that technological development, brought about by economic, social, and political change, constantly affects tactics and strategy. *On War* contains numerous references to this basic fact. Nor did he ignore the dependence of military institutions and of warfare as such on economic resources and policies, although he was too knowledgeable to equate mere wealth with military strength. The history of Prussia sufficed to indicate how many other factors might be at work.[27] A state's economic resources, together with its geography and its social and political conditions, according to Clausewitz, determine, or should determine, its military policies. As long as theory accommodates this truth and provides an appropriate place for it in its dynamic representation of war, a comprehensive treatment of economics is not necessary. If subsequently the relationship of economics to war is fully explored, the analysis can be fitted into the already existing theoretical scheme. Theories concerning the motives and behavior of individuals and of groups and societies need not, and indeed never can, address every variable of their subject; it is enough that the theory has the capacity to incorporate the new findings and investigations of new areas as these are developed without its basic hypotheses being proved inadequate or false.

Some readers have criticized Clausewitz for ignoring ethics in *On War*, for not thoroughly discussing the causes of war, and for not questioning the validity of policies that lead to war. These objections raise important issues; once again, however, they seem to derive from a failure to accept Clausewitz's intentions and to acknowledge the logical parameters of his work.

The morality of going to war, Clausewitz thought, was a question of political ethics, not one that concerned the theory of war. War is a social act, and the decision to resort to it lies beyond war itself. That remains true even if the decision is influenced, or wholly determined, by the military leadership, for in that case the soldiers share in, or assume, political authority. They step outside of war.

Ethical justifications for resorting to war may certainly influence the

[27] A good example of Clausewitz's awareness of the role of economic factors in war is his discussion of the nature of eighteenth-century warfare that begins with the sentence, "This military organization was based on money and recruitment" (ibid., Book 8, chap. 38, pp. 588–89).

conduct of operations. Insofar as they affect the governments of the warring powers and the international community, these justifications, too, lie
outside the theory of war. Their impact, if any, on the soldiers actually
engaged in the war is subsumed in Clausewitz's discussions of morale,
loyalty, and the psychology of the fighting man.

That is also true of the ethics of behavior in war. Codes of ethics, their
observance or transgression, may influence the soldier. They are part of
the values of society, which according to Clausewitz always affect war.
But *in themselves*, he thought, they have little substance: "Attached to
force are certain self-imposed, imperceptible limitations, hardly worth
mentioning, known as international law and custom . . . moral force has
no existence save as expressed in the state and the law."[28] In short, the
theory concerns itself with ideals only to the extent that these values actually influence behavior. *On War* seeks to understand the reality of war,
and to lay bare the logical demands of the forces involved in war; it does
not try to adjust this reality to a particular ethical system. Clausewitz, as
he himself recognized, is far closer to Machiavelli's position than to that
of the church fathers and moral philosophers who want to define the just
war and just behavior in war.

Policy in *On War*—the German word *Politik* may mean either policy
of politics—refers to those political acts that lead to war, determine its
purpose, influence its conduct, and bring about its termination. In his historical writings and political essays, Clausewitz frequently analyzed the
failings of policy, whether those of Prussia or of other states. In *On War*
he set himself a different task. Here the substance of policy is not at issue;
what matters is the effectiveness with which the government directs its
military resources to achieve the political purpose. That purpose Clausewitz assumes to be in general realistic and responsible. Policy, he wrote
in Book VIII, "is nothing in itself; it is simply the trustee for all . . . interests [of a particular society, including its 'spiritual' values] against the
outside world. That it can err, subserve the ambitions, private interests,
and vanity of those in power, is neither here nor there. In no sense can the
art of war ever be regarded as the preceptor of policy, and here we can
only treat policy as representative of all interests of the community."[29]
Because the theory of war deals with the use of force against external
enemies, Clausewitz was logically correct in not exploring the problems
caused by irrational or mistaken policies—questions he left to political
theory. In the illustrative, exemplary passages of his work he might, of
course, have expanded his brief references to the misguided policies of
such men as Napoleon and Charles XII, without doing damage to the

[28] Clausewitz, *On War*, Book 1, chap. 1, p. 75.
[29] Ibid., Book 8, chap. 6B, pp. 606–7.

theoretical structure. Whether he would have done so, had he lived to complete the revision of his manuscript, it is impossible to say.[30]

V

In the history of ideas, it is not unusual for an author's work to be widely discussed and to influence thinking on its subject—private morality, for example, or forms of government—while the subject itself is hardly affected by the work. Clausewitz is such an author. But perhaps because he wrote in a field in which the theoretical literature was almost entirely utilitarian rather than speculative in a philosophic or scientific sense, there has been no lack of effort to discover the impact his ideas have had on war in reality, on the manner in which wars are actually fought—an odd fate, it may be thought, for a writer who stressed the nonutilitarian nature of his work.

The influence of a theorist whose intentions in his major work are not prescriptive is perhaps especially difficult to determine. It is not surprising that the search for Clausewitz's influence, which began in the second half of the nineteenth century, has been confused and inconclusive. That one or two sentences from *On War* have entered common usage, or that some of its arguments have been misinterpreted to support the military fashions of the day, scarcely proves that the ideas have had a genuine impact. On the contrary, if we examine the conduct of war since Clausewitz wrote, we will find little evidence that soldiers and governments have made use of his theories. Wars have repeatedly demonstrated the relevance of Clausewitz's theories, but nothing has proved more elusive to discover than an application of "lessons" learned from *On War*.

The discussion of Clausewitz's influence may benefit from a temporary separation of two related aspects of the issue: how he has influenced the manner in which people think about war; and how and to what extent he has influenced the actions of soldiers and statesmen. Reading Clausewitz seems, for example, to have helped Marx, Engels, and Lenin to clarify their ideas on the political nature of war; but it is far from certain that their encounters with Clausewitz's work were essential to the development of their thought. Nor is it clear whether other political figures gained insights from *On War* that they might not have acquired elsewhere. Points of view may agree without one having influenced the other. The close interaction of war and politics, to give only the most obvious

---

[30] James E. King, in a personal communication, observes that Clausewitz "left the analytic questions as to why and how political values (the objective) control the armed forces and their employment in war (the means) to be answered by a political theory as sophisticated as his theory of war. That task has still not been accomplished."

example, is after all not a program but a piece of reality, a process that in some societies is more readily understood and better managed than in others. Abraham Lincoln or Georges Clemenceau did not need to read Clausewitz to discover the relationship between the military objective and the political purpose of the wars they were fighting. Some people reached conclusions similar to Clausewitz's without reading On War; on the other hand, many of his readers either did not understand or did not agree with him.

In his own society it is precisely the political aspects of Clausewitz's theories that were given what was at best an ambiguous reception. Until the 1930s, his most significant German readers were either unwilling or unable to accept his thesis of the close integration of politics and war and of the primacy of political considerations even during the fighting. Instead, throughout the nineteenth and early twentieth centuries, the chiefs of staff and commanders-in-chief of the Prusso-German army thought of war, once it had broken out, as an essentially autonomous activity, and they did everything in their power to protect the army, its strategy, and its operations from political interference. Even the close partnership between Bismarck and Moltke was at times shaken by the soldiers' efforts to preserve their autonomy. Hindenburg and Ludendorff finally achieved a very considerable measure of independence during the First World War, until the failure of the spring and summer offensives in 1918 caused them to drop responsibility into the lap of a now-helpless government. The instinctual sense of the permanent interaction of politics and war that Clausewitz had developed as a young man and that guided his thinking throughout life was no longer as comprehensible to Germans as their society became industrialized and entered the era of imperialism. In a culture increasingly shaped by specialists and technocrats, with an assertive but anxious military unchecked by the political leadership, the universalistic outlook that Clausewitz expressed in On War dimmed and was lost.

Perhaps the two most important legacies that German soldiers accepted from Clausewitz, two strands in the army's doctrine well into the twentieth century, were his agreement with Napoleon that a major victory was likely to be more important than many small successes, and his concept of imponderables. Not to be overwhelmed by the unforeseen demanded flexibility in all aspects of war, from grand strategy (though the decision to stay with the Schlieffen plan in 1914 cannot be regarded as an example of flexibility) to tactics. One result was the development of Auftragstaktik, the policy of issuing directives stating the overall intentions of the supreme command, while leaving a high degree of initiative and the issuance of specific orders to subordinate commands. Shortly before 1914, the distinguished French officer and historian Jean Colin still found a pronounced utilitarian benefit in this aspect of Clausewitz's writings: Clausewitz had "the incomparable merit of driving formalism out of military education."[31] In Colin's view, the belief that a theory of action should not lay down rules, which Clausewitz first expressed in his criticism of Bülow, was in itself a practical lesson of the greatest significance.

But with such exceptions, Clausewitz's influence on the manner in which wars are prepared for and fought is difficult to discern and even harder to verify. It is easier to see his impact on more theoretical or historical thinking about war; although even among scholars he cannot be said to have founded a school. He did, however, strongly influence some historians of war, notably Hans Delbrück. In many disciplines and fields of study—ethics or political theory may again serve as examples—general analyses of a discursive, speculative nature are not rare; but the subject of war still tends to evoke works that condemn or try to eliminate war or that seek to improve the effectiveness of the means and strategies of conflict. That war can be studied in a different spirit is perhaps the most important lesson to be drawn from Clausewitz's work. He has given us a base on which to build. But the detached interpretation of organized mass violence continues to pose the greatest difficulties to the modern world.

Clausewitz stands at the beginning of the nonprescriptive, nonjudgmental study of war as a total phenomenon, and *On War* is still the most important work in this tradition. Even Machiavelli, whom he perhaps most resembles in his passionate interest in the actual functioning of politics and war, was more of an advocate. *The Prince* and *The Art of War* are informed by a view of the political conditions of Italy and by Machiavelli's dissatisfaction with them, but *On War* was not written to strengthen the Prussian monarchy. Clausewitz ranges far beyond the parameters of success and failure in which strategic thought moves to explore the ultimate nature and dynamic of war. It would be comforting to believe that this intellectual understanding not only forms the basis for effective strategy, but that it is also conducive to responsible military policy and statecraft. Clausewitz never made that assumption, and history before and since he wrote has demonstrated that the assumption would not invariably be correct. Nevertheless both as an issue that dominates our time and as a still-imperfectly understood force in our past, war demands much further exploration. That so few scholars and soldiers have taken it up in something of Clausewitz's spirit of objective inquiry, and with his ability to combine reality and theory, is not the least measure of his achievement.

[31] Jean Colin, *The Transformation of War* (London, 1912), 298–99. It is characteristic of the search for Clausewitz's influence that even this brilliant historian simply took for granted the impact Clausewitz's ideas had on Prussian strategy in 1866 and 1870 (ibid., 303–4), an assumption that would have puzzled the Prussian general staff and the commanders of the Prussian armies in these conflicts.

8

TWO LETTERS ON STRATEGY

I N CONTRAST to the comprehensive biographical and theoretical
character of the preceding essay, this brief paper addresses one particular episode in the development of Clausewitz's ideas. It started as an
introduction I wrote for two letters by Clausewitz, which Daniel Moran
and I translated and which the Art of War Colloquium of the Army War
College published as a pamphlet in 1984. Despite good intentions all
around, a series of extraordinary misunderstandings and breakdowns of
communication between sponsoring institution, the translators, the copy
editor, and the printer bedevilled the modest project, and the result was a
confused—and I imagine to most readers confusing—publication. The
outcome was the more regrettable because it obscured one of the most
interesting documents of the last phase of Clausewitz's theoretical work.

The two letters comment on strategic problems that were assigned to
Prussian general staff officers in 1827. Because the exercises dealt with
defensive operations, the first German publication of the letters in 1937
was given the title "Two Letters by General von Clausewitz: Thoughts
on Defense." As will be seen, their scope is actually far broader, and the
present title seems more appropriate.

The 1984 pamphlet printed the text of the letters in full—some eight
thousand words. For this version I have included merely the key section
of the first letter, which I have retranslated. I have also rewritten the essay's conclusion.

❧

In 1827 the Prussian general-staff officer, Major von Roeder, requested
Clausewitz's comments on solutions of two strategic problems that had
been set by his superior, Lieutenant-General von Müffling, chief of the
general staff. Müffling, best known for his service as Prussian liaison officer in Wellington's headquarters during the Waterloo campaign, never
freed himself from the cautious strategic concepts current in the Prussian
army before 1806. Position warfare and the occupation of territory dominated his thinking, rather than the defeat of the enemy's forces. But he
was an efficient peacetime chief of staff, who took the training of his officers seriously and whose operational exercises, war games on the map

and on the ground, and innovations in communications and mapmaking, contributed to the growing professionalization of the general staff.

At the time, the general staff was still far from the army's central planning and, in effect, executive organ that it became some forty years later under Moltke. In 1821 it had been detached from the Ministry of War; but the chief of staff continued to report to the minister on all major business, and his right to report directly to the monarch was strictly circumscribed; he was still an advisor who responded rather than initiated. The staff itself was small for a major power with a peacetime army of some 127,000 officers and men, which could be expanded to over four hundred thousand if the reserves were called up. The central body, or Great General Staff, in Berlin numbered nineteen officers, including the chief; twenty-seven officers served with the guards, the eight army corps, and the artillery inspectorate general. Five officers holding other assignments were attached to the staff and kept informed of its work, though they participated in it only when their special expertise was needed. The senior in this group was Clausewitz, since 1818 director of the War Academy. Trigonometric and topographic sections, an archive, and a duplicating office completed the organization.[1]

Roeder was the head of the general staff's "Central Theater of War," the section that dealt with operations against Austria. Born in 1787, seven years younger than Clausewitz, he had been Scharnhorst's student at the Academy for Young Officers in 1804 and 1805, during which time he first met Clausewitz. After serving in the War of 1806 he resigned his commission and studied at the universities of Berlin and Heidelberg, before reentering the Prussian army as a second lieutenant at the beginning of the Wars of Liberation in 1813. In the battle of Grossgörschen he was severely wounded, but he recovered to participate in the fighting that autumn and in the campaign of 1814. During the Hundred Days, Roeder, by then a captain on the general staff, was assigned to one of the brigades in III Corps, whose chief of staff was Clausewitz. He fought in the battles of Ligny and Wavre, in which the corps, by tying down Grouchy's far stronger force, helped make the victory of Waterloo possible. After the war Roeder continued to serve as a general staff officer and royal adjutant until he retired with the rank of major general in 1841. Six years later he was promoted to the nominal rank of lieutenant general.[2]

---

[1] The figures, which do not precisely coincide with the number of positions authorized at the time, are taken from the Army List for 1827: *Rang und Quartier-Liste der Königlich Preussischen Armee* (Berlin, 1827).

[2] Roeder's memoirs, *Für Euch, meine Kinder!*, published posthumously in Berlin in 1861, are an interesting source for the conduct of operations in the Prussian army from the perspective of a junior staff officer. They repeatedly mention Clausewitz; see, for instance, 56, 305, 306, 314, 315, and 319.

While not a man of striking originality, Roeder was an intelligent officer, broadly experienced as a planner and in the field. His early association with Scharnhorst and other members of the reform movement left a
permanent mark on his ideas and attitudes. He was one of the men who
carried a hint of the reform era's idealism and independence of judgment
to the army's peacetime routine in the sluggish, conservative decades after
1815. His memoirs indicate that he looked up to Clausewitz, who in turn
liked him and—as the following letters show—trusted him sufficiently to
express his opinions at length and frankly, to the point of openly criticizing Müffling's operational and strategic views.

The problems Müffling assigned to Roeder and others on the staff toward the end of 1827 were, like the majority of his exercises, defensive in
nature. Prussia had become a major power, her territory now stretching
from the Niemen and the Republic of Cracow in the east to the Rhine and
beyond in the west; but larger, richer, better armed neighbors lay on her
borders. Neither a preventive strike nor an offensively waged defensive
were part of Müffling's thinking. In any future war, he expected "an enemy to invade Prussia from west, east, or south. Political weakness
[would] compel Prussia to fight on the defensive on her own territory."[3]
Within these constraints, Roeder worked out his answers, and then for-
warded Müffling's exercises to Clausewitz, together with his solutions
and a solution to the first problem by another officer, who signed himself
merely with the initial M—possibly First Lieutenant Count Monts of the
Great General Staff.

In a first reply, dated 22 December, Clausewitz critically discussed the
terms of Müffling's problem and then turned to the solutions by M and
Roeder. In a further letter two days later, he analyzed Müffling's second
exercise and Roeder's solution. Together the two letters were well over
eight thousand words in length. Clausewitz never found it difficult to express his thoughts in writing, but the timing of Roeder's request may have
contributed to the extensiveness and thoroughness of his response. Only
a few months earlier he had decided that the manuscript of On War,
which had occupied him for nearly a decade, should be "thoroughly re-
worked once more." The revisions he had in mind, would, he hoped,
"bring out the two types of war with greater clarity at every point." By
this he meant, on the one hand, wars waged for major objectives, which
can be achieved only by the far-reaching destruction of the enemy's pow-

---

[3] Herbert von Böckmann, "Das geistige Erbe der Befreiungskriege," Von Scharnhorst zu
Schlieffen, ed. Friedrich von Cochenhausen (Berlin, 1933), 122. Böckmann's essay contains
a good analysis of Müffling's ideas. See also "C. v. W." [i.e., Phillip Friedrich Karl von
Müffling], Betrachtungen über die grossen Operationen und Schlachten der Feldzüge von
1813 und 1814 (Berlin and Posen, 1825); and the discussion of Müffling as chief of staff in
Kurt von Priesdorff, Soldatisches Führertum (Hamburg, 1937?), 4:313–18.

ers and will of resistance; and, on the other, limited wars waged for limited ends. He also wanted his revisions to develop more fully another, related point, "that war is nothing but the continuation of policy with other means."[4] Roeder's request thus reached Clausewitz during a period of intense intellectual reappraisal, and he seems to have welcomed the opportunity to apply his ideas on fundamental issues of war to specific operational situations.[5]

The opening paragraphs of Clausewitz's letter of the twenty-second, which are printed below, criticize Müffling's first problem for its failure to indicate the political purposes of the antagonists, and to establish the level of significance the military operations possessed for the opposing governments. Without this information, sensible strategic and operational planning was out of the question. That this was not mere pedantry on Clausewitz's part, that a limited conflict between Prussia and Austria lay as much in the realm of the possible as the desperate struggles of the Silesian and Seven Years' War, is shown by the campaign of 1778, the so-called Potato War, between the two powers, which consisted primarily in feints and armed demonstrations while a diplomatic settlement was worked out. Then, and at all times, political interest largely determined— or reasonably should determine—the scale and type of military effort. In the rather casual context of a private letter to a younger comrade, Clausewitz tests and applies hypotheses that eventually receive their ultimate formulation in the polished, compact prose of the revised opening chapter of Book I of *On War*:

> You have asked me, dear friend, to give you my opinion of the strategic problems and the two solutions you have sent me. I do so with the understanding that you will treat my communication, which is made purely in the interest of scholarship, as entirely confidential.
>
> Forgive me if I start at the very beginning; but nowhere is a basic understanding, the true and unambiguous recognition of *inescapable facts*, so lacking as in the so-called science of strategy.[6]
>
> War is not an independent phenomenon, but the continuation of politics by different means. Consequently, the main lines of every major strategic plan are *largely political in nature*, and their political character increases the more the plan encompasses the entire war and the entire state. The plan for the war results directly from the political conditions of the two belligerent

---

[4] Carl von Clausewitz, "Note of 10 July 1827," *On War*, trans. and ed. Michael Howard and Peter Paret, rev. ed. (Princeton, 1984), 69.

[5] For a more extensive discussion of Clausewitz's thinking at the time he received Roeder's letter, see my *Clausewitz and the State*, rev. ed. (Princeton, 1985), 378–81.

[6] Clausewitz writes "wie die sogennannte Strategie," which taken literally would make little sense. The rest of the sentence makes it apparent that he is referring to the "science" or "discipline" of strategy. The emphasis throughout this extract is Clausewitz's.

states, as well as from their relations to other powers. The plan of campaign results from the war plan, and frequently—if there is only one theater of operations—may even be identical with it. But the political element even extends to the separate components of a campaign; rarely will it be without influence on such major episodes of warfare as a battle, etc. According to this point of view, there can be no question of a *purely military* evaluation of a great strategic issue, nor of a purely military scheme to solve it. That it is essential to see the matter in this way, that the point of view is *almost self-evident* if we only keep the history of war in mind, scarcely needs proof. Nevertheless, it has not yet been fully accepted, as is shown by the fact that people still like to separate the purely military elements of a major strategic plan from its political aspects, and treat the latter as if they were somehow extraneous. *War is nothing but the continuation of political efforts by other means.* In my view all of strategy rests on this idea, and I believe that whoever refuses to recognize that this must be so does not yet fully understand what really matters. It is this principle that makes the entire history of war comprehensible, which in its absence remains full of the greatest absurdities.

How then is it possible to plan a campaign, whether for one theater of war or several, without indicating the political condition of the belligerents, and the politics of their relationship to each other?

Every major war plan grows out of so many *individual* circumstances, which determine its features, that it is impossible to devise a hypothetical case with such specificity that it could be taken as real. We are not referring simply to trivialities, but to the *most important issues*, which nevertheless have almost always been ignored. For instance, Bonaparte and Frederick the Great are often compared, sometimes without keeping in mind that one man ruled 40 million subjects, the other 5. But let me call attention to another, less noticeable and yet very significant distinction: Bonaparte was a usurper, who had won his immense power in a kind of perpetual game of chance, and who, for the greater part of his perilous career, did not even possess an heir; while Frederick the Great disposed of a true patrimony. Had nature given both men identical psychological qualities, would they have acted in the same manner? Certainly not, and that alone makes it impossible for us to measure them by the same standard. In short, it is impossible to construct a hypothetical case in such a way that we can say that what was left out was not essential. We can of course think of many characteristics of the opposing armies and states that are identical, and have the effect of canceling each other out; but solving such problems would be no more than a *useful exercise*. Our best solutions could not be applied to *real conflicts*.

If, therefore, such exercises allow us to leave many things out of consideration because we believe they neutralize each other, we still cannot ignore those conditions that have brought about the war and that determine its political purpose. The political purpose and the means available to achieve it give rise to the *military objective*. This ultimate goal of the entire belligerent act, or of the particular campaign if the two are identical, is therefore the first and most important issue that the strategist must address, for the main lines of the strategic plan run toward this goal, or at least are guided by it. It is one thing to intend to *crush* my opponent if I have the means to do so, to make him *defenseless* and force him to accept my peace terms. It is obviously something different to be content with gaining some advantage by conquering a strip of land, occupying a fortress, etc., which I can retain or use in negotiations when the fighting stops. The exceptional circumstances in which Bonaparte and France found themselves since the Wars of the Revolution, allowed him to achieve major victories on almost every occasion, and people began to assume that the plans and actions *created* by those circumstances were *universal norms*. But such a view would summarily reject all of the earlier history of war, which is absurd. If we wish to derive an art of war from the history of war—and that is undoubtedly the only possible way—we must not minimize the testimony of history. Suppose we find that out of fifty wars forty-nine have been of the second kind—that is, wars with limited objectives, not directed at the total defeat of the enemy—then we would have to believe that these limitations reside in the nature of war itself, instead of being in every case brought about by wrong ideas, lack of energy, or whatever. We must not allow ourselves to be misled into regarding war as a pure act of force and of destruction, and from this simplistic concept logically deduce a string of conclusions that no longer have anything to do with the real world. Instead we must recognize that war is a political act that is not wholly autonomous; a true political instrument that does not function on its own but is controlled by something else, by the hand of policy.

The greater the extent to which policy is motivated by comprehensive interests, affecting the very existence of the state, and the greater the extent to which the issue is cast in terms of survival or extinction, the more policy and hostile feelings coincide. As policy dissolves into hostility, war becomes simpler; it proceeds according to the pure concept of force and destruction, and satisfies whatever demands can be logically developed from this concept, until all its component parts come to possess the coherence of a *simple necessity*. Such a war may seem entirely *apolitical*, and on that account has been considered the norm. But obviously the political element exists here no less than it does in other kinds of war. It merely coincides so completely with the concept of force and destruction that it vanishes from sight.[7]

In light of this discussion, I have no need to prove that wars exist in which the objective is even more circumscribed[8]—a bare threat, armed negotiations, or in the case of alliances, the mere pretext of action [by one of the

[7] Compare *On War*, Book 1, chap. 1, sections 25 and 26, pp. 87–88.
[8] I.e., than in the limited wars mentioned two paragraphs earlier.

allies]. It would be unreasonable to maintain that such wars are beneath the art of war. As soon as we concede that logically some wars may not call for extreme goals, the utter destruction of the enemy, we must expand the art of war to include all gradations of military means by which policy can be advanced. War in its relation to policy has above all the obligation and the right to prevent policy from making demands *that are contrary to the nature of war*, to save it from misusing the military instrument from a failure to understand what it can and cannot do.

Consequently I must insist that the military goals of both sides are stated whenever a strategic plan is drawn up. For the most part these goals arise out of the political relations of the two antagonists to each other, and to other states that may be involved. Unless these relations are outlined, a plan can be nothing more than a combination of temporal and spatial relationships, directed toward some *arbitrary* goal—a battle, siege, etc. To the extent that this goal cannot be shown as necessary or superior to others, it can be challenged and contradicted by other projects, without these coming any nearer the absolute truth than did the first plan. That is, indeed, the history of all strategic discussions until today. Everyone rotates within some arbitrary circle. No one tries to push his argument back to the origins of the war that is to be fought, to its true motive, to the one and only point where the logical development and conclusion of the military operations can alone originate. Whatever correct and effective strategic decisions are made, result from the instinctive tact of talented commanders, who with a glance penetrate and assess a mass of circumstances. This instinct suffices for action, but obviously not for analysis, even though action is something far greater than the laborious unfolding and laying bare of facts.

You see from this, dear friend, how little I can make of your assignment.[9]

The remainder of the letter and the second letter, written two days later, enter into detailed operational and even tactical issues that can be followed only with the aid of large-scale maps. It is a striking illustration of Clausewitz's way of thinking that the general discussion with which the letters open is developed in conjunction with highly technical analyses of topographical features, road networks, and march schedules. These details no longer have much to say to anyone who is not a specialist in the methods and specifics of warfare in the 1820s. But like the plaster form that is knocked away after a sculpture has been cast they are an essential part of the working process. It is the interaction of technical military expertise with political and psychological understanding and the ability to abstract and generalize without ever departing from the facts that lie at the core of Clausewitz's unique achievement.

[9] "Zwei Briefe des Generals von Clausewitz: Gedanken zur Abwehr," special issue of the *Militärwissenschaftliche Rundschau*, March 1937, 5–9.

9

CLAUSEWITZ AS HISTORIAN

ONE SUMMER in the late 1950s when I was working in German archives on my dissertation, a fellow researcher mentioned that the library of the former Imperial and Royal War Archive in Vienna was selling the duplicates of its holdings. This led to my acquiring a set of the first edition of Clausewitz's posthumous works in ten volumes, published in Berlin between 1832 and 1837. The edition includes the larger part of his writings but leaves out many important manuscripts, numerous shorter pieces, and his correspondence. It merely suggests the full scope of his work. What particularly struck me when I first saw the volumes together on my desk was the proportion of historical to theoretical texts. I had read Clausewitz's famous account of Prussia before and during 1806, and vaguely knew that he had written other histories, but here was concrete evidence of the importance that the study of the past assumed in his work: the first three volumes of the edition contained *On War*, the other seven were filled with historical narratives and analyses.

Until recently Clausewitz's histories were largely ignored in the literature. *On War* loomed too large. When scholars began to move beyond it they first turned to his other theoretical manuscripts and articles, to some of his political essays, and from the 1930s on to other theorists of his generation, whose work they compared with his in order to trace influences and reactions. Nevertheless his letters and *On War* itself clearly indicate the decisive part that history played in the development of his theories.

If the relationship between theory and history in Clausewitz's thought has barely been studied, still less attention has been paid to his methods of historical research and interpretation. And yet anyone reading *Observations on Prussia in her Great Catastrophe*, the biography of his teacher and friend, Scharnhorst, or his history of the invasion of Russia—which combines a brilliant eye-witness narrative with characterizations of leading personalities, and sweeping reflections on the policy and strategy of the opposing sides—might have sensed the individual note that set their author apart from other historians of his generation.

Over time, as I wrote his biography and in other studies, I discussed many of the elements of Clausewitz's historical writings and became convinced that an interesting, in some respects highly original historian lay concealed in the many thousands of pages of his work. Eventually, for an edition of his historical and political texts, I wrote the following general, comprehensive analysis.

ॐ

In Clausewitz's thought, history and theory were closely linked. They did not, however, interact on a level plane. Clausewitz believed that a valid theory of such social phenomena as politics or war could be developed only by taking account of the past as well as of the present. Without the instrument of history, theory should not be constructed. On the other hand, he did not believe that a theoretical understanding of government and of armed conflict, although desirable, was essential for their historical reconstruction and analysis. Long sections in his historical works reveal neither theoretical arguments nor foundations. Theory might assist but did not direct Clausewitz's historical interpretations. History not only tested and validated his theories, it gave rise to some of them.

One reason for Clausewitz's elevated view of the importance of history may at first seem paradoxical: his conviction that theory must remain as close to reality as it was possible for an abstraction to be. In a comment on one of his theoretical studies that preceded *On War*, he noted that its

> scientific character consists in an attempt to investigate the phenomena of war and to indicate the links between these phenomena and the nature of their component parts. No logical conclusion has been avoided; but whenever the thread became too thin I have preferred to break it off and go back to the relevant phenomena of experience. Just as some plants bear fruit only if they don't shoot up too high, so in the practical arts the leaves and flowers of theory must be pruned and the plant kept close to its proper soil—experience.[1]

Put differently, Clausewitz's theoretical writings on war were based on the experience of war, his own experience and that of his generation, but also on another form of experience that only history can transmit. By opening up the past for us, history added to the fund of knowledge that we can acquire directly and also made possible universal concepts and generalizations across time. To enable history to do this, the historian must be as objective or—as Clausewitz would have said—as scientific or philosophical as possible.[2] In fact, the two latter qualities encompassed more than objectivity. They also represented the search for the essential

[1] Carl von Clausewitz, "Author's Preface," *On War*, rev. ed., trans. and ed. Michael Howard and Peter Paret (Princeton, 1984), 61.
[2] *Wissenschaftlich* or *Philosophisch*—terms that Clausewitz often used interchangeably.

quality of the phenomenon studied—violence in the case of war—and the consequential tracing of this quality in its changing forms through all parts of the subject. The theoretical reflection of this dynamic reality should focus on its basic structure rather than seek completeness. Clausewitz's comment on the scientific character of his theories, which I have just quoted, opens with the combative assertion that the "scientific approach does not consist solely, or even mainly, in a complete system and a comprehensive doctrine."[3] Even as a young man, in his first attacks on the convoluted military theories of the late Enlightenment, he argued that a closed system of laws, principles, and prescriptions could be achieved only at the expense of reality and of history, which represented past reality. History in the service of a philosophic worldview as Hegel encapsulated it, for instance, would not serve Clausewitz's purpose.

Clausewitz's demand for objective, analytic, nonteleological history gained further strength from the affinity between this ideal and the character of his theories. The purpose of his theoretical writings was not to teach a specific doctrine that would lead to successful strategies and increase operational effectiveness, but rather to contribute to an understanding of war as an apparently permanent element of human experience. By enabling the theorist to join past and present, objective history might make possible generalized insights into the timeless reality of war. Consequently historical study became a major component in Clausewitz's pursuit of theory.

Social scientists today might find little to disagree with in this position, although few would base their hypotheses and arguments as firmly on historical interpretations as Clausewitz did. But the reciprocal relationship between the effort to understand the uniqueness of the past and the effort to generalize and conceptualize is so pervasive in his writings that the reader soon comes to feel that more is at work than the belief that history must nourish and control theory. Clausewitz's writings reflect the mind of an author who is fascinated by the specific and unique as much as he is by the general. The study and writing of history, it might be said, responded directly to his need to understand, and indirectly by sharing in the development of theory. In consequence, his historical work assumed many different forms once it progressed beyond the school exercises that he wrote as a young officer, exercises that were not important in themselves but that accustomed him to think historically. *On War* and his other theoretical writings are filled with references to the past, discussions of past events, and even with more or less self-contained historical essays that analyze a development over time. An example is chapter 3B of Book

---

[3] Clausewitz, "Author's Preface," *On War*, 61.

VIII of *On War*, which traces the interdependence of military, political, and social forms from antiquity to the nineteenth century.

Clausewitz also wrote a large number of separate historical studies. In some of these the theoretical motive was important, perhaps even dominant, even if he did not always communicate this to the reader. He believed he could not draw theoretical conclusions from the available accounts until he himself had worked through and reinterpreted the material. Several of these studies were brief; a few were very long and demanded years of effort. The histories of the campaign of 1796 in Italy and of the War of 1799 in Switzerland and Italy fill three volumes in the posthumous collected edition of his works. Both were written in the second half of the 1820s, at a time when Clausewitz had decided to revise the manuscript of *On War* so as to strengthen the treatment of two concepts that he had come to regard as major themes of the work: the political nature of war and the distinction between absolute and limited war. Other works are marked by a strong personal element. The author reports and interprets events that he himself had witnessed or in which he had taken part, conditions that he had experienced, individuals he had known. Still other writings, which treat war only marginally or not at all, have a political motive. The past is drawn on to illuminate domestic politics and foreign affairs of Clausewitz's own day. Finally, some of his historical studies lack either a personal, a political, or a theoretical note; their sole motivation appears to be the author's fascination with the past.[4]

Clausewitz's ambition to see the past truthfully and objectively did not mean that he excised all personal opinions from his texts. On the contrary, the author is ever present as observer, commentator, even judge—especially when he writes about conditions or events he himself had witnessed. In the chapter "Critical Analysis" of *On War*, Clausewitz distinguishes between "the critical approach and the plain narrative of a historical event" and further identifies three paths that the critical approach might take: "The discovery and interpretation of equivocal facts . . . ; the tracing of events back to their causes . . . ; [and] the investigation and evaluation of means employed. This last is criticism proper, involving praise and censure."[5] In his previously cited essay on Clausewitz, Hans Delbrück argued that despite his "eminently historical bent" and his "extraordinarily rare faculty of absolutely objective perception," Clausewitz

---

[4] For general discussions of Clausewitz's historical writings, see Hans Delbrück, "General von Clausewitz," in *Historische und politische Aufsätze* (Berlin, 1887); Hans Rothfels, *Carl von Clausewitz: Politik und Krieg* (Berlin, 1920); Rothfels's introduction and notes to Carl von Clausewitz, *Politische Schriften und Briefe* (Munich, 1922), which discuss a number of historical texts; and Peter Paret, *Clausewitz and the State*, rev. ed. (Princeton, 1985), 78–89, 327–55.

[5] Clausewitz, *On War*, 156.

had chosen the last of these paths. "By vocation and intent Clausewitz was a military critic and solely a military critic."[6] This seems to confuse criticism with an analytic interpretation that goes beyond plain historical narrative and judges Clausewitz's writings from a historicist position of impossible purity. But undoubtedly Clausewitz was prepared to make sharp judgments, even if he always sought to understand the conditions obtaining at the time. Several of his works could not be published immediately after his death because they would have given offense to the court and to senior personages in the government and the army. Other manuscripts that were included in the first posthumous edition of his collected works or that appeared separately had their language toned down. Recently it has been recognized that editorial emendations and substitutions were far more frequent than had been supposed. Two motives are apparent from the changes: the replacement of unusual words and phrases to make the text stylistically more conventional and the reduction or even elimination of the author's criticism of personalities and of Prussian institutions and policies.

The restored texts not only reveal Clausewitz's individuality with greater precision, they also offer additional evidence for his political views, which in the sixteen years he was to live after Napoleon's downfall placed him among those groups in Prussia that favored a constitution, responsible ministerial government, equality or legal rights, and a degree of political participation of the upper classes. To the conservatives that regained full control of the government and army after 1815 he was a man of doubtful political reliability, who had never renounced the radical reformism of his earlier years. When the prospect arose of his being made minister at the Court of St. James, his conservative critics succeeded in reversing the appointment, because, as the British envoy reported to his government in Berlin, "There is not that confidence in his being wholly free from revolutionary views."[7] These views did not shape Clausewitz's historical interpretations, but occasionally they enrich them with a grace note.

His urge to explore past reality was strengthened by the succession of events that began with the fall of the Bastille a few days after his ninth birthday. Four years later, as an ensign in a Prussian infantry regiment, he first fought against the armies of the new republic, and until his thirty-fifth year, when he served as chief of staff of a Prussian corps in the campaign that ended with the battle of Waterloo, his existence was largely determined by the French Revolution and its political and military con-

---

[6] Delbrück, "Clausewitz," 218.

[7] Clausewitz's prospects for a diplomatic career between 1818 and 1820 and their eventual failure are discussed in my essay " 'A Proposition Not a Solution' " below.

sequences. In particularly intense form his career reflected a more general experience. The French Revolution was the central political and social fact of Clausewitz's generation. Its material and intellectual forces changed the political map of Europe, accelerated the opening up of society, and beyond these pressures and dislocations affected large areas of European thought. New possibilities emerged, but at the cost of old certainties. If this was at first especially marked in philosophy and political theory, it soon spread to the study of history—understanding the Revolution and its causes became an urgent necessity. In a more general sense, the fact that the Revolution had occurred at all altered people's ideas about the past as such, changed the character of historical enquiry and interpretation, and especially in Germany helped raise historical scholarship to a position of cultural dominance that it was to retain for several generations.

Among the great variety of reactions to the Revolution, Clausewitz's response stands out for its nonpartisan, complex realism. From the time when he began to set down his ideas on the history and present condition of Europe as a young officer of twenty-three, he seems to have been convinced that the Revolution had been inevitable, that the administrative system of the French monarchy and its economic and social institutions were so inefficient and inequitable that a violent correction had to come.[8] His view of a society regaining its balance and progressing toward its full potential of power was accompanied but not clouded by a strong distaste for revolutionary rhetoric and mob rule. On the other hand, his recognition of the need for change and his sympathy for the claims of at least the educated and commercial elements of the Third Estate did not weaken his sense of danger that a reformed, rejuvenated France posed to Europe. He never doubted that war alone could bring French expansion to a halt.[9] This way of looking at the Revolution as it blended into the Napoleonic empire, which emphasized the inevitable interaction and conflict of interests and energies instead of making moral judgments, was closely linked to attitudes that were to characterize his historical writings: a sense of impermanence in human affairs, disbelief in progress, denial that the social and political status quo reflected a God-given order, and rejection of any teleological force in history.

Revolutions demonstrate the reality of great and sudden change. In an unusually direct manner, the events of his youth and early maturity confronted Clausewitz with the need to explain the changes that were taking

---

[8] References to the French Revolution abound in his writings. The most important analysis of its causes occurs in the essay "Agitation," in Carl von Clausewitz, *Historical and Political Writings*, ed. Peter Paret and Daniel Moran (Princeton, 1992), 335–68.

[9] For a characteristic statement of this view, see his note of 1803 beginning "Whether the Franks are like the Romans?" ibid., 239–40.

place and offered him the choice between two different views of history. In the beginning the French Revolution presented itself to Clausewitz largely in military terms. It coincided with revolutionary innovations in military organization, tactics, and operations, first implemented on a large scale by the republican armies, and until the Napoleonic empire collapsed it was more urgent for Clausewitz to understand these innovations and turn them against the French than to fit the Revolution into the larger processes of European history. On a deeper level, he took for granted that, like the Revolution, the revolution in war could be accurately interpreted only if the conditions preceding it were also taken into account. To many of the more reflective soldiers of his day this posed no particular difficulty. Jomini expressed a widely held belief when he claimed that Napoleon, the heir of the Revolution, had discovered permanently valid principles of war, and that earlier wars were merely stages in a long, continuous development leading to the Napoleonic pattern of large armies launched on campaigns of deep penetration, aimed at destroying the opponent's forces and occupying his capital. According to this view, the most gifted commanders of the past, Frederick the Great, for example, acted whenever possible according to strategic principles that subsequently were fully implemented by Napoleon in a military environment that had changed little between the 1740s and 1815.

Clausewitz never questioned the links—ranging from the central element of all wars, organized mass violence, to the use of similar or even identical weapons—that joined warfare before and after the Revolution. But he also insisted on important discontinuities. The military institutions of the ancien régime, he wrote in an essay on the life of his teacher, Scharnhorst, "had collapsed in the wars of the French Revolution; its forms and means were no longer appropriate to the changed times and new political conditions."[10] The earlier period should not be dismissed as merely preparatory to the present, and the present was misinterpreted if it was regarded merely as the fulfillment of past strivings. This fundamental difference aside, individual human beings should not be regarded as interchangeable. Clausewitz noted the uniqueness of the creative personality—a historical force that in his theories reappeared as the concept of genius—each acting in conditions that could never be duplicated. Frederick the Great and Napoleon not only governed and waged war in dissimilar environments, they also differed in character and personal circumstances. That Napoleon reigned not by inheritance but as a newcomer who needed to establish his dynasty and demonstrate the permanence of his rule might compel him to take greater risks than a hereditary monarch was likely to accept. The norms of war that some writers thought they

[10] "On the Life and Character of Scharnhorst," ibid., 102.

had discovered were not only dependent on the circumstances of the times, they were derived from the unique situation and interests of one individual, which might not recur under altered conditions or in different personalities. Napoleon's mass armies and all-embracing strategic goals were made possible by new conditions and expressed a highly personal conception of war. In the same way, the society, economy, and politics of the ancien régime had been conducive to, and had justified, limited operations.[11]

In his differentiated view of the past and in his efforts to interpret each period according to its own measure, Clausewitz reveals certain affinities with Ranke and other scholars of the Restoration era who were introducing a new outlook to the study and writing of history. This marked a departure from nearly every historian he had read in his youth. Between his arrival in Berlin in 1801 and the outbreak of War in 1806, he made excerpts of Schiller's *Revolt of the Netherlands* and of Johannes von Müller's *History of the Swiss Confederacy*, which he read with sufficient care to recognize that a passage was paraphrased from Machiavelli. Notes from those years refer to Machiavelli's *Discourses* and *Art of War*. Among other historical works he read before 1806 were books and essays by Montesquieu, Robertson, Ancillon, and Gentz. Justus Möser's *History of Osnabrück*, themes of which reappear in an essay Clausewitz wrote in 1807, he had perhaps already encountered in the 1790s, and he had begun the intensive exploration of Frederick the Great's *History of My Times* and *History of the Seven Years War*, which resulted in important studies in the 1820s. The number of specifically military historians cited or referred to in his early writings is even greater.[12]

We can guess which aspects in the works of these writers were most interesting or appealing to him. Machiavelli's frank recognition of the primacy of political and military power might have had a liberating impact on his thought. He must have valued Montesquieu's skepticism, specificity, and recognition of the importance of irrational factors; years later Clausewitz singled out his work as a model for his own theoretical efforts. In the same way he valued Möser's belief in the individuality of historical epochs and his replacement of the Enlightenment's concept of progress with the more earth-bound, less abstract sense of historical evolution. That a historian need not express himself in convoluted, academic-bureaucratic German, but could develop ideas and narrate events in vigorous carefully structured prose he might have learned above all from Schiller, the author most frequently cited or referred to in his early

---

[11] Clausewitz's view of this issue is discussed more extensively in "Continuity and Discontinuity in Some Interpretations of Tocqueville and Clausewitz" below.

[12] On Clausewitz's early reading see Paret, *Clausewitz and the State*, 78–97.

manuscripts and correspondence. But particular influences are difficult to trace. Perhaps Frederick's irony and easy use of antithesis helped inspire similar characteristics of Clausewitz's prose, but he encountered such elements in other authors as well. Far easier to recognize are the important differences that distinguished Clausewitz even in his youth from writers who could stimulate, nourish, but not fully satisfy his intense wish to reach back and understand the past.

Above all, his historical writings are free of any teleological message. Much as he admired Schiller, he could not write history in order to celebrate the idea of freedom, or, indeed, the workings of any abstraction supposedly revealed through the realities of the past. In the same way, the patriotic, idealistic purposes of Müller's *History of the Swiss* could never have served as a model for him—neither in its purpose nor in its style—although this did not prevent him from studying Müller's works and learning from them. Schiller and Müller were born in the 1750s; their elevation of moral absolutes as the dramatic goals of social, political, and military events was an essential part of their struggle against narrowly rationalistic and judgmental tendencies of Enlightenment historiography. But even some scholars who were Clausewitz's exact contemporaries and who published their most important and influential works during the last decade of Clausewitz's life differed sharply from him in the concerns they carried to the study of history. Friedrich Christoph Schlosser saw himself as an educator of liberal Germany, and his histories as means of strengthening ethical values and building moral character. Heinrich Luden and Friedrich von Raumer both idealized the German Middle Ages, and Raumer in particular helped turn the Hohenstauffen emperors into heroic figures for the Germans of the Restoration, symbols of a past empire that held out the promise of renewed German unity in the future. They used history for purposes external to it. Clausewitz studied and wrote history to gain greater understanding of the past, and—by means of the contribution history could make to theory—of the past, present, and future phenomenon of war.

One author, Scharnhorst, whom Clausewitz not only read with the greatest care but who also strongly influenced his scholarship was not primarily a historian. Like Schiller and Müller, Scharnhorst was born in the 1750s, but he was never entrapped in the moralizing assumptions of late-Enlightenment historiography, nor did he seek to rise above them by writing history as a drama of ethical grandeur and conflict. In his voluminous theoretical and technical works on military institutions and war, the interpretation of the past is only one among several fields of study. He was nevertheless convinced that the study of history should be at the center of any advanced study of war, and the historical passages in his writings are anything but mere background or decoration. Historical examples fill his theoretical treatises and manuals and illustrate how the techniques under discussion functioned in reality. In *On War*, Clausewitz praises Scharnhorst's use of historical material even in manuals meant to be carried on campaign in the officer's saddlebag—examples drawn from earlier wars, whose analysis helped to bridge the ever-present, dangerous gap between theory and practice, and his own extensive use of historical examples owes much to Scharnhorst.[13] The expert, sober manner in which Scharnhorst outlined these circumscribed episodes of military history carried over to his more extended historical studies, whose subject was no longer the formation of combat patrols or the effectiveness of land mines but strategy and national policy. Particularly interesting in this group is a long essay of 1797 on the reasons for the French successes in the revolutionary wars, which Scharnhorst wrote as an analytic introduction to a history of these wars. The essay is an original and far-sighted effort to appraise the more important components of the French effort, from the republic's geographic position and her unified political and military command to ideology and psychological factors. That the author was a serving officer in the army of an absolutist state who had fought the French for years did not prevent him from emphasizing the importance of political and popular energies that were generated in a society more open than his own.[14]

Scharnhorst's thorough knowledge of military engineering, siege warfare, and the design and employment of firearms is often reflected in his historical works. Clausewitz's campaign histories contain little of this. They focus mainly on the relationship between government policy and military action, the psychology and ability of the commanders, and on the construction of often highly detailed analytic narratives of strategic decisions and their operational implementation. They are also more openly speculative and seek illustrations and comparisons across a wide spectrum of the European past. The writings of teacher and pupil nevertheless show a number of related traits. Some psychological and social affinities may have helped Clausewitz incorporate parts of Scharnhorst's historical style, and perhaps made the process of adoption possible in the first place. Like his teacher he valued the specific. If he could never quite attain Scharnhorst's profound realism, he always strove for it, and both men held nonpartisan, utilitarian views of the political and military forces whose histories they interpreted. Clausewitz developed even his abstractions in a remarkably concrete manner, surrounding them with examples and analogies drawn from the sciences and everyday experience; he liked

---

[13] Clausewitz, "On Historical Examples," *On War*, 170.

[14] On Scharnhorst's writings, see Rudolf Stadelmann, *Schicksal und Geistige Welt* (Wiesbaden, 1952); and the chapter "Scharnhorst's Mediation between Old and New," in Paret, *Clausewitz and the State*, 56–77.

to characterize states, armies, and the processes of conflict in terms borrowed from physics and mechanics.[15] Perhaps he borrowed this device from Enlightenment authors, and yet to imagine large institutions and their component parts as machines, levers, ratchets, or counterweights subject to the pull of gravity and the retarding force of friction might have contributed to the evenhanded, practical note that runs through his historical interpretations, an interest in understanding how things really work that was further strengthened by a social fact: like Scharnhorst, Clausewitz did not belong by birth to the traditional or even to the recently ennobled elites among whom he spent his life. Scharnhorst was an outsider, Clausewitz's background was only marginally more privileged. Each had made his own way, and each thought about society and his place in it in highly pragmatic, unideological terms.

Clausewitz's writings are marked by the struggle for an objective interpretation of the past, a quality he thought essential for its own sake as well as for enabling history to create theory. But what historian did not seek or claim objectivity, which in any case is an ideal of many meanings? In his *History of the Thirty Years' War*, Schiller tried to be evenhanded, and, Johannes von Müller thought, he succeeded; which did not prevent him from glorifying Gustavus Adolphus as the inspired champion of religious freedom, while condemning Catholic obscurantism and political ambition. Clausewitz's objectivity was more encompassing, and his rejection of myths in favor of more mundane realities perplexed many of his early readers. His evaluation of Frederick the Great became famous for its sober recognition of the king's superior qualities and its total lack of adulation; when one of his first, long manuscripts, "Gustavus Adolphus' Campaigns of 1630–32," was at last published in 1837, the editor felt compelled to note that "Clausewitz's characterization of the king [did not] sufficiently emphasize that the war was a matter of conscience for him, and that his true greatness had another basis than military ambition."[16] Perhaps ultimately Clausewitz's historical objectivity derived

---

[15] One of the most striking examples of this approach is the concept of friction, which Clausewitz describes in part in the following words:

> The military machine—the army and everything related to it—is basically very simple and therefore seems easy to manage. But we should bear in mind that none of its components is one piece, each part is composed of individuals, everyone of whom retains his potential for friction. . . . A battalion is made up of individuals, the least important of whom may chance to delay things or somehow make them go wrong. . . . This tremendous friction, which cannot, as in mechanics, be reduced to a few points, is everywhere in contact with chance, and brings about effects that cannot be measured, just because they are largely due to chance.

"Friction in War," *On War*, 119–20.

[16] "Gustav Adolphs Feldzüge von 1630–1632," *Werke* 9 (1837): v.

from his matter-of-fact belief that the urge for power and expansion was inherent in most political and social entities. Even if the scholar favored one side over the other, his recognition that the opponent also functioned according to his nature and interests served as a brake on partisanship. Clausewitz's refusal to judge the past by the standards or concerns of the present did the rest. Indeed, as his political essays demonstrate, he was far more critical of his own time than of any period of the past, and the evenhandedness that generally marks his historical writings is unusual not only in comparison with the historical literature of his day, but perhaps even more so in comparison with the historical literature of the following generation.

Ranke published his first books toward the end of Clausewitz's life. Clausewitz was familiar with at least some of them. He read the *History of the Serbian Revolution* shortly after it was published at the beginning of 1829, but we do not know his opinion of the work.[17] In his own historical writings, Clausewitz approaches his younger contemporary in his rejection of abstract and teleological elements in history, in his emphasis of the unique, and in his respect for the separateness and particularity of each epoch. Even their views of the state and of the European community of states reveal certain similarities, grounded in their understading of political and military power. But Clausewitz does not follow Ranke in combining a sense of the uniqueness of each age with a belief in God's immanence in historical forces, nor was he inspired by visions of large structures and patterns of history, akin to the unity and division of the Latin and Germanic peoples that for Ranke defined the European experience since the rise of Christianity and the decline of the universal empire of Rome. Equally, perhaps even more significant, Clausewitz's historical writings show no sign of the methodological revolution initiated by Ranke and by a few older scholars, whose work influenced or paralleled Ranke's: Savigny, Karl Ritter, Niebuhr—once again almost exactly Clausewitz's contemporaries. Nothing in Clausewitz's treatment of his material points to the new, more systematic comparative analysis of documents, accounts, and traditions that these men developed to reveal the genuine facts of the past and gain a firmer sense of the dynamic of events. He possessed only the most limited recognition of the importance of archival research and of the systematic exploitation of the available material and seems on the whole to have been prepared to accept published versions as faithful to the original manuscripts. His sources were other historical accounts and published memoirs, reports, and correspondence. His sparse references suggest that he based his works on a small number

[17] Clausewitz to Gneisenau, 8 July 1828, in Carl von Clausewitz, *Schriften-Aufsätze-Studien-Briefe*, ed. Werner Hahlweg (Göttingen, 1966–90), vol. 2, part 1, 549.

of sources, which he read critically and compared to each other. He put himself in the position of the writer, as he always tried to put himself in the position of the people that he and others wrote about. His treatment of Napoleon's memoirs in his history of the Italian campaign of 1796 is a good example: he uses the memoirs to help him understand events and compares the events with Napoleon's account to evaluate the memoirs, always conscious of the personality, exceptional ability, and the political and private motives of their author.

Taken together, these practices suggest a writer who in historiographical terms is a transitional figure: a rigorous thinker who has left past preconceptions behind but has not acquired the new methodological tools that are being developed; an amateur scholar, not an academic, untouched by the nascent professionalism of the discipline of history. We may regard him as a precursor of German historicism, whose work has not yet acquired scientific character. But as always when we are faced with a scholar who rises above the average, what is most interesting and valuable about his work transcends methodological and historiographical categories.

10

CONTINUITY AND DISCONTINUITY IN SOME

INTERPRETATIONS BY TOCQUEVILLE

AND CLAUSEWITZ

THIS ESSAY ADDS to and comments on the preceding discussion of Clausewitz's historical work. It may also be said to form a bridge between his histories and his theories because it points to some specific cases in which his historical studies contributed to the development of theory. Originally it was written for a seminar on methodology at Stanford; its intellectual starting point was a statement by Hans Delbrück in 1878 to the effect that Clausewitz's interpretation of the causes of the French Revolution was worthy of Tocqueville. The piece in which this comment appears—Delbrück's review of the first biography of Clausewitz—had been known to me for years, and I was surprised that no one had taken up the hint and pursued it. The comparison seemed appropriate for a seminar discussion; but as I returned to Tocqueville's and Clausewitz's works in preparation for writing the essay, it became apparent to me that the affinities between the two men went beyond their views of the French Revolution.

That is not to deny that the Revolution was the central historical event in their lives, though for each in somewhat different form. Leaving aside its direct impact on them, the Revolution changed Europe and released vast forces that set new problems for the analyst and theorist. Its military consequences—the wars of Napoleon—were as shattering as its political implications, the breakdown of the principle of legitimacy and the threat and promise of the opening up of society and of wider participation in the political process. But for Tocqueville and Clausewitz the Revolution did more than pose problems and present difficulties. They were among those of their generation for whom the destruction of old certainties in the culture, society, and politics of Europe—painful though this could be—proved psychologically and intellectually liberating. Both thought and wrote in ways that would not have been possible before 1789.

Ideas can take on lives of their own and function under conditions very different from those in which they had emerged. But even if they acquire a power independent of their original environment and we respond to them as pure abstractions, they are understood with greater precision if we return to their genesis and see how their creators transformed the specifics of their lives and experience into absolutes. Just as it is wrong to limit the value of psychoanalysis to middle-class Vienna before 1914, it would be a mistake to assume that Clausewitz's ideas had a special or even exclusive validity for Restoration Prussia or Tocqueville's for France in the years before and after 1848. But the historical seedbed of an idea and the undergrowth and weeds through which the idea forces its way to light tell us something important about it, and it seemed worthwhile to me not only to compare certain ideas of Tocqueville and Clausewitz, but also to discuss the two men and their thought in relation to their times and to the Revolution.

మ

The title of this essay tries to indicate its limited purpose. It is not my intention to present a comprehensive analysis of the explanatory concepts of continuity and cataclysmic change in Tocqueville's and Clausewitz's works. I merely want to compare the function of the two concepts in a few instances of their work, although, to be sure, these pertain to major themes: Tocqueville's thesis of the links between the ancien régime and the French Revolution; and Clausewitz's interpretation of this revolution, of Prussia's decline and revival, and above all his view of the revolution in war—a transformation that coincided with, and in part was caused by, the break-up of the French monarchy and its replacement by the First Republic and the empire.

Of course any comparison of Tocqueville and Clausewitz must acknowledge a large asymmetry. Although scarcely a typical historian of the July Monarchy and the Second Empire, Tocqueville wrote as a historian much of the time. He was and continues to be read as such. Clausewitz, on the other hand, is generally not thought of as a historian, and he himself regarded his historical work, with some important exceptions, not as an end in itself but as a stage in a process leading, by way of a better understanding of the past, to the development of theory. For Clausewitz, history possessed primarily a theoretical function, but it was a function of crucial significance: history stood for a part of reality, the many segments of which—past and present—it was the task of theory to comprehend and illuminate. Tocqueville also had pronounced theoretical concerns, but in his work the historical element is at once apparent: it forms the whitecaps and waves, in Richard Herr's metaphor, on the surface of the ocean, far beneath which runs the deep current of the author's theoretical purpose.[1]

The differences in Tocqueville's and Clausewitz's aims and achievements are great, but similarities also exist, and we may thus be justified in bringing together aspects of their work. To pass Tocqueville's *Old Regime and the Revolution* like a magnet over Clausewitz's writings and lift out some of their historical components should give us a better sense of Clausewitz the historian. It will also illustrate some of the meanings the concept of continuity had for the two men.

I

Even when they wrote on historical subjects, Tocqueville and Clausewitz addressed issues of their times. With an openness not commonly found in scholarly writing, they also linked their analyses to recollections of their family situation and childhood experiences. A glance at their antecedents is therefore appropriate.

Born in 1805, Tocqueville descended through his father from country nobles established in Normandy since the fifteenth century and on his mother's side from an important family of the judicial nobility. Her father was president of the Parlement of Paris; her grandfather, Lamoignon de Malesherbes, was a famous president of the same body, one of the leaders of the parliamentary opposition to Louis XV and, as director of censorship, a valued protector of the editors and authors of the *Encyclopédie*. In 1792, at the age of seventy-two, Malesherbes volunteered to defend Louis XVI at his trial before the Convention. The following year he was guillotined, together with his daughter and son-in-law, Tocqueville's grandparents. Tocqueville's father and mother were imprisoned and not released until after Thermidor.

His family history thus linked Tocqueville to some of the most important forces in French history, and his pronounced need to understand the attitudes and actions of his ancestors as well as his family's tragic fate during the revolution lay at the roots of his most important scholarly interests. In one form or another the power of the state, the freedom of the individual, their interdependence and antagonisms, occupied him throughout life. His two major works are distinguished by an unusually open personal engagement, which is made even more explicit in his correspondence. The history of France, as it moved from feudalism to the

---

[1] Richard Herr, *Tocqueville and the Old Regime* (Princeton, 1962), 35.

unifying, centralized state, held the explanation for the history of his family.

Tocqueville's social position opened the doors to a judicial career and eventually to high political office. When he began to write he did so not only as a noble whose antecedents gave him an almost proprietary sense of the French past but also as an official who understood the machinery of the state. He lived and wrote as an insider. In the simpler, more controlled environment of Prussia, so did Clausewitz. His origins, however, were considerably more modest. Far from the center of an established elite, the bourgeois family into which he was born in 1780 occupied a position barely at its margin. Parsons and landowners were among his paternal and maternal ancestors. His father's claim of nobility was based on little more than family legend, but it carried the Clausewitzes into the ranks of officers and officials who rose in the world as they served the expanding Prussian state. Tocqueville would have regarded Clausewitz as a member of that aristocracy of achievement that, to his regret, the French nobility had ceased to be.

Unlike Tocqueville, for whom the values of his family remained the touchstone of intellectual independence and principled action, the young Clausewitz rebelled against much that he had learned as a child. His ambivalence toward his early environment came to affect his view of the state and also of the nobility, whose privileges he opposed and whose role in the modern world he examined with notable detachment in his writings. In his history of Prussia before and during 1806, he went so far as to detail his own background to ensure that his highly critical analysis was not dismissed as the view of an embittered outsider and to demonstrate that his family held attitudes which, multiplied many times, were one cause of the state's collapse: an arrogant confidence in the Prussian military and political system, which kept men from moving with the times. My father, he writes, "was filled with the prejudices of his class; in [my] parents' house [I] saw almost no-one but officers, and not the best educated and most versatile at that."[2] He soon questioned their assumptions. But he would never have been able to analyze war and policy with the same kind of detailed knowledge had he not become part of the Prussian military caste.

His many years of military service, and his administrative and political duties during the Reform era and later, never carried Clausewitz to a position of eminence comparable to Tocqueville's frustrating but instructive tenure as foreign minister. Still, Clausewitz very nearly became Prussian minister at the Court of St. James, and he ended his career as chief of

[2] Carl von Clausewitz, "Observations on Prussia in Her Great Catastrophe," in *Historical and Political Writings*, eds. Peter Paret and Daniel Moran (Princeton, 1992), 40.

staff of the forces Prussia mobilized during the international crises of 1830 and 1831. The immersion of the two men in the business of government, their exposure to the cross fire of policies and personal ambitions, helped give their thought its eminently realistic and practical cast.

II

It was Tocqueville's understanding of the institutions and dynamic of centralized government that freed his interpretation of the French Revolution from dependence on its rhetoric and on the rhetoric of its opponents. Neither revolutionary assertions of liberty and fraternity nor counterrevolutionary accusations of anarchy and godlessness could blind him to the degree to which governments after 1789 carried forward and expanded the policies of their absolutist predecessors. A supreme effort of the historical imagination was still needed to link the evolution of administrative centralization with his thesis of a centuries-long tendency in French and European history toward social equality, the destruction by kings and their ministers of the intermediary powers in the state, and the decline of the French nobility, and to conclude from the sum of these forces that the revolution, far from being the explosive beginning of a new age, merely gave expression to earlier intentions and processes, under which Frenchmen might become more equal but less free. In a famous chapter of Book II of *The Old Regime and the Revolution*, he wrote that under the Bourbon monarchy, as today, "The central administration held all Frenchmen in tutelage, and if the insolent term had not yet been invented, at least the reality already existed."[3] The revolution, he declared in an earlier chapter, "took the world by surprise, nevertheless it was nothing but the completion of a long development." Indeed, not even that, because the development had not yet come to a halt.[4]

Tocqueville's thesis of continuing or permanent revolution is one of the many indicators of the contemporary orientation of his book. The difficulty of categorizing Tocqueville's political views is well known. He was anything but dogmatic, an analyst rather than partisan, whose pessimism about the future of European society may have made it easier for him to be critical of both conservative and liberal thought. *The Old Regime* was a corrective of received opinions on both sides. But potentially—had nineteenth-century radicals paid more attention to historians who were not in their camp—the book might have been more damaging to the left.

---

[3] Alexis de Tocqueville, *L'ancien régime et la révolution*, ed. André Jardin; vol. 2 of *Oeuvres complètes*, ed. J.-P. Mayer (Paris, 1952), part 1, p. 122.
[4] Ibid., 96.

Its continuity thesis denied the concept of the new and would have deprived the left of an idea of tremendous psychological power, which Tocqueville, pointing to the continuing administrative centralization under the First Republic, dismissed as inapplicable. Perhaps the book made its strongest impact on the politically moderate bourgeoisie, more comfortable with the ideas of 1789 than 1794, who, a contemporary critic noted, were astonished to learn from M. de Tocqueville "the extent to which nearly every result of the Revolution already existed in the ancien régime."[5]

The continuity thesis also responded to Tocqueville's need to make sense of the fate of his family. If the revolution was not a conflict between repression and freedom but rather between two forms of increasingly authoritarian government—the monarchy and the republic—its execution of such a representative of the traditional intermediary powers as Malesherbes was merely necessary and logical.

III

Tocqueville's life and thought were dominated by the French Revolution. For Clausewitz, too, the revolution constituted a force of the first magnitude, but in his mind its general significance was linked to the decline and revival of Prussia. Discussions of these episodes in French and German history are found throughout his writings on war, but he also treated them in several long essays, which were to remain unpublished for fifty years or more. One essay of the early 1820s, with the faintly ironic title "Umtriebe"—which might be translated as "Political Agitation" or simply "Agitation"—denied the fear of some conservatives that the political unrest then current in Germany would lead to revolution.[6] The essay opens with a reconstruction of the background of the French Revolution to show that major political upheavals tend to be caused not by conspiracies or treason but by social and political developments lasting over generations. When the essay was at last printed in 1878, it elicited from the young Hans Delbrück the admiring comment that Clausewitz's interpretation of the limited historical evidence available in the 1820s might be compared to the result of Tocqueville's later detailed research—a comment that students of the history of history were to ignore for the next century.[7]

[5] J. J. Ampère, quoted by André Jardin, ibid., 339.

[6] Carl von Clausewitz, "Agitation," in *Historical and Political Writings*, 359–60. See also my discussion of the essay in *Clausewitz and the State*, rev. ed. (Princeton, 1985), 20–21, 298–306.

[7] Hans Delbrück, "General von Clausewitz," first published in 1878, reprinted in Delbrück's *Historische und politische Aufsätze* (Berlin, 1887), 214.

What is it in Clausewitz's essay that may be said to foreshadow Tocqueville? For one, the author's insistence on the force of historical continuity. Not that he emphasized the revolutionary governments' continuation of earlier policies. The element of continuity that he developed concerned causation rather than content. But he also denied that the revolution was an absolute break with the past. Arbitrary rule, he writes, was replaced by a "mixed form of government. . . . The philosophers wanted to base everything on the rights of man"—but that was only one of the bases of the new system.[8]

A second part of the essay that more closely parallels Tocqueville's ideas is a careful analysis of the political and spiritual decline of the French nobility, a wasting away that Clausewitz declares occurred everywhere else as well, though at a somewhat slower rate. A few quotations and paraphrases will suggest the character of his treatment of the caste that he himself had recently entered: With the rise of the absolute monarchy, "the noble, while still lord over the peasant and privileged above the bourgeois, no longer shared in the power of the state; the noble had become a subject like everyone else."[9] As soon as the nobility ceased to possess a true political and social function, it was bound to decline. In outward appearance it grew somewhat closer to other groups in society;

> internally it took on the character of a ruin, undermined by time. . . . The totally altered condition of the nobility, the ambiguous place it assumed in the new political community, and the rise of the bourgeoisie, generated a high degree of tension, which had to be resolved in one way or another—gradually, through voluntary change, or at once, violently. This tension we regard as one, and the primary, cause of the French Revolution. The other is the misuse of administrative power.[10]

In his study of Prussia's decline, Clausewitz points up the contrast between revolutionary France and the post-Frederician monarchy: Prussian society was not allowed to play a role in public affairs. The state's achievements under Frederick the Great now actually worked against it. The expansion of its territory made Prussia more difficult to govern, and while the bureaucratic structure continued to grow in complexity, it was no longer infused with its former energy. The traditional military institutions of absolutism were unlikely to prove a match for the "energies released in a *revolutionary war*."[11] Prussian diplomacy and strategic planning were feeble, but the consciousness of past triumphs gave government and army a false sense of confidence. We might note that these and similar

[8] *Historical and Political Writings*, 346.
[9] Ibid., 153.
[10] Ibid., 157, 162.
[11] Ibid., 32.

judgments in other essays written during the Restoration were not merely the result of hindsight reinforced by scholarship; they echo and expand on the criticisms and presentiments of the young Clausewitz in the months before Prussia's collapse twenty years earlier.[12]

In the essay "Agitation," Clausewitz writes that great revolutions do not come from petty causes—and he implied, neither do great defeats.[13] He believed that particular events or individuals could not by themselves bring about major change. In his view of the past nothing is isolated. Even Napoleon—for him the personification of creative energy—needed the long evolution of French history to make him ruler of Europe. "Mother Revolution" was Clausewitz's characteristic term; but, he added, once Napoleon gained power, he knew how to keep his foot on her neck.[14] His historical studies always assume the strength of long developmental processes. He does not, however, interpret these causal forces extending over generations and centuries as the expression of divine will or as part of a general force for progress. Progress might occur in some areas, other fields might experience decline: in world history the lines of causal development move through an environment of social and political energies that rise and fall. All products of human endeavor, he noted in a letter written in his early twenties, carry within themselves the element of their own destruction.[15] By this he seems to have meant not merely that organisms age and die but also that their qualities generate contrary forces with which they exist in a symbiotic relationship and by which they may be defeated—just as in war such elements as attack and defense or intention and friction coexist and interact.

Clausewitz's belief in the power of historical continuities was perhaps less common among historians of the 1820s than it subsequently became. Today we find it unexceptional, the more so since his sensitivity to connections and implications was combined with a strong awareness of the unique. It is this aspect of his historical sense that caused him to dismiss claims of continuity which assumed, if they did not openly assert, an absence of change. A particularly significant example is his rejection of the view, propounded by Jomini among others, and widely accepted at the time, that in his wars Frederick the Great acted whenever possible according to strategic principles that subsequently were fully implemented by

---

[12] On Clausewitz's pessimistic appraisal in 1806 of Prussia's political and military prospects, see my *Clausewitz and the State*, 110–19.

[13] *Historical and Political Writings*, 359.

[14] Ibid., 348.

[15] In a discussion of organized religion and the constitution of Sparta as instances of impermanence, letter to his fiancée, Marie v. Brühl, 5 October 1807, in *Karl and Marie von Clausewitz: Ein Lebensbild in Briefen und Tagebuchblättern*, ed. K. Linnebach (Berlin, 1917), p. 142.

Napoleon in a military environment that had changed little between the 1740s and 1815. From this perspective Frederick, having merely dominated central Germany rather than the whole of Europe, appeared as a miniature Napoleon or as Napoleon's predecessor. Clausewitz, on the contrary, saw a radical discontinuity. The military institutions of the ancien régime, he wrote in an essay on the era of Prussian reform, "had collapsed in the wars of the French Revolution; its forms and means were no longer appropriate to the changed times and new political conditions."[16] The result was a revolution in war. In Book VIII of *On War*, Clausewitz concludes the best-known of his many discussions of this revolution with the apocalyptic statement: "War, untrammeled by any conventional restraints, had broken loose in all its elemental fury." In the following passage he summarizes the most important instruments of this change: mass armies, drawn from populations that were beginning to take part in the affairs of their nations, an involvement that resulted "partly from the impact that the [French] Revolution had on the internal conditions of every state, and partly from the danger that France posed to everyone."[17]

Frederick and Napoleon not only acted in different environments, Clausewitz insisted, but they also differed in character and personal circumstances. For example, the fact that Napoleon reigned not by hereditary right but as a new man whose throne lacked the authority derived from tradition was likely to affect his strategy.

This discriminating view of the past meant better history. It also helped Clausewitz develop his most important theoretical concepts. To continue with our example of Frederick and Napoleon: In agreement with Jomini many soldiers of Clausewitz's generation equated the emperor's increasingly expansive wars with modern war as such, and interpreted the history of war as a slow—often blocked or diverted—advance toward this goal. Clausewitz, too, thought it probable that in future conflicts states would tend to mobilize all possible resources to gain total victory. He even argued that logically no force existed within that body of social activity called war that could prevent the escalation of violence toward totality. Finally, he suggested that Frederick and Napoleon might be taken to represent two stages in the history of war, which he sometimes called "princely war" and, emerging in the 1790s, "national war." But the change from princely to national war did not signify an inevitable progression toward the unlimited use of violence. If in the past, many—indeed most—wars had fallen short of totality, it was not because soldiers

[16] Carl von Clausewitz, "On the Life and Character of Scharnhorst," *Historical and Political Writings*, p. 102.

[17] Carl von Clausewitz, *On War*, trans. and ed. Michael Howard and Peter Paret (Princeton, 1984), Book 8, chap. 3, p. 593.

or governments were unenlightened, but because generally the purposes for which the wars were fought did not warrant extreme efforts, or because the social and political conditions of the warring powers made such exertions impossible. Two kinds of war had always existed, and would always exist: total war, which responded to the philosophic ideal of unalloyed violence, and limited war. Not only did the study of history enable Clausewitz to place the military experience of his generation in perspective; it helped him avoid the error of defining Napoleonic war as the "correct" war. Instead he was able to give theoretical expression to the common-sense observation, confirmed by history, that the intensity of any particular conflict tended to reflect the political forces that had given rise to it. Consequently Frederick and Napoleon do not represent stages in a progression from inferior to superior ways of fighting; rather the two men personify the permanent duality of war. Total (Napoleonic) wars had occurred in the past, and limited (Frederician) wars would occur in the future. Positing a measure of discontinuity between Frederick and Napoleon helped Clausewitz create a unified, all-encompassing theory of war.[18]

IV

To conclude, let me once more pick up the Tocquevillian magnet, with which we drew historical interpretations out of the compact mass of Clausewitz's writings—a process of extraction that was aided by certain similarities in their approaches to the past. I commented on the importance the two men attributed to the concept of continuity and on the strong personal note found in their work. The two may be linked. Too often, when we discuss theses of continuity, we think of ideologies, interest groups, and other general factors and ignore the experiences of individuals, which may bracket very different times. That certainly was true for the generations of Tocqueville and Clausewitz. The revolution, empire, and restoration were made by men of the ancien régime. Of the Prussian generals who faced the Napoleonic torrent in 1806, at least fifty had fought in the Seven Years' War.[19] Not everyone who experiences change is prepared to analyze it; but in different ways Tocqueville and Clause-

[18] The most comprehensive exposition of the theory of limited and unlimited war and of the main lines of the historical analysis on which it is based is given in Book VIII, chaps. 1–8 of *On War*. Concise statements of the duality of war derived from its political, social, and intellectual context may be found, for example, in Book 1, chap. 1 of *On War*, and in "Two Letters on Strategy," above, pp. 127–29.

[19] Since most of the Prussian army archives for the period have been destroyed, this estimate, derived from army lists and extracts of service records, may slightly understate the total.

witz came to terms in their writings with their families' past and with forces they themselves had experienced.

We also noted that even their historical works openly or indirectly addressed concerns of their times and gave voice to their own reactions to aspects of the age—for instance, to the phenomenon they both called the "democratization of society." But their responses were given a unique weight by their interest in universals and general developments. They thought conceptually, and not only Tocqueville but to a lesser extent Clausewitz as well wrote history that often assumed the character of comparative political sociology. By chance we have two comments they made about their work that help us see the similarity of the goals they set themselves. When Tocqueville first conceived the plan of *The Old Regime* in the 1830s, he wrote to a friend: "I have in mind a work like Montesquieu's *Considerations on the Causes of the Grandeur and Decadence of the Romans*," a statement he repeated in similar terms fourteen years later.[20] Clausewitz cited the same model when he began the manuscript that eventually became *On War*: "The manner in which Montesquieu dealt with his subject was vaguely in my mind."[21] Both men were inspired by Montesquieu's effort to interpret his own times and explain general phenomena with the help of history.[22]

It is in their use of continuities as explanatory concepts that they approach each other most closely. Clausewitz would have approved of Tocqueville's emphasis on the presence of earlier forces in the French Revolution and might even have agreed that this constituted its central truth. His comparable interpretive achievement is the discovery of two opposites in the web of historical continuities: limited and unlimited war, which together encompass all of war.

Of the two interpretations, both of which profoundly marked subsequent thought on their subjects, Clausewitz's is the more immune to de-

---

[20] Alexis de Tocqueville to Louis de Kergorlay, 10 November 1836, *Oeuvres et correspondance inédites*, ed. Gustave de Beaumont (Paris, 1861), 1:338; and 15 December 1850, *Nouvelle correspondance entièrement inédite*, ed. Gustave de Beaumont (Paris, 1866), 268.

[21] "Author's Comment," *On War*, 63.

[22] A more wide-ranging comparison of the two men than is attempted here would reveal any number of additional similarities and affinities, some incidental and of no significance—both Tocqueville and Clausewitz married older women, neither had children—others perhaps worth further analysis. For example, both men developed literary styles that moved easily between the abstract and the specific, excelling equally in creating miniature portraits of contemporaries and in the exposition of complex ideas. Both *Old Regime* and *On War* are based on insights their authors had already gained—though not yet fully developed—in their youth, and both works were left incomplete. Both Tocqueville and Clausewitz opposed dominant political forces of their time and place; both were skeptical of the idea of progress, distrusted ideological thinking, and defended their intellectual and political independence against left and right.

tailed criticism. Explaining much of the revolution through the continuing accretion of administrative power is a magnificent thesis, which retains its explanatory vitality to this day. But is it not the case that Tocqueville slights the reality of changes that did occur, for instance the creation of legal equality for all, even if this equality went hand in hand with the loss of freedom for some? To millions who had very little freedom before 1789, this loss may have appeared insignificant. Tocqueville laid bare the false side of revolutionary equality but found it difficult to acknowledge that for many Frenchmen the closer control government now exerted over all of society mattered far less that it did to an aristocratic intellectual.

We have seen such writers as Jomini reduce the idea of continuity to one of changelessness, relieved only by the teleological concept of progress. On a far higher and richer plane, Tocqueville also suggested an absence of change between the ancien régime and the revolution, which can be true only if we agree that a process once begun is as good as completed. At critical junctures the historian in Tocqueville gives way to the political sociologist tracing large patterns from the middle ages to his own day, to the pessimistic observer of the decay of French freedom and individuality, to the grandson of victims of the Terror. Family antecedents, ethical and social values, and his conception of political development in Europe shaped his view of the French Revolution. Similar personal elements in Clausewitz's histories and especially in his theoretical writings were less distorting of the evidence. But the degree of one-sidedness in the views of the two men matters less than does their creative potential. All historians are captives of their own times and conditions, and their personal histories always impinge on the histories they write. To our good fortune a few among them also possess the genius to turn their subjective personal concerns into interpretations that, although partial and incomplete as all interpretations must be, open up new lines of inquiry into the past, for the rest of us to learn from, explore, and expand.

11

KLEIST AND CLAUSEWITZ:

A COMPARATIVE SKETCH

IN DISCUSSIONS of Clausewitz's work it is not uncommon to encounter references to his links with poets, philosophers, and the high culture of his time. Often these allusions are motivated by a wish to explain and justify aspects of his thought that the modern reader might consider odd. If this seems an expedient of doubtful value, it nevertheless points in the right direction. Clausewitz was a man of broad cultural and scientific interests, who read very widely and personally knew or corresponded with many academics and literary figures. He lived in a preindustrial, preprofessional society that still enabled and even encouraged its members to range beyond the boundaries of their particular occupations, and their intellectual associations and mutual borrowings ran far deeper than was to be the case even a few generations later.

In *Clausewitz and the State* I traced some of these relations, especially as they affected the development of Clausewitz's political views and his ideas on the historical and theoretical study of war. It would have skewed the structure of the book to expand my analysis into contacts and similarities that did not bear directly on his work. Nevertheless it was apparent that these were numerous and that they held out the possibility of casting further light not only on Clausewitz's general attitudes and ideas but also on his hypotheses and on the methods of reasoning by which he arrived at them. An invitation to give a talk to the German Studies Association, an organization that counts more literary scholars and teachers of German among its members than historians, provided the occasion for a closer discussion of Clausewitz's relations with a writer of his generation. For his counterpart I might have chosen among such associates as the patriotic poet and pamphleteer Ernst Moritz Arndt, the literary theorist August Wilhelm Schlegel, or the political writer Joseph von Görres. Instead I decided to talk about Clausewitz and Heinrich von Kleist, even if it cannot be documented that the two ever met or read each others writings. I did so because they moved in the same society and served the same state, and because I vaguely felt that a comparison of their works might reveal affinities. A third reason had to do with the fragmented nature of Kleist's biography. He is one of the great figures of German literature, but important periods of his life remain closed to us or are known only in outline. It seemed worthwhile to trace even the faint ties and simultaneities that could be expected to exist between two intellectually aware Prussian officers of the Napoleonic era. Although I did not then foresee it, I was not surprised when in the course of preparing the talk I encountered far more than the few biographical parallels that had served as my starting point.

વે

Neither Heinrich von Kleist nor Carl von Clausewitz mentions the other in his surviving letters, and the vast scholarly literature that has grown up around each has little to say about the other.[1] But they were contemporaries living in sometimes identical, sometimes related segments of a small society and must have shared not only certain cultural affinities, but also personal links—connections that may be worth tracing.

One justification for the comparative sketch that this essay will attempt lies in our continued ignorance about many stages in Kleist's life. Even if it bears on Kleist's immediate environment rather than on him directly, additional information is worth pursuing. A syncretic approach to the two men may also bring out the characteristics of each more sharply. Finally, such a confrontation may uncover similarities in their intellectual positions, a discovery that could advance the analysis of their work.

If Clausewitz were only the author of an opaque classic on war, the usefulness of comparing him and Kleist might nevertheless be doubted. But he was, of course, far more than a military theorist. His numerous histories reveal him as a creative if still insufficiently recognized member of the first generation of German historicism. Delbrück compared his interpretation of the French Revolution to that of Tocqueville, and Dilthey has gone so far as to assert that "no German historian can compare with this brilliant pupil of Scharnhorst."[2]

No less remarkable than Clausewitz's histories are his political essays. Their lack of ideological partisanship and their understanding of the re-

---

[1] The most striking attempt to link the two men occurs in Reinhold Steig, *Heinrich von Kleist's Berliner Kämpfe* (Berlin and Stuttgart, 1901). Steig claims that in 1811, as members of the christlich-deutsche Tischgesellschaft, Kleist and Clausewitz worked for a national uprising against Napoleon. While there is no doubt that Clausewitz belonged to the Tischgesellschaft, it has long been recognized that Steig seriously misinterpreted the group's political character and significance as well as Kleist's political position. More recently, Hans Joachim Kreutzer has argued that the documentary evidence leaves it uncertain that Kleist was even a member. Hans Joachim Kreutzer, "Heinrich von Kleists Lebensspuren . . . ," *Euphorion* 62 (1968): 210–12.

[2] Wilhelm Dilthey: "Scharnhorst," in *Zur Preussischen Geschichte* (Leipzig and Berlin, 1936), 120.

ality of power make them stand out in the political writings of Restoration Germany—or would have done so if censorship had permitted their publication. Finally, his theories on war are never narrowly military but interpret war as an act of political and social intercourse that combines the rational with the irrational. To Clausewitz war is a mirror, a prism in which all of life is refracted. Even at his most detailed he conveys a sense of the endless interrelations that he finds in the physical, intellectual, and emotional world. But perhaps there is no need further to justify a comparison of the two most original writers to emerge from the Prussian military nobility in its long history.

In the following pages I propose, first, to indicate certain parallels and even links between their lives. Having sketched their dual biography, I want to proceed to their work and raise some questions concerning the interaction between their writings and their times. How did the poet and how did the theorist respond to, and make use of, the events that occurred around them? And I shall suggest that their very different writings give expression to a number of similar concerns and assumptions.

I

Kleist and Clausewitz, the younger by three years, were sons of Prussian officers; but while Kleist belonged to the country's oldest nobility, although to an impoverished branch of his extensive family, the Clausewitzs were bourgeois. Clausewitz's great-grandfather was a Lutheran pastor, his grandfather professor of theology at Halle. His son, Clausewitz's father, assumed the title of nobility and during the Seven Years' War served in the Prussian army, from which he was retired because he could not authenticate his noble descent.[3] Not until the less restrictive conditions after Frederick the Great's death were three of his sons admitted to the army as cadets, to begin careers in which all three rose to the rank of general. The Clausewitzs followed a characteristic eighteenth-century path from parsonage to state service, bringing with them an infusion of energy and talent that helped make possible the growth of Prussia to a modern power, while the Kleists belonged to an old elite that neither in numbers nor perhaps psychologically could meet the demands of the expanding state. In June 1792 Kleist was appointed to the Potsdam footguards. A few weeks earlier Clausewitz had been accepted in the thirty-fourth Infantry Regiment, stationed in the nearby town of Neuruppin. Between 1793 and 1795 the two young men saw active service in the war

---

[3] Eberhard Kessel: "Carl von Clausewitz: Herkunft und Persönlichkeit.," in *Wissen und Wehr* 18 (1937): 763–74.

against the French Republic.[4] But even then neither could be called typical of his station. In one of his earliest letters, Kleist wrote to his sister; "May Heaven bring us peace, so that with more humanitarian deeds we can make up for the time we are here killing so immorally."[5] Clausewitz's letters from this period are lost, but in a diary entry some years later he recalled the conclusion of his first campaign, comparing the "thickly wooded, and thus raw, poor, and melancholy mountains" of the Vosges, in which the fighting took place, with his own sadness and anxiety:

> With a kind of resignation our eyes had already grown accustomed to see no more than a few steps of the path that we followed. Our psychological existence was much the same; the physical surroundings perfectly reflected our mood. His extremely limited horizon barely permits the soldier to survey the next few hours of his existence. Often he hears the voice of battle, which is near and yet remains invisible, and he approaches his fate as he approaches danger in a dark night.—Finally, after an arduous march we suddenly had reached the crest of the last ridge of the Vosges mountains, and before and beneath us, from Landau to Worms, stretched the magnificent Rhine valley. At that moment life seemed to me to change from ominous gravity to friendliness, from tears to smiles.[6]

Clausewitz expresses himself less critically than does Kleist, but he, too, even in his youth, responds to war with a mixture of feeling and realistic analysis, acknowledging his feelings and subsequently reconstructing with great frankness what clearly had been a powerful emotional experience.

Although younger, Clausewitz was promoted more rapidly—to ensign in 1793, and at the age of fifteen, two years later, to lieutenant, a rank that Kleist attained only in his twentieth year. By then Kleist was already preparing himself, perhaps not yet consciously, to leave the army. With

---

[4] It is conceivable that Kleist and Clausewitz met during these years. Their regiments took part in the siege of Mainz in the spring and summer of 1793 and fought in the battle of Kaiserlautern and in one of the engagements near Trippstadt (2 and 3 July) the following year. In the spring of 1795 both units were stationed in Westphalia before returning to Prussia. See Günther Gieraths, *Die Kampfhandlungen der Brandenburgisch-Preussischen Armee*, (Berlin 1964), 56–57, 113, 421, 461.

[5] Heinrich von Kleist to Ulrike von Kleist, 25 February 1795, Heinrich von Kleist, *Briefe 1792–1804*, ed. Helmut Sembdner (Munich 1964), 12. It should be noted that Kleist wrote this sentence, which is not infrequently quoted in the modern literature, after the preliminary armistice between Prussia and France had been signed in January 1795. Kleist may therefore refer to life in bivouac—at the time his regiment was stationed near Frankfurt a. M.—rather than condemn war as such. His criticism of military life in his letter to Martini of 19 March 1799—"my innate distaste for the profession of arms" also refers to the routine of drill and discipline rather than to fighting.

[6] Carl von Clausewitz, "Journal einer Reise von Soissons über Dijon nach Gent," in Karl Schwartz, *Leben des Generals Carl von Clausewitz* (Berlin, 1878), 1:90.

close friends—one of whom, Rühle von Lilienstern, became Clausewitz's fellow student in Berlin and, still later, his colleague—Kleist played chamber music and took private lessons in mathematics and philosophy. Since my return to Potsdam, he wrote, "I have been a student rather than a soldier"—behavior that led to conflicts with his commanding officer, General von Rüchel, whom Clausewitz in his history of Prussia's decline before 1806 was to caricature as "a concentrated distillate of pure Prussianism."[7]

In 1799 Kleist resigned his commission to devote himself, as he put it, to scholarship and the search for happiness. During the following six years he briefly attended a university, applied for a post in the Prussian administration and withdrew his application, traveled extensively, suffered severe intellectual and psychological crises, and began to write. His early faith in reason and human perfectibility was overcome by determination to identify and interpret the force and dynamic of emotion. When he was twenty-five his first play was published, and the following year— 1804—it was even performed in a provincial Austrian theater. But by then he had reached the devastating recognition that he could not complete the drama *Guiskard* on which he had been working for two years and which he had expected to bring him instant fame. He responded to this shock with a suicidal attempt to join the French army in its invasion of England, but he was stopped at Boulogne and forced to return home. There he gave in to family pressure and his own sense of failure and entered the Prussian financial administration.

During these years, while Kleist's genius fought to free itself from psychological inhibitions and the restraints of upperclass expectations, Clausewitz's life moved undramatically from success to success. At the age of twenty-one he was sent from his provincial garrison to Berlin to attend a school for gifted junior officers. There he did undergo a crisis: he was overcome by a sense of inadequacy and wanted to leave the school; but he soon recovered confidence. Berlin gave him what he needed: the opportunity to immerse himself in the study of history, mathematics, and philosophy under the guidance of an inspired teacher, Scharnhorst. By the time he was twenty-five his exceptional abilities had become apparent. His early writings are already touched by an element that was to dominate his mature work—a rejection of intellectual systems that are more concerned with their own ideals and logic than with the brute reality of their subject matter. Examples are an essay that attacked contemporary theorists for squeezing the boundlessness and violence of Napoleonic warfare into highly artificial categories and a history of the Thirty Years'

[7] Carl von Clausewitz, "Observations on Prussia in Her Great Catastrophe," in *Historical and Political Writings*, ed. Peter Paret and Daniel Moran (Princeton, 1992), 46.

War, which neither condemned the war in the manner of the late Enlightenment as an especially irrational, anarchic struggle, nor regarded it with Schiller as an episode "in which the fight of powerful men for an important goal rages before our eyes." Instead he tried to reconstruct the war by putting himself in the place of its protagonists and victims.

His professional success opened Clausweitz the door to those circles in which Kleist moved by right of birth. He was appointed adjutant to a royal prince. He met his future wife, Marie von Brühl, a lady-in-waiting of the queen mother and a good friend of Marie von Kleist, Kleist's cousin and one of the most important women in Kleist's life. His fiancée introduced Clausewitz to the family of Prince Radziwill, whom in later years Kleist hoped to gain as a patron. Clausewitz became even more intimate with the king's younger brother, Prince Wilhelm, and with his wife, Marianne, to whom Kleist dedicated *Prinz von Homburg*, and whose rejection of the play—or at least disinterest in it—proved to be one of his last deep disappointments. Marie von Brühl's brother, Karl, many years later staged the first Berlin production of the play, in a heavily edited version that unsuccessfully tried to make the drama palatable to the Prussian court.

Kleist did not take part in the War of 1806 but had the bad luck of being arrested by the French as a suspected spy. Clausewitz fought in the autumn campaign and was captured. Both men were imprisoned in France, and for both their return to Germany in the second half of 1807 ushered in a period of intense creativity. Kleist wrote *Penthesilea*, *Amphytrion*, *Hermannsschlacht*, and his greatest stories. In December 1807, together with Adam Müller, he launched the journal *Phöbus*. Clausewitz became an influential assistant to Scharnhorst and other leaders of the Prussian reform movement, deeply involved in the administration and politics of modernization. At the same time he was perfecting the analytic method he needed to interpret that aspect of human activity, war, that had now dominated Europe for nearly two decades—a method that combines the concepts and values of German idealism with a new realism. The outbreak of fighting between France and Austria in spring 1809 interrupted and diverted these efforts. Both men at once offered their services to Austria. Kleist, who for some months had drawn closer to the anti-French network of Prussian patriots in which Clausewitz was very active, wrote his "Songs of War" and political essays and petitioned Vienna to sponsor a new patriotic journal, *Germania*, under his editorship. Clausewitz applied for a commission in the Austrian army. The defeat at Wagram and the subsequent armistice not only shattered their hopes that Europe would liberate herself from Napoleon, but also dealt a blow to their personal prospects, from which Clausewitz recovered more quickly and fully than could Kleist. Clausewitz did not give up his plans for leaving Prussia to carry on the fight against France elsewhere, but in the meantime his part in the military regeneration of the country grew in importance. By 1810, at the age of thirty, he was a member of the general staff and a lecturer at the War Academy. He sat on government commissions and was military tutor to the crown prince. Kleist's position, on the other hand, was deteriorating. Behind him lay the collapse of *Phöbus*, the failure of *Der Zerbrochene Krug* in Weimar, and the terrible shock of Goethe's antagonism. In the summer of 1810 Queen Louise died, and with her Kleist's best prospect of royal patronage. Futhermore, Iffland rejected *Käthchen von Heilbronn* as unsuitable to the Berlin stage. Kleist's finances were nearly exhausted. The start of a newspaper in Berlin was a desperate attempt to earn a living and regain a foothold with the public, and its end after six months could have been predicted.

If Kleist and Clausewitz had not met before—and some encounters are likely, although we cannot document them—they almost certainly did come to know each other in 1811. In Berlin both moved in small, overlapping social circles; Clausewitz joined the christlich-deutsche Tischgesellschaft, an association to which Kleist either belonged or that sought him as a member. We know of Kleist's contacts with several of Clausewitz's closer associates: with the Radziwills, with Prince Wilhelm and his wife. Kleist writes about a long talk with Clausewitz's close friend Gneisenau, on whom he called to advance his plan to reenter the army, and also mentions a visit to the estate of Ludwig von der Marwitz, another member of the Tischgesellschaft and Clausewitz's brother-in-law.[8]

Had Prussia gone to war with France in fall 1811, Kleist might not have committed suicide in November. An appointment in the army would have restored his finances and rescued him from the terrible isolation into which he had fallen after the *Berliner Abendblätter* ceased publication and the manuscript of *Prinz von Homburg* was ignored. When the Prussian government decided—no doubt correctly—that the country was still too weak to stand up to Napoleon, the last external prop of Kleist's existence gave way. Clausewitz's reaction to Prussia becoming a French satellite was not physical suicide but nevertheless extreme. He submitted three memorandums to the king, which in violent language protested the Franco-Prussian alliance, resigned his commission, and entered the Russian army, for which a Berlin court tried him in absentia—behavior that turned the king against him and compromised his career when he eventually returned to Prussia.

[8] Marwitz's first wife, Franziska von Brühl, was the younger sister of Marie von Clausewitz.

II

It is not necessary to outline the remaining twenty years of Clausewitz's life or to mention further acquaintances common to Clausewitz and Kleist, although more could be named. Nor have I even alluded to the opportunities their work affords for stylistic and thematic comparisons. It would be enlightening, for instance, to contrast Kleist's patriotic appeals of 1809 with Clausewitz's "Bekenntnisdenkschrift" or to compare their analyses of Parisian society and of the French character, which borrow similar concepts and phrases from the extensive contemporary German literature on France. But perhaps enough has been said to suggest certain parallels and even links in the lives of the two men from childhood on. They also shared a number of personal attitudes: an intense desire for fame—according to Kleist "the greatest of all earthly goods"—their disappointment with Prussia or the mixture of hatred and admiration they felt for Napoleon. These similarities are largely of biographical interest, although obviously they may have broad implications. A further and more significant bond between the two men is their fascination with violence. For Clausewitz that interest goes without saying; but warfare is, of course, also a condition common to Kleist's drama and prose. War is central to four of his eight plays—*Guiskard, Penthesilea, Hermannsschlacht,* and *Prinz von Homburg*; it is a determining force in *Marquise von O . . . ,* in *Michael Kohlhaas,* and in *Die Verlobung in Santo Domingo*; and violence on a smaller scale, between families and individuals, occurs in nearly all of Kleist's works.

I am very far from suggesting that the revolutionary and Napoleonic wars provided a significant stimulus to Kleist's treatment of individual and mass violence. It would be absurd to impose such narrow determinism on an original and creative mind. What can be said, however, is that the external violence, the political and military struggles that accompanied Kleist throughout life, matched the violence that existed within him from very early on. The Napoleonic age was Kleist's natural environment. In the events that he witnessed and in which he sometimes took part he could find reflections and confirmations of his own feelings and insights. With Clausewitz the connection is even simpler. War was his special sphere of activity, and soon war also became that segment of life that he chose to study and through which he sought to interpret life in general.

But of course war is not merely violence. Among much else it is also an expression of uncertainty, and it is an agent for change: the uncertainty of success, of physical and social survival; the change that comes with the destruction of traditional authority—the French monarchy, the Holy Roman Empire—and the emergence of new, unknown forces. There is no doubt that Kleist as well as Clausewitz was profoundly impressed, perhaps even inspired, by this overwhelming fact of the times. In his twenty-second year Kleist declared, "It would at least be wise and advisable in these changeable times to count as little as possible on the accustomed order of things;" and in various formulations the idea of the world's frailty and ambiguity—what he sometimes called "the world's fragile condition"—recurs throughout his works.[9]

In their response to this cosmic uncertainty Kleist and Clausewitz differed from many of their contemporaries. They neither tried to evade the insecurity that enveloped them by ignoring it or by minimizing it as an exception to the norm; nor did they join the Romantics in setting up the ideal of an earlier stable and just order of things that ought to be restored. Instead they immersed themselves in the reality of uncertainty, insisting— Kleist sometimes with terror—that it had to be faced, accepted, and understood, which did not mean smoothing it over or surrendering to it.

Obviously there is a point beyond which a poet and a scholar cannot be compared, and I don't mean to exaggerate the affinities that do exist between them. But in two respects the manner in which Kleist and Clausewitz transform their recognition of uncertainty into poetry or into theory is strikingly similar. One similarity grows out of their sense of ambiguity and paradox that I have just mentioned, and that is their dialectic. Both think in thesis and antithesis. And for both the dialectical progression of their argument finds its justification in itself; it rarely moves toward a synthesis. The judge in the *Zerbrochene Krug* is the criminal. The Marquise von O. would not have regarded Count F. as a devil if earlier she had not admired him as an angel. In Günther Blöcker's phrase, "Kleist's harmony asserts itself in the undiminished awareness of dissonance. It rests on the recognition that a resolution is not always possible."[10] Much the same holds true for Clausewitz. The often tragic history of the misinterpretation of his works derives largely from the inability of his readers to proceed beyond his thesis to its antithesis and to understand that he usually locates the truth in the tension between the two. The most obvious example of this is Clausewitz's dialectic description of war: war is distinguished from all other human activities by the fact of organized violence. Therefore war should ideally consist of nothing but violence—a truly Kleistian demand. But, Clausewitz continues—and in this continuation has lost thousands of his readers—since war is an expression of politics it ought rationally to be guided by political considerations, which may properly demand the least degree of violence needed to attain the

[9] Heinrich von Kleist to Christian Ernst Martini, 19 March 1799, *Briefe 1792–1804*, 25.
[10] Günther Blöcker: *Heinrich von Kleist, oder das absolute Ich* (Berlin 1960), 92.

goal. Theory must recognize that in the real world wars tend to be torn between the opposing impulses of escalation and limitation. In Clausewitz's work, as in Kleist's, polarity is a central concept.

No doubt their sensitivity to the fact that a single phenomenon may contain diametrical opposites springs from the writers' own psychological experiences and reactions. In Kleist's works this personal element is turned into a persuasive if implicit psychological interpretation. Appearances are emphasized just because the contrary reality that underlies them is so powerful. Michael Kohlhaas, the reader is told in the opening sentence of the novel, is not merely a decent human being—he is one of the most righteous men of his time, and, the author immediately adds, one of its most terrible criminals as well. Indeed, Kleist asserts, it is his pronounced sense of justice, repeatedly insulted by powerful men and by agencies of the law and of government, that makes Kohlhaas rob and kill. Clausewitz, more interested in the behavior of societies than of individuals, treats this theme with greater detachment but also more explicitly. War is not what it appears to be at first sight—merely a sequence of destructive acts—but the continuation of politics by other means. That idea is, of course, reversible. Politics, the peaceful ordering of relations within society and between states, easily turns to violence, even total violence.

But this fragile, violent, paradoxical world, which both men depict and interpret dialectically, contains a firm element, and it is the second striking similarity in Kleist's and Clausewitz's writings that for both this element is the same: the exceptional individual—whatever his position in life—who trusts his instincts and holds fast to his values. Nearly all of Kleist's works are concerned with the ability of men and women to recognize their true natures and their ability to remain true to their nature or to find their way back to it in the face of uncomprehending or hostile world. Sometimes it is a matter of God-given or Rousseauan, animal-like innocence: Käthchen von Heilbronn knows, all evidence to the contrary, despite the blindness of the man she loves and the barrier of his social superiority, that she and he belong together, and in the end she is revealed, to her own astonishment, as socially—and emotionally—not only his equal but his superior. Even more impressive than such representatives of instinctual self-knowledge are those of Kleist's characters who through the hard school of experience and self-analysis achieve what Max Kommerell in his Kleist essay calls "loyalty toward the unconscious."[11] For them, understanding of their unconscious and loyalty to it are the results of emotional maturity, as they were for the Marquise von O., who knows herself to be innocent even though she cannot deny her pregnancy, and

---

[11] Max Kommerell: "Die Sprache und das Unaussprechliche," in: *Geist und Buchstabe der Dichtung* (Frankfurt a. M., 1944), 309.

who gains the courage—defying her parents, society, and her own conventional scruples—to advertise in the newspapers for the unknown man who had made her a mother. That Kleist's vision of the individual isolated in a frivolous, cruel society—and sometimes corrupted by it—is essentially autobiographical does not diminish the strength with which he interprets the human condition in a revolutionary world. And he never hesitated to universalize his personal insights: in his final masterpiece, the essay on the puppet theater, he explicitly defines recovery of the unconscious as the goal of mankind: "We . . . [should have to] eat again from the tree of knowledge in order to return to a state of innocence."

Clausewitz seeks to catch the same qualities and make them subject to analysis in his concept of genius. It was one of his most important achievements that his theories for the first time in history placed psychological factors at the center of the study of war. In *On War* he accuses the military analysts of the Enlightenment of surrendering to the mystery of the human psyche: "Anything that could not be reached by the meager wisdom of such one-sided points of view was held to be beyond scientific control: it lay in the realm of genius, *which rises above all rules*." On the contrary, "what genius does is the best rule, and theory can do no better than show how and why this should be the case."[12]

By genius Clausewitz means not only what he calls "a very highly developed mental aptitude for a particular occupation," but also explicitly a combination of abilities that overcome the impediments of the spirit and of matter on any level of activity. He employs the concept of genius to describe the recovery of the unconscious, the understanding of motives and powers that enables the psychologically mature and honest individual, whether a general or a common soldier, to transform his knowledge into instinctual ability—"Knowledge must become capability"—until like the fighting bear in Kleist's essay on the puppets, he triumphs over opponents who can act only according to rote, who inadequately tap their inner resources, who are dominated by laws external to them.

III

I can suggest no hypothesis that might explain why Kleist and Clausewitz followed paths that diverged so greatly from the aesthetic and intellectual norms of their environment. Many Prussian officers of the time attempted

---

[12] Carl von Clausewitz: *On War*, trans. and eds. Michael Howard and Peter Paret, rev. ed., (Princeton 1984), 136. On Clausewitz's use of the concept of genius to make possible a systematic analysis of the psychological factors in war, see my *Clausewitz and the State*, rev. ed. (Princeton 1985), especially 157–61, 372–75.

poetry or wrote on war, but none moved in the direction they did.[13] Possibly their early experience with war made them more sensitive to certain themes. That their lives, though very different, reveal any number of connections and corresponding elements was, of course, a matter of chance. And it must also have been accidental that their works are marked by intellectual affinities and at times show a similar response to the historical situation. Perhaps all that can be said is that each man, for his own emotional reasons, was fascinated by the ambiguity and violence of human nature and of the world, and insisted on interpreting these facts without shutting his eyes to their frightening or disgusting features—in contrast to so many of their gifted contemporaries, who either wallowed in the horrors of life or did their best to deny them. One result, incidentally, of their striking out on their own was that neither attracted disciples, neither established a school; their works gained acceptance only very gradually, decades after their deaths.

In their determination to acknowledge a basic element in their own natures, which was also a basic condition of the times in which they lived, both may be called realists—even if Kleist had little of Clausewitz's practicality and historical understanding. Their pronounced psychological realism, however, continued to be suffused with the impulses of German idealism toward a universe with immanent ethical demands, demands that can be met only if man strives to fulfill his moral and intellectual potential. Their psychological insights coexist oddly with an ideal vision of the reciprocity of man and nature, a vision they adapted to new interpretive tasks, but never abandoned. Their ideas sweep in great curves between the real and the ideal. For our brief sketch, the conception that Clausewitz had of his work may serve as a final summing up of both men's positions. To interpret the behavior of individuals and societies one must free oneself from the straight jacket of dogma, doctrine, so-called scientific laws. Instead one's interpretation should match the fluidity of its subject. It must seek to identify the various, often conflicting elements in war and in life, and appraise their dynamic interaction, without masking their ambiguities and their unpredictability. In both Clausewitz's and Kleist's thought these elements make up an intensely dangerous universe, but a universe in which the individual who knows himself, accepts his duties, and follows his convictions can act with greater certainty, with less confusion, than do his peers. Even he may not survive, but both Clausewitz and Kleist were confident that if the universe survives as more than a conglomerate of material phenomena and brute sensations, it is because of such men.

---

[13] Clausewitz occasionally wrote verse, but never rose above the average educated poetizing of the times.

12

CLAUSEWITZ'S POLITICS

THIS ESSAY AND THE TWO that follow address Clausewitz's conception of politics and his positions on specific political issues. The first essay attempts an overview; the other two discuss particular episodes in the second half of his life.

When we speak of Clausewitz's politics we need to distinguish between his picture of basic political forces and their workings throughout history, and his opinions on political conditions and questions of his day. Each influenced the other; but it is not the case that his general hypotheses and convictions merely reflected whatever partisan attitudes he held. It may be true, as has been suggested, that no one has yet developed a theory of politics that is the counterpart of *On War*; certainly Clausewitz never attempted to do so. On the other hand, *On War* expresses a firm view of states as political organisms and of the ways they deal with each other, and the work is filled with political observations and allusions. One example is the brilliant discussion of alliances in Book VI, chapter 6, which moves from a consideration of their military potential to an analysis of their political motives and from there to the workings of the balance of power. It would not be unreasonable to regard *On War* as a part—the military part—of an encompassing if unwritten general theory of politics.

When I decided to write a biography of Clausewitz, I realized that his political ideas and his political behavior would occupy a large place in any study that tried to do justice to his theories as well as to his life. In the course of writing their significance became even more apparent, and in the end I chose a title for the book—*Clausewitz and the State*—that pointed to the interaction between the man and the political institution that in its Prussian guise was a decisive force in his emotional development and his career, and that as a general phenomenon exerted a strong impact on his theories. Two events after the book was published led me, after a few years, to return to the subject of Clausewitz's politics. One was a thoughtful review by the British historian C. B. A. Behrens, who questioned my characterization of Clausewitz's views of domestic affairs in Prussia after 1815 as approaching those of early German liberalism. The other was an invitation by the German Clausewitz Society to take part in a program marking the two hundreth anniversary of Clausewitz's birth. Raymond Aron contributed two papers on related themes to the conference: in one he discussed the conception of political strategy in *On*

War, the other analyzed the international system since 1945 with reference to Clausewitz's theories. Clausewitz's influence and the contemporary relevance of his theories are interesting topics, but there is still much
to learn about the ideas in their original form. I saw it as the main task of
my paper, of which the following is a shortened English version, to open
a broader discussion of Clausewitz's political views as he expressed them
in his writings and actions. Recently Daniel Moran has developed a more
detailed interpretation in his introduction to the political part of the edition of Clausewitz's historical and political writings on which he and I
have collaborated. I hope, nevertheless, that my brief reflections on Clausewitz's basic ideas on politics and on foreign policy may still have their
uses.

ॐ

War as a "True Political Instrument"

Clausewitz's analysis of the political character of war is among his most
significant and potentially most fruitful achievements. When he identified
the state's political intentions and energies as a basic element of war he
did not, of course, reveal anything that was unknown to soldiers and
statesmen, even if they did not always fully understand the implications
of this identification. Nor did earlier political or military theorists ignore
the links between policy and war and between military organization and
economic, social, and political conditions. But Clausewitz was the first to
place politics at the center of an analysis of what he called the "total phenomenon" of war and to develop concepts and methods that made possible the systematic study of the interaction of politics with other basic
components of organized violence. In the expansive definition of war that
he proposes at the end of the first chapter of *On War*, politics and policy
are in constant interaction with the other two dominant tendencies of the
"remarkable trinity" that according to Clausewitz makes up war: emotion and violence, and the play of chance and probability.

War is not waged in a military vacuum. At every point it touches on
political interests or on elements that may quickly become political, and
strategic planning as well as the operations themselves must be mindful
of these links and consequences. War is an expression of the state's political will. It is therefore only rational to insist that the soldier be subordinate to the political leadership—or more accurately, because direct political and military authority may rest in the hands of one man, like
Napoleon, or of a group, like the Committee of Public Safety, military

action should express policy as closely and effectively as possible. In turn the government owes it to the state and to society to use its military instrument sensibly and, whenever possible, to assign missions to the armed forces that are not beyond their capacity. This demands true cooperation between the political leadership, its military advisors, and the commanders in the field. In *On War* Clausewitz proceeds on the assumption that governments would act rationally and represent the true interests of the state as best they could. He has been criticized for this. But since *On War* is neither a historical analysis of wars as they have actually occurred, nor a work of political theory, he felt justified in leaving the problems of irrational or immoral policy out of account. Just as he analyzed instances of inadequate military leadership in *On War*, so inadequate political leadership should be discussed in works of political theory or in historical works, as it often was in his own histories. He would in any case never measure the justice of resorting to war against some general ethical and political standard, other than that of the right of self-defense. He rejected the universal validity of ideologies and political ideals and instead sought the standard of appropriate action in the rational self-interest of specific political societies, each existing in its own unique circumstances—which did not exclude a sense of international responsibility and adherence to such supranational concepts as the balance of power. Consequently he could believe that war might be generated by a clash of opposing but similarly valid interests.

Clausewitz's View of International Relations

A similar absence of ideological preconceptions marks his views of foreign policy in general, of which war is only one among many possible expressions, and of domestic politics in Prussia.

Clausewitz's view of international relations was based on the concept of a community of states, each in more or less enlightened fashion pursuing its own interests, and at the enlightened end of the spectrum acknowledging that the wish to increase one's own power must take account of the interests of one's people and of the international community. Unlike many statesmen and political writers of his time, Clausewitz did not think that this community of states expressed or should express a particular ideology, whether of Christianity or legitimacy, on the one hand, or of the social contract or democracy, on the other. A variety of beliefs and goals was the natural result of the world's historical development. Each state, each ethnic or social group might push its claims to the utmost; but any assertion that its beliefs had universal validity should be rejected. From the perspective of the French government in the 1790s, the occupation of the Rhineland was an understandable goal; for the German states along the Rhine it was appropriate to defend themselves. The Poles naturally wanted to rescind the partitions and regain their independence; their neighbors just as naturally opposed them. Ultimately the maintenance of the balance of power should assure a solution that though far from ideal would satisfy the largest range of interests.[1]

The pronounced realism and pragmatism of his thought made Clausewitz an unforgiving critic of political rhetoric. That he first encountered its force in all its virulence emanating from the revolutionary governments in Paris, and later from the Napoleonic empire, only reinforced his disdain of exaggeration and fantasy. But it could also blind him to historical forces that lay buried in the seemingly irrational—not so much of the individual leader, but of the mass of the people.

The Just Society and the Authority of the State

The realistic if increasingly icy manner in which Clausewitz viewed foreign affairs became more complex when he turned to the internal conditions of his own country. Here, too, he was remarkably untouched by ideological preconceptions. As a young man he had been among the more radical members of the reform party, but he had worked for pragmatic changes rather than for an overall political program. Once his youthful idealization of the Prussian state faded and the emergence of a repressive conservatism after 1815 forced him to renounce his hopes for further innovation, he became a skeptic rather than a believer. He had a sense of social justice that was uncommon for the time and for his social milieu; but his humanitarian instincts and even the egalitarian note that frequently sounded in his comments on society were qualified by his belief that every state must above all see to its own security and that in a state that like Prussia was surrounded by powerful neighbors efficient centralized government and a strong army took precedence over other domestic considerations.

Even after 1815 the concept of the state assumed a position of greater authority in his thought than it was usually accorded in the contemporary political theories of Western Europe and the United States. But even in Germany his position never wholly coincided with those that could be regarded as typically liberal or typically conservative. Despite some obvious similarities, Clausewitz never corresponded to the type of liberal

---

[1] I have discussed Clausewitz's conception of the balance of power in greater detail in an article, "Gleichgewicht als Mittel der Friedenssicherung bei Clausewitz und in der Geschichte der Neuzeit," *Wehrwissenschaftliche Rundschau* 29 (May–June 1980): 83–86.

Prussian official for whom the essence of the state lay in its educational function and in efficient, progressive administration. He could never separate his view of the state from the dynamic and drama of power. For a man of his generation he possessed an unusually well developed appreciation of the state as a historical individual, an organism, which, to survive and prosper, must above all gather and maintain power. He held similarly clear ideas on the international political context of the state and the state's dependence on the balance of power, which limited its freedom of action but without which most states could not exist. He accepted as inevitable that the machinery of the balance could not function without consuming some raw material—German and Italian principalities and occasionally even such a large entity as Poland. Foreign policy was the sum of the state's interests, its power, and its sense of the interests and power of its neighbors. These ideas did not differ greatly from Frederick the Great's conception of raison d'état. But Clausewitz's understanding for the dynamic, growth, and decline of a state was more comprehensive and historically better grounded than that of the High Enlightenment.

How should the state acquire the degree of power needed for its security and for an effective foreign policy? This question touches on the entire complex of issues in the relationship between state and society. For most Prussian conservatives, even after 1815, monarchical absolutism and a legally defined hierarchic society was far more important than the continuing increase in the power of the state could exert in foreign affairs—the more so because the administrative, financial, and military power of centralized government grew at the expense of local and regional interests. Clausewitz, on the other hand, had no difficulty in rejecting remnants of the ancien régime that survived into the nineteenth century—corporative privileges, and certain demands for social subordination and deference—because he recognized that in the modern world these could continue only at the cost of a healthy society and the power of the state. He himself was largely untouched by social prejudice. The privileges of the European nobility, he wrote in the early 1820s, had once been justified by service to society and the state, but were no longer appropriate and defensible in modern times.[2] That did not mean that he favored the leveling of social groups and classes. He believed in an elite of education and achievement. But every able individual deserved access to this elite, for reasons of plain justice, and because it would make for a healthier society and thus add to the power of the state. Education, cultural sophistication, a sense for the demands of the modern age—so his ideas might be paraphrased—were valuable for society and the state. But

---

[2] "Agitation," in Carl von Clausewitz, *Historical and Political Writings*, eds. Peter Paret and Daniel Moran (Princeton, 1992), 338–44.

they were not the monopoly of traditional hierarchies, and the military and administrative institutions of the state should not continue, let alone further increase, the unequal treatment of its citizens. On the contrary, as the achievements of the bourgeoisie increased, the old forms of precedence, privilege, and rank should be abolished. Even the mass of the population, which until now had not grown far—if at all—beyond its age-old subordination and dependence, should no longer be treated as an inert, passive mass. To continue the old conditions would gradually poison and fragment society. Repeatedly Clausewitz expressed his aversion to the "ignoble profits" sought by the nobility, and the attempts by the well-to-do and influential to escape military service filled him with disgust: "The end result of our miserable system is always that the poor man becomes a soldier, the rich man remains free," which was just in the eyes of neither God nor man.[3]

It was perhaps inevitable that as a serving officer Clausewitz showed his opposition to the social and political forces that came to dominate Prussia in the Restoration most openly in a conflict affecting the armed forces: the fight over the future of the Landwehr. Boyen, the minister of war, who had played a major role in establishing the Landwehr during the Wars of Liberation, wanted to turn it into a permanent force, its officers largely members of the middle range of urban and rural society. In peacetime as well as in war it was to be one of the principal tasks of the Landwehr to strengthen that sense of mutual allegiance and responsibility in state and citizen that had been one of the main goals of the reform movement. In Restoration Prussia an institution that bridged social classes and reduced the nobility's preponderance in the officer corps was no longer welcome, and by 1819 the special character of the Landwehr, even its very existence, were threatened. In letters and memorandums to critics as well as supporters of the Landwehr, Clausewitz argued that Prussia could not afford to renounce the military and psychological strengths that rested in the people in arms. Objections to the Landwehr's social egalitarianism and fears that it might become a revolutionary force, he dismissed as expressions of caste egotism. He acknowledged that the Landwehr was not as effective a military force as the regular army but denied that this was the true reason why conservatives hated it: "Opposition is caused not so much by patriotic concern for the technical inadequacy of Landwehr officers as by the disagreeable feeling of seeing the former character of the officer corps changed by so many alien additions, to see the son of a nobleman serve with the son of a grocer, or even under

---

[3] Ibid., 343; Peter Paret, *Clausewitz and the State*, rev. ed. (Princeton, 1985), 291.

him."[4] The Landwehr, he wrote to a friend at this time, "remains a horror to the more elevated classes of our state."[5]

To sum up, Clausewitz believed that all citizens owed the same duties toward the state, that all should be equal before the law, and that all careers should be open to talent. Although he accepted social differences as inevitable and appropriate, the history of the past two centuries had taught him that all classes were drawing closer to each other. To fight this development was futile. It was the task of government and society to guide it into healthy channels, away from rigid conservatism, on the one hand, and, on the other, from the radicalism of the French Revolution at its zenith.

Between Liberalism and Conservatism

With these views Clausewitz approached the position of early liberalism. But he rejected the liberal argument that the individual's liberty and legal rights were assured only when at least the educated and well-to-do possessed political rights that the executive had to respect. Instead he put his faith in an efficient and honest administration, carefully trained and relatively independent judges, ministers with executive responsibility, and a council of state to advise the crown. During the Reform era both he and his friend Gneisenau had hoped that the king would grant a constitution. They had supported a limited franchise, without precisely defining its extent, based on residence, income, and profession, as well as a parliament of two chambers, for the time being without significant legislative powers, but with the right to debate and advise.

These ideas were not that different from the provisions of the French *Charte* of 1814 or from the programs generally advocated by early liberalism in Germany. But parliamentary institutions were far less important to Clausewitz than they were for French and German liberals. After the Carlsbad Decrees of 1819—of which Clausewitz disapproved as much as he despised the student agitation and the murder of Kotzebue that helped bring them about—he had no difficulty in arguing that parliamentary institutions might be best suited to countries that derived a degree of security from their geography—for instance, Great Britain, the Netherlands or the United States. Only determined policies of a firm executive, he believed, could maintain the German states against the dangers by which they were surrounded.[6]

---

[4] "Our Military Institutions," *Historical and Political Writings*, 327.

[5] Quoted in Paret, *Clausewitz and the State*, 297.

[6] "Agitation," *Historical and Political Writings*, 351–52.

Clausewitz's conviction that Prussia above all needed a strong executive and that this executive could be trusted to defend civil rights has led some historians to speak of his conservatism or of his "more pronounced aristocratic attitude" after 1815.[7] The most comprehensive and differentiated version of this view was developed by the Cambridge historian C. B. A. Behrens, whose analysis of Clausewitz's politics concluded that although Clausewitz

> objected as strongly as anyone to what it became the fashion to call the "mechanischer Staat" or the "Maschinenstaat" of Frederick the Great's day—a state in which human beings were treated as if they were cogs in a machine— it seems clear that he was strongly influenced by the tradition of enlightened despotism as it developed in Prussia in the second half of the eighteenth century. This tradition, notwithstanding the legal barriers between the various groups in the population that existed until 1807, laid far more stress than did the Western thinking of the time on the obligations of both the ruler and his subjects to the community, whose interests were identified with those of the state.
>
> The tradition of enlightened despotism could be adopted to permit administrative and economic reforms in some respect more drastic than those achieved by the Revolution in France, but it was hardly compatible with the kind of individualism that found expression in the West in the demand for civil and political liberty. In the first half of the nineteenth century the Prussian administration and the Prussian army became the most efficient in Europe, and the Prussian economy began to make the strides that led to its overtaking first the French and then the British. Politically, however, Prussia was the bulwark of reaction. It does not seem possible to absolve Clausewitz from having contributed to these developments even though he deplored some of them. There can be no doubt about the side on which he would have found himself had he escaped death from cholera in middle age and lived until 1848.[8]

It would certainly be difficult to imagine Clausewitz as a supporter of the Frankfurt Parliament, but Miss Behrens's hypothesis might be enlarged by noting that German history could have taken a different course if Frederick William III had fulfilled his promise to grant the country a constitution and expanded political life even to the limited extent that Clausewitz at the time considered desirable and feasible. The weakness she finds in his political judgment is to a large extent the result of his political environment and experiences, and her conclusion may say less

[7] Friedrich Meinecke, *Das Leben des Generalfeldmarschalls Hermann von Boyen* (Stuttgart, 1896–99), 2:285.

[8] C. B. A. Behrens, "Which Side Was Clausewitz On?" *New York Review of Books*, 14 October 1976, 44.

about Clausewitz than about the history of Prussia with its tragic under-valuation of representative institutions. Miss Behrens uncovered a feature of his thought that German scholars have ignored only too often; but despite her reference to the tradition of enlightened despotism, her con-clusion tears Clausewitz out of his historical context. It is risky to mea-sure ideas held in 1820 by the standards of 1848. How many leaders of the British reform movement of the 1830s would have advocated an ex-pansion of the electorate and its redistribution by region and class in 1805? Clausewitz's contemporaries, in any case, drew very different con-clusions about his politics. Frederick William III and his conservative ad-visors worried that he harbored revolutionary thoughts, and their suspi-cion of his outlook handicapped his career during the final wars against Napoleon and after Waterloo. It characterizes the oppressive atmosphere of restoration Prussia, but also Clausewitz's ability to retain a degree of political independence, that his views, which would have aroused little concern in Western Europe, were feared as dangerous in his own country.

Clausewitz's Political Views and *On War*

Clausewitz never developed his political views into a systematic theory comparable to *On War*. He expressed them in essays, official and unoffi-cial memorandums, and letters in response to particular events and as part of his historical studies. At times he tried to win over others to his position; often he merely attempted to clarify his ideas to himself. A num-ber of general principles may be extracted from this mass of observations and comments: The essence of the state is power. Because it guarantees the state's existence, power in relation to other states is the ultimate stan-dard by which the internal affairs of the state must be measured. (At least that is the case with major states. Smaller entities must safeguard their independence by ensuring pacific relations between social groups, effi-cient administration, and sensible alliances.) Domestic policies must cre-ate the means of political and military power, but at least in states that are surrounded by powerful neighbors their particular character matters less than their efficiency. However, social change is inevitable and should be reflected in the country's political institutions. The readiness to fight and the readiness to compromise lie at the core of politics. These ideas and even principles recur throughout Clausewitz's writings but he rarely generalized them or analyzed them in detail as he did his ideas on war. Quite apart from their different content, his views on politics and his ideas on war and on the conduct of war differ in his manner of developing them and of giving them their ultimate form.

Nevertheless we can recognize some parallels between them. It is not a question of matching a particular political or social opinion to a specific argument in *On War*. As long as Clausewitz was not so conservative as to deny the significance of a population's attitudes and feelings in war, or so liberal as to reject the necessity of military power, he might have held any political opinions whatever without influencing his theories. Whether or not we agree with its particular hypotheses, the undogmatic universality of *On War* transcends specific ideologies. The parallels or relationships that may exist have to do with the emotional and intellectual bases and tendencies of his thought.

Obviously Clausewitz's hypotheses of the interaction of politics and war were influenced by his historical studies, his observations of the political and military conflicts of his time, and his personal experiences. Politics not only were an important component of his theories, they also played a role in their development. To Clausewitz politics represented a large part of the reality of earlier ages and of his own time, which often enough led to war. It was politics above all that lent wars their varied character, ranging from the extreme of attempting to destroy the enemy to such a minimum of violence as an armed demonstration. Clausewitz had to come to terms with politics if he wished to solve the theoretical task he had set himself. Consequently he tried to see political issues not as a partisan, which would have inhibited the objective understanding he needed.

For this reason his conclusions in both the military and the political area reveal some similarities. The fragmentary, incomplete expressions of his political views contain a component that suggests that had Clausewitz expanded them into a systematic analysis he could have proceeded according to methodological principles that we know from *On War*. The conception of the state as an organism that seeks the greatest degree of power accords with the hypothesis of absolute war. In *On War* the conflict that achieves the highest degree of violence is postulated as the extreme necessary for theory, the ideal condition that enables us to identify and understand the various and generally not absolute forms that war assumes in reality. In life the absolute—whether total violence in war or the state's unlimited drive for power—is usually limited both by innate and by external forces, a reduction that is realistic and beneficial for the state and society. Clausewitz's essays and correspondence plainly show that this was not merely an intellectual construction or recognition, but that it represented a firm belief. Unlike Napoleon he respected the community of states. He opposed the unlimited accretion of internal as well as external power by any of its members, and he wished that the state that meant most to him would break out of the rigid authoritarian mold that enveloped it after 1815. The best course for Prussia, he continued to think, was to open herself cautiously to the opportunities and uncertainties of a political system for which the energies of society meant more than simply the state's military and economic potential, but were also a force that would gradually invigorate the country's political life.

13

"A PROPOSITION NOT A SOLUTION"—

CLAUSEWITZ'S ATTEMPT TO BECOME PRUSSIAN

MINISTER AT THE COURT OF ST. JAMES

FOR A TIME after his promotion to the rank of major-general in 1919, Clausewitz hoped that he would be seconded to the diplomatic service. The wish demonstrates not only his distaste for the administrative duties of his new assignment as director of the War Academy in Berlin, and probably an urge to escape from the narrow military world of senior officers in the capital, but also his abiding fascination with political issues and questions of foreign policy.

In my book *Clausewitz and the State*, I traced the course of his campaign for the appointment on the basis of published correspondence, references in letters and diaries of contemporaries, and other printed sources. After the book went to press I came across previously unknown documents on the episode in the Public Record Office and the British Museum. The new material did not alter the general outline of my account but added much interesting information on Clausewitz's actions and those of his opponents, especially of the British minister in Berlin, who was able to orchestrate the conservative opposition that eventually blocked the appointment on the ground that Clausewitz was too liberal to be entrusted with a major diplomatic post. In their specificity and detail the documents stand out among the sources for Clausewitz's life during the time he was writing his major theoretical and historical works, and I happily used them for a much more extensive narrative and analysis of the episode. The text appeared in a German historical journal. I thought of giving it the title "A Proposition Not a Solution"—the British minister's rendering of Frederick William III's comment that although Clausewitz's appointment had been proposed he had not yet resolved to make it. The English phrase seemed a little obscure at the head of an article in German and I did not use it; but as title of the English translation it may be appropriate.

❧

When Clausewitz was appointed director of the War Academy in 1818, he regarded the transfer from Coblentz to Berlin as a step toward a more important assignment. At the very least he hoped that the scope of the "Military Directorate" would be sufficiently enlarged to give him a voice in the educational policy of the academy and in the work of the general staff, of which he was made an associate member. In March 1819, three months after he had arrived in the capital, he sent the minister of war a radical reform program for the academy, an indication that he was not prepared to wait passively until he was given more important duties. By that time he had already been proposed for an appointment that fully responded to his interests and ambitions, and would have taken him away from Berlin: the position of Prussian minister at the Court of St. James. The chancellor, Prince Hardenberg, and the new foreign minister, Count Bernstorff, favored his appointment, as did Humboldt, Gneisenau, Boyen, Grolman, and others associated with the reform movement that had recast Prussian institutions between 1807 and 1814. Conservatives at court, in the army, and in the bureaucracy were equally strongly opposed, and could count on the unwillingness of the king to choose for the post someone he had disliked since the beginning of 1812, when Clausewitz had demonstratively resigned his commission and joined the Russian army to avoid having to take part in the invasion of Russia as a member of the Prussian contingent of the Grande Armée. In the conflict that now began and that was to continue for two years, the issue of Clausewitz's fitness for the post was entwined with doubts about his political views and became linked with the larger struggle between constitutionalism and a rejuvenated absolutism in Prussia.

The general course of the conflict over Clausewitz's appointment, which political circles at the time followed attentively, is well known. Dispatches between Rose, the British minister in Berlin, and the Foreign Office in London, contain much additional information on foreign as well as Prussian aspects of the episode. In particular, the new evidence confirms the major part in blocking Clausewitz's appointment played by the British envoy, who did not hesitate to engage ambassadors of other powers as well as Prussian officials in his campaign.[1] It is worthwhile to quote Rose's dispatches and letters extensively. Not only do they convey a detailed if unfavorable portrait of Clausewitz and illuminate an episode that might have become a turning point in his life and work; they also illustrate the workings of conservative cooperation across frontiers in the first years after the collapse of the Napoleonic empire.[2]

---

[1] Already Clausewitz's first biographer, Karl Schwartz, held Rose responsible, but he offered no evidence and said nothing about Rose's motives except that he found Clausewitz's personality too rigid. Karl Schwartz, *Leben des Generals von Clausewitz* (Berlin, 1878), 2:255.

[2] The dispatches are catalogued in the Foreign Office papers of the Public Record Office under F.O. 64/120, 64/128, and 64/131. F.O. 245/8 contains Rose's copies of his dispatches. The Rose Papers in the British Museum, Additional Manuscripts 42:781, and in the Lon-

Sir George Henry Rose—he was knighted in the course of the conflict—had assumed his post in Berlin after the Battle of Waterloo, and apart from long leaves was to remain in Prussia until 1823. He could look back on a varied diplomatic career on the continent and in the United States, but he did not figure among the more distinguished members of the foreign service. Charles Webster's description of British diplomatic representatives under Castlereagh characterizes Rose as a "dear middleaged gentleman, who took his duties very seriously, but had not much ability."[3] His father, vice-president of the Board of Trade and for some years during the Napoleonic wars paymaster of the navy, was a devoted follower of Pitt and a friend of Canning. The son, however, was a high Tory; it characterizes the man that Humboldt's appointment as Prussian minister in London in 1816 struck him as politically dangerous.[4] Not only Castlereagh but also the prince regent seem to have had confidence in him, but he was particularly close to another member of the royal family, the duke of Cumberland, a man much disliked in England, who after the House of Commons refused to increase his annual allowance moved to Berlin in 1818, and whose ultra conservatism fully coincided with Rose's views.[5] The connection with the duke of Cumberland afforded Rose a degree of access to Frederick William III and to the inner circles at court that otherwise would have been denied him. The duke had married a sister of the deceased Prussian queen and thus was a brother-in-law of the king and of Duke Charles of Mecklenburg-Strelitz, commanding general of the guards, who in these years increasingly stiffened the king's resistance to any further step of modernization and liberalization. As soon as Clausewitz was mentioned as Humboldt's possible successor, the duke of Cumberland with Rose in attendance, Duke Charles and his political ally Prince Wittgenstein, minister of the royal household, united in opposing him. They seem to have suspected Clausewitz as a secret radical, and feared that the appointment of such a man would not only place the government's communications with its most powerful ally in unreliable hands, but might also encourage the constitutional party in Prussia.

The legation in London had been vacant since Humboldt's departure

---

donderry Papers, vols. 31–32, now in the Public Record Office of Northern Ireland, include additional correspondence by and to Rose.

[3] Charles K. Webster, *The Foreign Policy of Castlereagh* (London, 1925), 40.

[4] Rose to Castlereagh, 28 September 1816, in code, Londonderry Papers, vol. 31, no. 1070.

[5] For instance, Cumberland to George IV, 31 March 1820: "And you are perfectly correct in all you say of our friend G. Rose for whom I profess the sincerest regard, as there does not exist a more honourable better man or a more truly zealous servant and subject of the Crown, or more faithfully attached personally to you than he is; This I can affirm, he & I think alike and we are most cordial and confidential together." A. Aspinall, ed., *The Letters of George IV* (Cambridge, 1938), 2:315.

in September 1818 for the Congress of Aix-la-Chapelle. Clausewitz was responsible for military arrangements and security at the congress and probably took the opportunity to discuss with Humboldt the chances of succeeding him in London. A somewhat ambiguous dispatch from Rose to Castlereagh at the beginning of 1819 suggests that at that time Rose was already aware of Clausewitz's interest in the appointment.[6] On 12 May Gneisenau suggested to Hardenberg that Clausewitz be sent to London, and after the meeting reported to his friend that the chancellor seemed not unwilling and had asked Gneisenau to discover whether "you would be prepared to accept the position."[7] The matter rested during the summer. In September Humboldt once again assured Clausewitz of his support.[8] It must have been around that time that Hardenberg and Bernstorff submitted Clausewitz's name to the king. On 6 November Rose wrote to Castlereagh: "Major General Clausewitz owes his nomination to General Count Gneisenau who earnestly recommended him to Prince Hardenberg as an Officer of first rate Merit. . . . His manner is cold and by no means popular; his temper is said to be vehement. He was considered to be a member of [the] Tugendbund, and the Party opposed to him deem him to be still such, but I imagine the Count to have been certain that at any rate such are not his Principles at present."[9] Two themes are developed in the dispatch that will run through the entire episode: Clausewitz's reserved behavior, which some people could interpret as arrogance; and his association with the Tugendbund, a fairly innocuous patriotic society of the Reform era, which both Napoleon and Prussian reactionaries took to be a revolutionary group but which had ceased to exist long before and of which Clausewitz had, in fact, never been a member.

Over the following two months, Rose engaged in remarkable exertions to prevent Clausewitz's appointment. On 7 November he asked the Prussian minister of foreign affairs whether it was true that Clausewitz was to go to London, rather that Baron Werther, a diplomat whose name had also been mentioned for the position. When Bernstorff answered affirmatively, adding that Clausewitz was by far the abler of the two men, Rose responded with a weighty indictment: Nothing was further from his

[6] Humboldt to his wife, 4 November 1818, A. v. Sydow, ed., *Wilhelm und Caroline von Humboldt in ihren Briefen* (Berlin, 1913), 6:369. Rose to Castlereagh, 1 January 1819, Marquess of Londonderry, ed., *Correspondence of Viscount Castlereagh* (London, 1853), 12:98–99.

[7] Gneisenau to Clausewitz, 12 May 1819. George Heinrich Pertz and Hans Delbrück, *Das Leben des Feldmarschalls Grafen Neithardt von Gneisenau* (Berlin, 1880), 5:370.

[8] Humboldt to his wife, 8 September 1819, in *Wilhelm von Humboldts politische Briefe*, ed. W. Richer (Berlin, 1936), 6:611. On the same day Humboldt wrote Hardenberg that the English would appreciate Clausewitz's balanced and intelligent character. Ibid., 2:329.

[9] Rose to Castlereagh, 6 November 1819, in code, Public Record Office, F.O. 64/120.

intention than to comment on the Prussian government's change of mind, however:

> Tho' General Clausewitz has been frequently at my house . . . the coldness of his manners has prevented my having any personal knowledge of him upon which I can depend, but that I hear his honor and probity spoken of as unexceptionable; knowing him however as slightly as I do, I am compelled to judge him according to what others do, who have better means of forming correct opinions respecting him; and according to the decided majority of those opinions there is not that confidence in his being wholly free from revolutionary views on which such a nomination can safely repose in the present state of things, in which the tendency to anarchy and the destruction of all that is dear and sacred to man can be averted by no other means whatever than by the most cordial, energetic and simultaneous cooperation of the great Powers of Europe; that unless they can communicate together with the utmost confidence these qualities of the cooperation must be wanting; and that the mission of a person from this Court to that of London in whom complete reliance could not be placed as to his views and principles on that essential point, which is the basis and soul of the Alliance, could not but tend to inspire the most mischievous mistrust; that it is possible that the opinions of the General's political leanings may be in some degree erroneous or excessive, but they exist; and whilst they exist the degree of confidence indispensable for the utility of his mission cannot be attained.[10]

Bernstorff admitted that he "was aware that opinions unfavorable to General von Clausewitz of the nature I had specified exist, but that he fully believed them to be unfounded; that he [Clausewitz] as well as General Count Gneisenau belong to what is called the moderate military party, and are considered as deserters by the vehement military party . . . that the heat of party occasions very unjust imputations of political tendencies to be thrown on many persons." Rose countered with the complaint that it was not his fault if Clausewitz's taciturn personality made it impossible to judge him correctly. He added: "As an instant of the opinion of his tendency, a very sensible, well disposed, and honorable man, Minister of an important German Court, respecting which it is essential that it should not suppose that [the Court] of Berlin to make concession to the innovators, announced this nomination to me in dismay as a triumph of what is called the German Cause [Deutschheit]."[11] In a subse-

---

[10] Rose to Castlereagh, 9 November 1819, in code, ibid.

[11] A coded letter by Rose to Castlereagh of 6 November 1819 identifies the diplomat: "The Bavarian Envoy C[oun]t Rechberg came to me today to represent that his brother the Minister for Foreign Affairs at Munich complains to him that he is misleading him as to this [Prussian] Government which he hears is about to make essential concessions to the Revolutionists and that he learns that the English Gov[ernmen]t is about to do the same. His

quent letter Rose informed Castlereagh that he had taken care to report his conversation with Bernstorff in an uncoded dispatch, "which would of course be opened and perused by the Chancellor of State," so that Hardenberg, who at this time told the Austrian ambassador that Clausewitz's appointment was a settled matter, would be fully aware of Rose's fears.[12]

Bernstorff's open support for Clausewitz made it seem advisable to Rose not to take further steps to block the appointment without reinforcements from other quarters. On 11 November he wrote Castlereagh: "As in my conversations with Count Bernstorff respecting the nomination of Major General v. Clausewitz I acted on general views directed to the common interests of the Powers, who have established a concert for the maintenance of the tranquility of Europe, I have felt it my duty not only to communicate to their Ministers here what I said, but also to seek their opinion on it, and on the whole matter."[13] He was relieved to discover that the Austrian, Russian, and French envoys shared his views, although the French ambassador had not intended to raise questions about Clausewitz's appointment.

That Rose had been acting without explicit instructions from London becomes apparent from the dispatch he sent Castlereagh two days later by special courier. The message of twenty-three pages opens with the assurance that only a pressing sense of duty had led him to express himself on a matter, "on which otherwise I should have felt myself bound by the strictest silence unless directed to make communications by your Lordship's orders."[14] Numerous reasons not mentioned in his dispatches had led him to take such unusual steps. He felt somewhat encouraged when on 10 November Bernstorff, who was about to leave for Vienna, informed him that Frederick William III had characterized the suggestion to appoint Clausewitz as "a proposition not a solution." The king's comment, Rose continued, convinced him that "the only safe way, and that promising the best success, of endeavoring the abandonment of the intention of sending Monsieur de Clausewitz to London would be through Prince Wittgenstein." He persuaded the Austrian ambassador, Count Zichy, to act as spokesman for his colleagues and inform Wittgenstein that not only he but also the British and Russian envoys were deeply troubled by Clausewitz's views. Wittgenstein assured Zichy that he had already warned the king against appointing Clausewitz, but that he was prepared

---

conclusion seems to be that it will be useless of him to attempt a stand. I have told him everything I could to keep him to the Collar but it is material that we should aid in giving courage and right impressions at Munich itself. Bavaria is now of the greatest importance." Londonderry Papers, vol. 32, no. 1275.

[12] Rose to Castlereagh, 13 November 1819, Public Record Office, F.O. 64/120.

[13] Rose to Castlereagh, 11 November 1819, ibid.

[14] Rose to Castlereagh, 13 November 1819, ibid.

to take the further step of informing the king of the ambassadors' doubts before Hardenberg reported on the matter, as he was scheduled to do on the following day. Rose continued:

> That Prince Wittgenstein's mind should be impressed, as those of the great majority of persons here are, respecting General v. Clausewitz's political leanings is the strongest evidence that I did not act on light grounds. His situation about the King and in society here, and his post of Minister of the Police during many years in which he bestowed an especial attention on the state of the public mind and on the proceedings of the innovators, give him unrivalled means of forming a sound opinion on the point on which I had to judge.
>
> Major General von Clausewitz, who, I apprehend, has never yet been employed in diplomacy, was for a time Preceptor to Prince August of Prussia, when France was about to attack Russia and Prussia allied herself with that former Power he went into the service of the latter, and his sovereign conceived much displeasure at this part of his conduct, and so much so that it has excited surprize that He assented to Prince Hardenberg's present recommendation of him. He returned to this service in 1813, and was employed on the staff; after the war he was chief of staff at Coblentz, then commanded the garrison of Aix-la-Chapelle, was made a Major General after having been frequently disappointed in his hopes of that promotion, and nearly a year since was named Head of the Military School at Berlin. This situation he dislikes, and therefore, and being ambitious, he sought the English Mission. . . . When he lived at Coblentz he was, I am told, notoriously in habits of intimacy with Mr. Görres, who has long been in his writings and periodical publications an ardent advocate of the Revolutionary Party; and it is on this account, no doubt, that he a few days since, to the astonishment of a friend of mine, who knew not his hopes, broke through his accustomed silence and reserve, and declared against Mr. Görres's recent conduct. I had observed him for some time forcing through his usual cold and distant habits and paying great attention to Count Bernstorff; and he did it with such success and putting so much constraint upon himself as to have persuaded the Count that he has great mildness in his Character.

The report concluded with the observation that "Prince Hardenberg in this matter is the dupe of the man in the world he should have mistrusted the most, Baron Humboldt," and with a renewed defense of the writer's action in "this matter, which has been of much delicacy and embarrassment and in which nothing but a positive sense of duty could have led me to take any part whatever."[15]

Rose continued his offensive some days later with an interview with

[15] Ibid.

Bernstorff's deputy, Ancillon, who conducted the affairs of the Foreign Ministry in Bernstorff's absence. He went so far as to assure Ancillon that Humboldt had falsely informed the Prussian government in claiming in 1818 that the prince regent desired a Prussian officer as Humboldt's successor in London. Whether Rose's accusation was true or not, it removed one of the strongest arguments in favor of Clausewitz's appointment. Ancillon lost no time in conveying this disclosure to Hardenberg, and the tone and content of the letter in which he informed Rose of his step indicate how closely Clausewitz's Prussian enemies now worked together with the British minister.[16]

It was in these days that Clausewitz called on Rose. He probably already suspected what was to become certainty in the following month, that Rose and the duke of Cumberland opposed his appointment, together with most Prussian diplomats, who could hardly be pleased to see one of the senior positions in the service fall to an outsider.[17] Clausewitz must have hoped to win over the minister, but his visit was not a success. He came, in the words of Rose's report to Castlereagh,

to inform me confidentially that Prince Hardenberg destines him to fill the Post of Prussian Envoy in London, and to request that I would bespeak your Lordship's confidence in him, assuring me that the honor and frankness of his character render him not undeserving of it. He spoke modestly of his want of qualifications such as diplomatic habits would give, and expressed the esteem he has long felt for the British nation. I said that I must of course conceive that His Prussian Majesty in making his choice had ascertained him to possess the qualities fitted for a due discharge of duty; that I had described him to your Lordship as a man of unsullied honor. He said that he had never borne arms in the cause of the enemies of Great Britain [evidently an effort to emphasize that unlike most Prussian officers he had resigned his commis-

[16] Ancillon to Rose, 22 November 1819: "Comme vous le désirer Monsieur, j'ai instruit le Prince Chancelier d'état, du mal-entendu qu'on a relevé de la part de votre Ministère, et j'ai tâché en le lui écrivant d'observer sévèrement la nuance que Vous m'avais indiqué. Je lui ai dit 'on sait à Londres qu'il s'est & répandu à Berlin que S.A.R. le Prince Régent avoit témoigné le désir que ce fut un militaire qui remplacât Msr. de Humboldt; Le Ministre Anglois a cru devoir dans un dépêche à M. Rose assurer que S.A.R. le Prince Régent n'avoit jamais ni eu ni exprimé une prédilection de ce genre et que c'étoit uniquement à Sa Majesté à juger de ces convenances.

Je crois que cette manière ne dit ni trop ni trop peu et je serais charmé d'avoir rencontré vos intentions." Rose Papers, British Museum, Add. 42:781. Rose continued to refer to Humboldt's possibly mistaken report that the prince regent hoped a Prussian officer would be given the London legation. See, for instance, his letters to Castlereagh of 1 and 18 January 1820, ibid.

[17] Clausewitz to his friend Carl von der Groeben, 26 December 1819, in Eberhard Kessel, "Zu Boyens Entlassung," *Historische Zeitschrift* 175, no. 1 (1953): 51.

sion in 1812 rather than fight for Napoleon.] I begged leave to inform him that I had stated the circumstance to your Lordship.

General Count Gneisenau made a similar communication the next day.[18]

The remainder of the dispatch consisted of a labored protestation that Rose was not opposed to Clausewitz out of a preference for Werther. An appendix in code explained the reason for this denial: "The latter part of this Dispatch is solely intended to deprive Prince Hardenberg of the only excuse which I am informed he alleges for persisting in a Nomination which created a sensation beyond what I could have imagined, and which excuse has not the shadow of foundation."

Although the alliance of ambassadors and Prussian conservatives, which Rose had helped mobilize and which he led, should have sufficed to block Clausewitz's appointment, the outcome remained in doubt during the last weeks of 1819. Clausewitz's future was scarcely a matter of great moment for Hardenberg and Bernstorff, although the latter found him very likeable, and in later years the two men became friends. But the appointment had become a factor in the ideological and political conflicts in Prussia, and in the hope of maintaining a moderate course between the various factions the chancellor might have hesitated to sacrifice Clausewitz. His room for maneuver was, however, contracting. Encouraged by the Carlsbad Decrees that had just been issued and by the rising conservative tide throughout Europe, Prussian conservatives were now turning against a major achievement of the reformers, the Landwehr, which they attacked as a socially dangerous and politically unreliable force. Clausewitz's determined and open defense of this Prussian version of the National Guard during these weeks could only increase their antagonism. Rose was unable to predict the king's decision. In an alternately optimistic and pessimistic dispatch he reported:

It is generally supposed, and chiefly, I believe, if not entirely from the delay of the signature of Major General von Clausewitz's appointment, that it will not take place; such delays however constantly occur here without being indicatory of such an effect, and I learn indirectly from Prince Wittgenstein that it certainly will be signed by the King, as Prince Hardenberg persists in soliciting it. . . . I understand that the signature has been deferred in consequence of official arrangements and that the amount of money for outfit has not yet been determined with him [d.h., Clausewitz]. I am told that the King is desirous of removing him from the direction of the Military School. . . .

Mr. Ancillon, who complains more loudly of the appointment of General von Clausewitz than anyone, assures me that his understanding is by no means of a superior cast, and that conscious of it, he adopts the reserved and

---

[18] Rose to Castlereagh, 20 November 1819, Public Record Office, F.O. 64/120.

dogmatical manner peculiar to him to conceal it, and this opinion I find prevailing generally.[19]

Ancillon went so far as to tell Humboldt that the choice of Clausewitz was the worst that could be made. Humboldt, Rose commented on 12 December, "replied almost [sic] in my hearing, that it was true, with the exception of Monsieur de Werther," an ironic twist that seems to have escaped Rose for he continued:

The fact is that he [i.e., Humboldt] does know that Monsieur de Clausewitz's appointment to be most unsuitable, but that he wishes it to take place to mortify and weaken Count Bernstorff, and because he probably attributes to Monsieur de Clausewitz a tendency of political opinions to the party he has espoused. General de Clausewitz's appointment was not signed four days since; and it is now conjectured that the delay arises from the wish to know what is thought of it by His Majesty's Government. The only personal motive with the King of Prussia for wishing it to take place can be His desire to remove him from the direction of the Military School.[20]

During the following week he repeated that Clausewitz's appointment had not yet been signed, "and I know that on Sunday last the English Correspondence had not been put into his hands. I am told that His Prussian Majesty said lately, 'I know not why I should name as my Envoy a man who has always been in opposition to me.' "[21]

One or two days later Rose received instructions from Joseph Planta, one of the two undersecretaries of state at the Foreign Office, not to intervene further in the conflict over the London appointment: "As to the proposed appointment of General Clausewitz, L[or]d Castlereagh hopes that as you have called the attention of the Pr[ussian] Ministers and of your colleagues to the difficulties you see in it you will now have the former [i.e., the Prussian ministers] make their own decision and not bring forward any official representation without hearing from His L[ordshi]p."[22] In his reply Rose defended himself heatedly against the suspicion that he had acted indiscreetly or with excessive energy: "I could

[19] Rose to Castlereagh, 30 November 1819, *ibid.*

[20] Rose to Castlereagh, 12 December 1819, *ibid.* Rose repeated Humboldt's statement in a private letter to Castlereagh two days later. Rose Papers, British Museum, Add. 42:781. In 1818 the king had only reluctantly decided to appoint Clausewitz as director of the War Academy. On 23 February 1818, Gneisenau wrote to Clausewitz that the king wished to know "whether young officers could be safely entrusted to you because of your political attitudes, and whether you too possibly belonged to the republican innovators, who are now threatening the thrones." Pertz and Delbrück, *Das Leben*, 5:292.

[21] Rose to Castlereagh, 18 December, 1819 Public Record Office, F.O. 64/120.

[22] Planta to Rose, 30 November 1819, in code, Rose Papers, British Museum, Add. 42:781.

offer sufficient testimonies to shew my moderation and circumspection in this matter, but I had rather trust to his Lordship's good opinion of me than to them." But he was unable to restrain himself from adding: "I have been informed, and I believe correctly, that the King waits but for the least word from us to refuse the signature on the General's appointment, desirous of having an ostensible ground to do so; but this I state simply as intelligence and not as a suggestion, as I am fully aware of the extreme delicacy of his Lordship's position in this affair."[23]

Despite Rose's anxieties and his disgust at the indecisiveness of the Prussian government, Clausewitz's prospects were fading. On 3 December, the Danish diplomat Eugen von Reventlow, who as Bernstorff's son-in-law was well placed to follow the nuances of views in the ministry of foreign affairs, informed Copenhagen that the matter was likely to be resolved in favor of the conservative party:

> I was assured yesterday that it was very possible that the designation of General Clausewitz to the London position will be withdrawn. The Duke of Cumberland has repeatedly declared his strong opposition, nor has M. Rose for his part painted the most favorable portrait of him. Not to mention other factors that could fault this choice, M. de Clausewitz is reputed to have belonged at all times to the democratic party, and to have been, for example, one of the foremost partisans of the Tugendbund.[24]

It was in these weeks that the remaining reformers in senior positions in government left office: Boyen, the minister of war, resigned because he would not further subordinate the Landwehr to the regular army; he was followed by Grolman, director of the second department in the ministry; two days later Humboldt was dismissed. The conservative and reactionaries at court and in the ministry had won a decisive victory, the consequences of which were to influence the history of Germany until 1945. That in this crisis a member of the reform party, for years closely allied with the men who had just been forced out of office, should be given an important diplomatic post was most unlikely. Clausewitz's name was not withdrawn, but by March 1820 when the duke of Cumberland wrote about the still unfilled position to his brother, who had just ascended the throne as George IV, he could treat Clausewitz's appointment as a possibility that had long been rejected:

> I take it for granted you have heard that a certain Major General Clausewitz was talked of for that place to the astonishment of all the world here, when I say this I beg leave not [to] be understood as meaning any thing in prejudice

---

[23] Rose to Planta, 21 December 1819, in code, Public Record Office, F.O. 64/120.

[24] Eugen von Reventlow to minister of foreign affairs, 3 December 1819, Dept. f. u. A. 1771–1848, Preussen II, Depecher 1819, Rigsarkivet, Copenhagen.

to his personal character, for I know him not sufficiently to form any opinion of him, but the choice of a man for such a high position as Minister at the Court of St. James, who is hardly a Major General of a year's standing & never employed before in diplomacy, did surprize every one. When I first heard it I could not believe it, but upon seeing Rose he said he was equally surprized, and I know he acted most honourably & zealously, at the same time with very great prudence & delicacy. To be plain & fair with you I am clearly of the opinion he would *not do for he is not* made for society or would be the sort of man either to suit you or anyone there. . . . It is generally believed that his nomination was owing to Gneisenau who is his great patron, and he is also connected with Lt. General Boyen and Grollmann [*sic*]. Certain it is that since the dismissal of these two latter gentlemen the report of the nomination of Clausewitz has subsided.²⁵

For some time the duke, seconded by Rose, had put forward his own candidate: Count Tauenzien von Wittenberg, a senior general of unblemished absolutist convictions.²⁶ When George III died in February 1820 and the Prussian court needed to send a special envoy to London to express the government's good wishes to the new monarch, Castlereagh wrote that the king hoped the choice would fall on Tauenzien, although he knew that Tauenzien would not be able to remain permanently in England.²⁷ Consequently Tauenzien was entrusted with the mission, and Cumberland and Rose suggested that he be appointed minister as well.²⁸ Soon Rose was compelled to inform Castlereagh that Tauenzien had declined the offer, and that it was likely that the chancellor would again put Clausewitz's name forward. But, he added, this did not worry him because Bernstorff now knew that London did not favor Clausewitz's appointment.²⁹ Rose's rejection of Clausewitz had evidently become the policy of the British government. For the time being, the Prussian legation in London remained in the hands of subordinate officials. Clausewitz was not told that his appointment had been withdrawn, but he could scarcely doubt that he was no longer in serious contention, the more so since an attempt of his friends to gain him the less important post of envoy to the Swiss Confederation also failed. Finally, on 10 August 1821, Baron Werther, the same man whom Clausewitz two-and-a-half years earlier had seemed to displace, was named to the post.³⁰ Clausewitz remained

²⁵ Cumberland to George IV, 31 March 1829, *Letters*, 2:315–16.
²⁶ For instance, Rose to Castlereagh, 12 December 1819, and Rose to Planta, 21 December 1819, Public Record Office, F.O. 64/120.
²⁷ Castlereagh to Rose, 20 February 1820, Rose Papers, British Museum, Add. 42:781.
²⁸ Cumberland to George IV, 3 and 31 March 1820, *Letters*, 2:311, 315; Rose to Castlereagh, 4 March 1820, *Correspondence of Viscount Castlereagh*, 12:216–18.
²⁹ Rose to Castlereagh, 10 August 1829, Public Record Office, F.O. 64/120.
³⁰ Rose to Castlereagh, 11 August 1821, Public Record Office. F.O. 64/128.

director of the War Academy—a position he was to retain almost to the end of his life—without having his authority and responsibilities enlarged. In 1822 he was decorated with the Order of the Red Eagle, Third Class—Rose surmised that the order was intended as a compensation for the failed diplomatic appointment, but in reality it was the customary decoration for a major general of Clausewitz's seniority.[31]

We may ask whether Clausewitz's enemies were justified in claiming that his personality and his politics made him unsuited for a diplomatic appointment. Certainly he would not have been a second Lieven or Esterhazy in London—he lacked the aptitude and wealth to turn the Prussian legation into a center of aristocratic and political society. We cannot imagine him as a member of George IV's "cottage coterie," although he might have got on better than most with the French ambassador, Chateaubriand, whose broad literary interests matched his own. But the diplomatic corps did not consist only of grandees. Among the men of affairs who represented the interests of their governments and reported on the political developments of the capital, Clausewitz would not have been out of place. It goes without saying that he would not have been able to pursue an independent course. His political views—reformist, not revolutionary—would in any case never have made him an unreliable link in the diplomatic intercourse of the two governments. On the contrary, free of ideological prejudices and with his pronounced sense of realism, he better than others might have explained to Berlin the United Kingdom's gradual detachment from continental ties throughout the 1820s.

That an extended stay in London would have influenced Clausewitz's view cannot be doubted. The fact that he sought a diplomatic appointment and continued to pursue it despite his increasingly embarrassing position demonstrates the strength of his interest in issues of foreign policy. His speculations on Europe's past, present, and future would have been enriched had he become acquainted with the kind of intense political and economic life that did not exist in Prussia. New experiences and perspectives might have expanded his theories of war. With the collapse of his English plans he lost the last possibility of breaking out of the narrowness of German conditions. But the duties of Prussian minister in London would never have allowed him the time and leisure that he possessed as head of the War Academy, years of undemanding routine that alone enabled him to write his major historical works and the incomplete theoretical manuscript *On War*.

[31] Rose to Castlereagh, 11 February 1822, Public Record Office, F.O. 64/131.

14

REACTIONS TO REVOLUTION

N EARLY THIRTY YEARS AGO when I began to study Clausewitz's political ideas and tried to understand their development
over the course of his life, it seemed to me that his essays and
other writings of 1831, the last year of his life, deserved more attention
than they were usually given. My discovery of a previously unidentified
and ignored letter by him led me to attempt a first analysis of these final
expressions of his political views, which appeared in 1970.

Clausewitz set down his opinions in response to a series of political
crises. Beginning in the summer of 1830, civil unrest and revolutions
broke out across Europe: the July Revolution in Paris, the Belgian revolt
against the Dutch-Belgian union; demonstrations for constitutional
change in the Swiss Confederation; disturbances in Germany, Italy, and
the Iberian Peninsula; and in November the Polish insurrection against
Russia, which affected Clausewitz directly when he was appointed chief
of staff of a Prussian observation corps on the eastern frontier. Clausewitz
had grown up as a witness of the French Revolution and began his military career by fighting against it. Now he seemed to be facing a repetition
of the earlier threat.

Although the various conflicts resulted from internal dissension, most
had international implications, and it is to be noted that Clausewitz analyzed them almost exclusively from the perspective of foreign policy. He
was primarily interested in the threat they posed to Prussia's security and
to the balance of power. In that respect his writings continued a process
that had begun some ten years earlier. As a young man Clausewitz had
been fascinated by politics as much as by foreign affairs. During the era
of reform and later, he had taken a decided stand on a number of political
issues. But now his attention was concentrated on foreign affairs. Presumably this shift was caused by the rise of an aggressive conservatism in
Prussia after 1815, the stunting of the reform movement and the failure
of constitutionalism, which isolated men with Clausewitz's reformist
views. Blocked on the domestic front, his pronounced interest in politics
now focused on foreign affairs, which he came to analyze in terms of an
increasingly harsh, aggressively anti-ideological realism. In the political
literature of the time, preoccupied with causes and doctrines ranging
from legitimacy to republicanism and national self-determination, his insistence on the supremacy of power is close to unique.

It was interesting to discover Clausewitz as a precursor of Bismarckian *Realpolitik*. But I now see that the comparison is flawed. Society and politics in Bismarck's Prussia were far more complex than anything known to Clausewitz. One of Bismarck's great strengths lay in his understanding and manipulation of the interaction of domestic and foreign affairs, while Clausewitz was still able to criticize and correct domestic political opinion in his analyses of the international situation as something beside the point. Less than two decades later the Revolution of 1848 was to demonstrate that this separation and detachment was no longer possible even in Germany.

We may perhaps conclude that in politics as in war Clausewitz lived in a period of transition. Forces that soon gained great significance were still in their infancy or stood out clearly because their essential characteristics were not yet obscured by later developments and accretions. Clausewitz's ability to identify the basic elements in war and trace their dynamic enabled him to create a theory of exceptional comprehensiveness and interpretive force. His political recognitions were equally sharp, and not inaccurate, but they were one-sided.

ॐ

Early in August 1831 Clausewitz wrote to his wife that a letter by him—refuting claims that Prussia, in violation of her announced policy of nonintervention, was aiding Russian forces against the Polish insurgents—had appeared in several newspapers.[1] The literature on Clausewitz has ignored this hint, and yet the letter—the last of his writings to be published while he was alive—is worth resurrecting. At the time, it gave the German public a glimpse of Clausewitz's ideas on political affairs, which apart from this brief emergence were to remain buried in manuscript for another fifty years; to the later reader it suggests a change in emphasis of much of the political energy generated by the Prussian reform movement, which was to prove increasingly significant in the course of the century.

The outbreak of the Polish insurrection at the end of November 1830 had caused Prussia to assemble an observation corps on the Polish frontier. To command this force, her greatest military figure, Gneisenau, was recalled from retirement, and on his request Clausewitz was designated as his chief of staff. This returned to prominence two men who had been among the most uncompromising reformers in the years after Jena, and who subsequently were excluded from any position of influence for fear

---

[1] Letter of 2 August 1831, in K. Schwartz, *Leben des Generals Carl von Clausewitz* (Berlin, 1878), 2:375.

of their supposed Jacobinism. In the second week of December, Clausewitz arrived in Berlin, where he spent the next four months assisting in the partial mobilization of the army, drafting plans for its employment in possible campaigns east or west, and incidentally in clarifying his own thoughts on the political situation. Both his strategic planning and his political reflections benefited from his longstanding friendship with the minister of foreign affairs, Bernstorff, whom during this period he seems to have seen every few days, and from his contacts with some of Bernstorff's senior officials, such as Eichhorn.[2] When in the previous July Charles X had unilaterally tried to increase the power of the crown in France, and in turn had been deposed, Clausewitz had longed for an army of 150,000 men with which to snuff out the revolution. But since an immediate response of the powers was impossible, if only because they were militarily unprepared, he came to favor a policy of nonintervention, condemned Russian pressures on Frederick William III to restore Charles by force, and opposed the related urgings by some members of the Prussian royal family to aid Holland in her campaign to recover Belgium. He hoped that Louis Philippe would succeed in establishing his regime firmly while refraining from foreign adventures; but he did not hold this hope very strongly in view of the radical opposition in Paris, the bellicosity of some members of the new government, and the departure of French volunteers for Belgium. What was more, he feared not only a revolutionary France, but the power of France in general. He felt certain that any French government, whatever its complexion, was tempted by the increase in strength that incorporation of Belgium would bring. The storm of support that the Polish insurrection aroused in France deepened his anxieties. Throughout the autumn he thought it almost inevitable that France would start war in the spring of 1831.[3]

Early in the new year, after he had familiarized himself with the information and views of the foreign ministry, Clausewitz wrote two papers on the international situation. The first, "The Condition of Europe since the Polish Partitions," was apparently intended for private circulation; the other, "Reduction of the Many Political Questions Occupying Ger-

[2] Clausewitz's life in Berlin during the early months of 1831 is discussed in my *Clausewitz and the State* (rev. ed., Princeton, 1985). J. A. F. Eichhorn, at this time *Vortragender Rat* for German affairs in the foreign ministry, had been active in the reform movement, served as Stein's secretary in the *Zentralverwaltungsdepartment*, and was a friend of Gneisenau and Schleiermacher. He became Prussian *Kultusminister* under Frederick William IV.

[3] For Clausewitz's political views at this time, see especially his diary, in Schwartz, *Clausewitz*, 2:298–318, and his correspondence with Gneisenau printed in G. H. Pertz and H. Delbrück, *Das Leben des Feldmarschalls Grafen Neithardt von Gneisenau* (Berlin, 1880), 5:606–48. Clausewitz's diary and correspondence do not support Treitschke's assertion in his *Deutsche Geschichte im Neunzehnten Jahrhundert* (Leipzig, 1889), 4:45, that Clausewitz favored a preventive war against France.

many to the Basic Question of Our Existence," Clausewitz hoped to publish.[4] He anonymously submitted his manuscript to the most prestigious newspaper in Germany, the *Augsburger Allgemeine Zeitung*, which, however, rejected it. A second attempt by Eichhorn to place the piece in the *Augsburger Allgemeine* also failed. The specific grounds for the rejection are not known, but, as Hans Rothfels suggests, at a time when most educated Germans tended to interpret international affairs as a conflict between the principles of autocracy and liberalism, an analysis based wholly on the concept of *raison d'état* would hardly be welcomed.[5]

That Clausewitz wished to influence German liberal opinion is evident both from his sending the manuscript to the *Augsburger Allgemeine Zeitung*, which enjoyed a large readership among the educated middle classes in all German states, and from a comment in his diary: "I sought to make it clear to the good people [Leutchen] that something besides cosmopolitanism should determine our position on the Belgian, Polish, and other questions, that German independence was in the gravest danger, and that it was time to think about ourselves."[6] The condition of Europe, he wrote in the first of the two essays, had undergone a change since the disappearance of Poland; not, however, because of the partitions, but because of the concurrent growth of French power. The widespread support that the Polish cause enjoyed among Germans was a fad, based less on moral than on aesthetic principles, neither of which should be substituted for one's political interests. The restoration of Poland was possible only at the expense of Austria and Prussia; any future war with France would involve these powers in a conflict with Poland and thus impose the strategic handicap of a two-front war on Prussia. Since 1789 French aggressiveness had rarely abated; today France continued to be the preponderant power on the continent, facing states with separate interests, which in turn were threatened by Turkey, Poland, and Sweden.

Clausewitz returned to the relation between French power and Prussian raison d'état in the manuscript submitted to the *Augsburger Allgemeine Zeitung*: Ever since the Burgundian buffer had disappeared, Germany had been under attack by France. Belgium, as long as Austria was in control, had served as a bastion for Germany and Europe, and as a

[4] The essays were first printed in Schwartz, *Clausewitz*, 2:401–17. English translations may be found in Carl von Clausewitz, *Historical and Political Writings*, ed. Peter Paret and Daniel Moran (Princeton, 1992), 369–84.

[5] Carl von Clausewitz, *Politische Schriften und Briefe*, ed. H. Rothfels (Munich, 1922), xxxii–xxxiii.

[6] Diary entry for 21 February 1831, Schwartz, *Clausewitz*, 2:313 (see also the letter of 18 March 1831 to his wife, ibid., 2:325). Months later Clausewitz was still toying with the idea of publishing the manuscript as a separate pamphlet (see the letter of 13 August, 1831 to his wife, ibid., 2:379–80).

foothold for England, whenever the British wanted to defend the threatened continent. German policy toward the new Belgian state must be guided by concern for German security, which should also determine policy in the questions of Italian and Polish independence. A free Italy would undoubtedly ally herself with France, as would a free Poland. The Poles claimed that they could serve as a buffer against Russia, but this required two conditions that did not exist: Poland was not a modern state, and would not be for many years; and the Poles would have to establish friendly relations with Germany, which was unlikely for psychological as well as for political reasons. In any case, "so long as *everything* must be feared from France, nothing is to be feared from Russia." Poles and Frenchmen always regarded themselves as natural allies, and the object of their alliance obviously was the man in the middle, Germany. France, on the other hand, had nothing to fear: England, Austria, and Prussia would never launch a preventive war against her because, among other reasons, a struggle with France could not be waged as a cabinet war but must be imbued with the same just enthusiasm that motivated the German people in 1813. Clausewitz ended by seeking to allay two misconceptions that, he claimed, were frequently expressed by liberal writers: he assured them that if it should become necessary to fight a defensive war, France would again be defeated because, in the first place, German military institutions had improved since the Napoleonic period, and, further, the French were no longer united—the radicals in Paris not being representative of the French people as a whole.

Had Clausewitz's appeal for the primacy of state power over ideology and cosmopolitan sympathies appeared in print, it would no doubt have been quickly submerged in the flood of enthusiasm for Polish independence that swept central and southern Germany, and would have even managed to express itself in Prussia where, particularly in the eastern provinces, it was strongly admixed with dislike and fear of Russia. Popular feeling did not, of course, alter the Prussian government's policy of benevolent neutrality toward her eastern ally. Both Prussia's freedom of action in foreign affairs and her administration of the former Polish territories, which she had acquired in the past fifty years, seemed best served by the rapid defeat of the insurgents. This, however, was not forthcoming. By March, when Gneisenau and Clausewitz established their headquarters in Posen, near the theater of operations, the Russian campaign of reconquest had made little progress. Even more effective than Polish resistance proved to be the inadequacy of Russian administration and supply, which was further hampered by early thaws and the spreading incidence of cholera. Under these circumstances the Russians felt compelled to ask Berlin for support. Requests deemed politically too compromising, such as one for permission to cross Prussian territory at Thorn, were denied; but as their troops slowly advanced toward the west and north, the Russians were allowed to purchase supplies in Prussia and in effect establish supply bases under Prussian protection. On 19 June, the Polish commander-in-chief, Skrzynecki, addressed a letter of complaint to Frederick William. After his note had been rejected on the grounds that the king could not accept communications from an authority whose position he did not recognize, it was published in Warsaw, and reprinted in several German newspapers.[7] The burden of Skrzynecki's complaint was that despite Berlin's stated policy of neutrality, Prussian officials on the Polish border supplied Russian forces with food, ammunition, and uniforms; that a Prussian engineer was helping the Russian command to construct a bridge across the Vistula; and that Prussian gunners had been detached to serve with Russian units. That some of his accusations were without foundation did not invalidate Skrzynecki's main point: the Russians were obtaining valuable support from Prussia. Clausewitz replied with an anonymous letter, which disingenuously minimized his government's role in the matter while pointing to the weaknesses and inconsistencies of the Polish arguments. His letter first appeared in the *Zeitung des Grossherzogtums Posen*, and was immediately reprinted in other journals:

This letter is apparently a device to renew certain ridiculous and wholly imaginary assertions, and serve them up to a credulous public. Nothing is true in these statements except that the Russians bought provisions and supplies for cash from private dealers in the Prussian provinces—mainly grain, hay, and straw—that they shipped their purchases on rented barges and wagons to the points where they needed them, that in addition they wanted to use the barges to transport troops across the Vistula, and now have in fact done so. Everything else is a deliberate lie. One must be very ignorant in the history of international law to find a breach of neutrality in such actions, if, indeed, it is possible to apply the concept of neutrality to an insurgent power that is not recognized by a single government in the world. When the French army crossed the Rhine during the Seven Years' War, it employed vessels of the neutral Dutch Republic, and subsisted on Dutch wheat. When, in turn, Duke Ferdinand of Brunswick crossed the Rhine in 1758, he did exactly the same. It is probably asking too much that a Warsaw journalist should be aware of such matters. But the Poles must know little of their own history, or be deeply ashamed of certain pages in it, if they can't recall the depots that Russia established on the territory of their magnificent, neutral republic during the Seven Years' War. At that time, after all, Poland was still a populous

---

[7] The official text is published in D'Angeberg (J. L. Chodz'ko), *Recueil des traités, conventions et actes diplomatiques concernant la Pologne* (Paris, 1862), 825–26. For a contemporary German version see, for instance, the *Staats und Gelehrte Zeitung des Hamburgischen unpartheiischen Correspondenten*, no. 174, 26 July 1831, 2–3.

nation; the partitions had not yet occurred. Indeed, the partitions were made necessary by the disorderly, almost Tartar-like administration of the vast areas the Poles possessed. The commercial dealings with Prussian subjects to which reference is made, in no way involve the Prussian government. If such traffic were to be in the nature of an intervention, how would one have to categorize the active help by means of money, arms, and volunteers that other countries have tolerated in order to give a boost to the Belgian and Polish rebellions?[8]

The arguments that Clausewitz had put forward in his two essays were here applied to a specific situation. In smaller matters as in large, he judged the internal occurrences in Poland, in Belgium, and indeed in Prussia, according to the effect they might be expected to have on Prussia's position in Europe. This single-mindedness, which gave his arguments their unusual sharpness, was the outcome of a change in emphasis, a shift of priorities, in Clausewitz's approach to politics, which had taken place over the preceding fifteen years and which can also be traced in the attitudes of many of his associates during the years of reform—for instance, in Gneisenau, in Grolman and Boyen. The reformers had pursued two aims: the modernization of Prussia's social and governmental institutions and the creation of sufficient power to enable the state to act vigorously on the international stage. The former, they held, was essential for bringing about the latter. Though they might differ on specifics, all were agreed on the need to increase the accountability of the monarch and his advisors, and to strengthen and formalize the political influence of certain groups in society—the nobility, the bureaucracy, segments of the educated middle classes—backed by efforts of the state to develop an educated and self-reliant people. The resurgence of the ultraconservatives after 1815 prevented the reformers from turning their many sympathizers in the army and administration into a true political base, and eventually—immobilized by an opposition in which political antagonism and personal vindictiveness were inextricably combined—they were no longer willing to press for further change. But in view of the substantial improvements that had been achieved between 1807 and the Congress of Vienna, did the subaltern conservatism that now dominated internal affairs necessarily rule out a freer style abroad? It is not difficult to see how the reformers' impotence at home might be compensated for by greater concern with foreign relations. Here too, however, their activism was stifled by a system whose immobility recalled to them the disasters of the Third Coalition and the days of 1809 and 1812. Clausewitz could still scoff bitterly at the legitimist fantasies of a Radowitz or the naive liberalism of journalists who knew nothing about the ways of government and the great

[8] I have based my translation on the text published in *Staats und Gelehrte Zeitung des Hamburgischen unpartheiischen Correspondenten*, 26 July 1831, 3.

world, but his diary and correspondence show clearly that he had lost heart, and that his political imagination now was mainly engaged by Prussia's foreign relations. It can hardly be denied that his analysis of the European system of 1830 was distinguished by a pronounced sense of realism; but his realism was suffused with ideas that were shaped—and to some extent falsified—by the experiences of his youth and early maturity: the Revolution, the French invasions of Germany, the Napoleonic domination of Europe. Even if France had been another tsarist autocracy, he would have seen her as the major source of danger to Prussia; the continuing vitality of her republican traditions added in his eyes a dynamic and unpredictable element to the workings of the French raison d'état. Political self-determination and the extension of political authority in society had to be opposed abroad if they promised to strengthen France, and restricted or postponed at home if they threatened to confuse the purpose and sap the energy of Prussia's dealings with her neighbors.

On 20 August Clausewitz received a Cabinet Order from Frederick William, praising the "content and form" of his defense of government policy.[9] Three days later Gneisenau died of cholera, which was now replacing Polish independence as the major problem facing Prussia in the east. By the end of the summer the Russians had reestablished their control over Poland. Clausewitz left Posen early in November, and on the sixteenth himself fell victim to the epidemic. Had he lived even a short time longer he would have witnessed the increasing currency that opinions related to his were gaining among the German public. Already in 1833 the classic formulation of the uniqueness of each nation's political development and of the primacy of foreign affairs was achieved when Ranke's *Historisch-politische Zeitschrift*, which had been founded under the sponsorship of Bernstorff and Eichhorn, printed its editor's essay on "The Great Powers." In the previous year Ranke had published Clausewitz's first posthumous work in the *Historisch-politische Zeitschrift*, a long study on the life and character of Scharnhorst, which Clausewitz's widow accompanied with an appreciation of the strength and distinctiveness of that earlier phase of Prussia's history. The essay indicates the changes Clausewitz's political interests had undergone. Written soon after the Wars of Liberation and still imbued with the convictions of those days, it defended the liberalization of the state's institutions, which Scharnhorst had championed and which for a time seemed to open the way for a significant extension of political responsibility in German society.

[9] The text of the order is quoted by Clausewitz in a letter to his wife of the same date (see Schwartz, *Clausewitz*, 2:384).

15

AN UNKNOWN LETTER BY CLAUSEWITZ

THE DOCUMENTARY SOURCES on Clausewitz's life are uneven. We are able to construct a reasonably detailed account of his military career on the basis of official correspondence, reports, and service data; but we know much less about his private affairs, and far too few of his reflections on his scholarly work have come down to us. His earliest surviving letter dates from his twenty-sixth year; were it not for a few recollections in letters and diaries written years later, we would know nothing about his thoughts and feelings as a boy and a young man. From 1806 on the situation is reversed. Together with other sources, the extensive correspondence with Marie von Brühl, whom he married in 1809, and with Gneisenau, after Scharnhorst his closest friend, affords us access to his ideas and emotions during the Reform era, the Russian campaign, and the Wars of Liberation. After 1815 the correspondence with Gneisenau remains an important source, while that between husband and wife, now no longer separated by war, comes almost to an end. Other letters to men in government and the army, to scholars and other social acquaintances, complete the picture. From the summer of 1830 on, when husband and wife were again separated, their letters reappear as a major source of information on the last year and a half of his life.

Many of Clausewitz's manuscripts and letters were destroyed or lost during the Second World War, and the few documents that have resurfaced have been mostly strength reports and service correspondence of little interest except for his signature. It was therefore an unusual event when a private letter appeared on the autograph market in 1990, and though hardly more than a note, its evidentiary value increased on examination. In it Clausewitz discussed his own work, and as it is the last document in his hand that we now possess, the letter may be said to have both substantive and symbolic significance.

When I came across the letter I was working on another subject. Despite a looming deadline, however, I found it impossible not to interrupt what I was doing and write an analysis of this new biographical source. I was not unaware of the danger of overinterpreting the brief document, but each of its sentences was charged with ideas that had occupied Clausewitz for years, even decades, and I found the page and a half—covered with his symmetrical script, which had scarcely faded after 150 years—a firm bridge over which to return to the past.

❧

On 7 November 1831, Clausewitz returned to Breslau from Posen after disbanding the headquarters of the army Prussia had mobilized to guard her eastern provinces during the Polish uprising. For the preceding eleven months he had served as chief of staff of this force, which was commanded by his close friend Gneisenau, until Gneisenau died in August of the cholera epidemic that the Russian reconquest was carrying into Poland and farther west. Clausewitz remained in Posen until the last Polish units ceased fighting in October. The Prussian army was demobilized, and he resumed his regular duties as commanding officer of the Silesian artillery inspectorate. On 9 November his wife joined him in Breslau, and they passed, she later wrote, "eight on the whole very happy days together."[1] Not only were husband and wife very close, Clausewitz looked forward to completing his manuscript *On War*, which he had been compelled to lay aside for the past year, and he received intimations of a new assignment, which together with his seniority could be expected to bring him promotion to lieutenant general. If, as his wife seems to suggest in the passage quoted above, his days were not entirely unclouded, it was because he worried over the political consequences of Gneisenau's death, which had deprived him and the progressive wing of the army in general of a powerful champion.

Between 1807 and the Wars of Liberation, Gneisenau had been a leader of those officers—Clausewitz among them—who against strong conservative resistance modernized the army. To many of the conservatives who regained dominance in the country after Napoleon's downfall, Gneisenau was and remained a secret Jacobin. In 1830 they disapproved of his appointment to command the army on the Polish frontier, the more so because it allowed him to choose as his chief of staff yet another officer suspected of liberalism. The secret relief felt in these circles at Gneisenau's death may have contributed to the restrained official reaction to the event. The king barely went beyond a few conventional phrases in acknowledging the passing of a man to whom the state owed much. It was Frederick William's coldness that particularly upset Clausewitz—unduly so, his wife thought: "Perhaps he took these things too tragically, and made

---

[1] Marie von Clausewitz to Elise von Bernstorff, undated, written soon after 20 November 1831, cited in my *Clausewitz and the State*, rev. ed. (Princeton, 1985). On Clausewitz's last year, see ibid., 396–430, where sources for Marie von Clausewitz's statement and for her other writings mentioned below will also be found.

them out to be worse than they were meant to be." But Clausewitz always remained an outspoken, even passionate defender of the reform program and would have been sensitive to any perceived slight to one of its leading figures. He may also have suspected that the meager acknowledgment of Gneisenau's services signaled a new isolation for himself and others like him in the army. These concerns apart, the life into which he was now settling held out the promise of a renewed spell of intellectual effort and creativity. Whether he actually took up the manuscript of *On War* is not known. On the morning of 16 November he dealt with business of the inspectorate in his study at home, then felt unwell and soon began to show signs of cholera. He died shortly before nine o'clock in the evening, probably of a heart attack brought on by the disease.

Until 1990, our knowledge of the last week of Clausewitz's life derived entirely from his wife, the main sources being two letters that she wrote to a friend within a week of her husband's death. Some time later she again referred to his last days in her editorial note to Clausewitz's essay on Scharnhorst, a strong defense of the reformers that Ranke published in 1832, and in her preface to *On War* when that work appeared—not least through her efforts—in the same year. Recently a new source, in which Clausewitz's voice is heard directly, has become known and adds a few further strokes to the outline drawn by Marie von Clausewitz. In the spring of 1990 a German autograph dealer sold at auction a previously unknown letter by Clausewitz.[2] The letter, dated 12 November 1831, is now the last document in his hand we possess, and although it was certainly not written with future generations in mind, it refers to the writer's theoretical and historical work in terms that are in the nature of an intellectual testament.

The letter—a page and a half written in Clausewitz's customary firm, flowing hand—was addressed to Prince August of Prussia, son of the youngest brother of Frederick the Great, a man who on and off for twenty-five years played an important role in Clausewitz's life. In 1803 when Clausewitz was still a student in Scharnhorst's Institute for Young Officers in Berlin, he had been seconded as temporary adjutant to Prince August, an assignment that was changed to a regular appointment when Clausewitz graduated at the head of his class the following year. In the War of 1806 the prince, accompanied by Clausewitz, commanded a grenadier battalion, which was cut off by French cavalry during the retreat from Auerstedt and surrendered after repelling seven cavalry charges. Much against his will Clausewitz was compelled to follow the prince into

² J. A. Stargardt, Marburg, Auction of 27 and 28 June 1990, nr. 1154. Copies of the letter have been deposited in the Wehrgeschichtliches Museum, Rastatt, Germany, and in the Hoover Institution, Stanford University.

internment in France, an episode that threw the two men into closer contact than ever before. The prince was a cosmopolitan extrovert, dedicated equally to his military duties and the good life, which as one of the richest men in Prussia he was able to enjoy to the full. He had a clear, practical mind but was only intermittently interested in the issues of theory and scholarship that preoccupied his reserved and almost penurious adjutant. During their forced sojourn in France each had occasion to be irritated with the other. On their return to Prussia the prince was appointed inspector-general of the Prussian artillery to assist Scharnhorst in modernizing this branch of the service, the status of which would also be raised by placing a member of the royal family at its head. Clausewitz did not wish to continue as his adjutant and succeeded in being reassigned to the War Department. It called for some tactful maneuvering to ensure that the prince did not resent his leaving, but the two men parted on good terms. Some ten years later, when many of the changes that had reformed the Prussian army after 1806 were under attack, Clausewitz did not hesitate to solicit the prince's support for the Landwehr, which with its heavily bourgeois officer corps and organizational separation from the line was a prime target for conservative reaction. The prince did not share Clausewitz's high regard for this Prussian version of the National Guard, but that Clausewitz felt free to turn to him suggests that their relations remained cordial, even if each was at times critical of the other.[3] Throughout the 1820s Clausewitz served as commandant of the War Academy, until at his request he was transferred to the artillery in 1830, a reassignment that would not have been made against Prince August's wishes and probably could have been made only on his recommendation.

The letter Clausewitz wrote on 12 November 1831 is a covering letter for a manuscript he was sending to Prince August. Since it comes to the point without preliminary explanations, it evidently followed on earlier correspondence between the two men. The manuscript—354 pages in print when it was published as the fourth volume of the posthumous edition of his works—was a history of Napoleon's campaign of 1796–97 in Italy.[4] Clausewitz never sought publicity through his writings, but he was not reluctant to show his manuscripts to people whose thinking he wanted to influence and whose judgment he respected. From a biographical perspective it is interesting to have evidence that in November 1831 he did not react passively to signs of further strengthening of conservatism in Prussia, but reached out to men like Prince August who might be

[3] See, for instance, Clausewitz's comment on the prince's pedantry in his letter to Gneisenau of 8 June 1830, in Carl von Clausewitz, *Schriften-Aufsätze-Studien-Briefe*, ed. Werner Hahlweg (Göttingen, 1990), vol. 2, part 1, p. 578.

[4] Carl von Clausewitz, *Der Feldzug von 1976 in Italien*, vol. 4 of *Hinterlassene Werke* (Berlin, 1833).

helpful in any political difficulties ahead. It has sometimes been suggested that Clausewitz died a deeply disappointed, depressed man, but the letter indicates nothing of the kind.

The letter is not only of biographical but also of theoretical relevance; it is a document in the history of Clausewitz's thought. In the first sentence following the letter's polite opening phrases, Clausewitz explains the approach he has taken to his subject: "I must observe that the campaign is treated mainly from the strategic point of view, and that it was my intention to pursue the strategic argument everywhere to an absolute conclusion, a conclusion that may indeed be wrong and mistaken, but at least isn't drawn out of thin air."[5] As he had occasionally in the past, Clausewitz here points out that his military histories are essentially strategic histories. Tactical and operational events are analyzed, if at all, in the context of the antagonists' strategic concerns and decisions. If this was onesided, it was so by choice, not through ignorance. Clausewitz had served as an infantry subaltern against the French in the 1790s and again in 1806, and later as a field-grade officer in the Russian campaign and the Wars of Liberation. In his youth he had published an important article that clarified the meaning of strategy and tactics; during the Reform era he had lectured on small-unit tactics and served as member of the commission that modernized the Prussian infantry regulations. But in his historical writings he sought above all to uncover the strategic intentions of the two sides and explain how they were translated into action. To Prince August, Clausewitz acknowledged that his conclusions might be mistaken, but they resulted logically and realistically from an analysis that kept the political elements basic to every conflict steadily in view.

Clausewitz's acknowledgment carries implications that are as important to his theories as they are to his histories. It expresses a covert criticism of other military theorists of his time, whose work he found inadequate. On the one hand, so the two main points of his critique may be summarized, such writers as Bülow and Jomini claimed to be scientific but actually were more interested in discovering the keys to victory than in understanding war in its many forms; they fashioned their keys from so-called principles that were not the result of logical and historical thought but expressed ideas haphazardly arrived at—"drawn out of thin air." As might be expected from intelligent and experienced observers, their ideas could be stimulating, sometimes even valid, but they did not come from a comprehensive view of war that integrated historical fact with contemporary reality. Instead, operational techniques of at best temporary validity, interpreted without sufficient attention to the dynamics

---

[5] Clausewitz writes *Anhalt*, meaning "conclusion" in the sense of reasoned judgment.

of policy and of events in the field, were presented as fundamental elements of war.

The emphasis Clausewitz places on strategy is reinforced by his next sentence: "Tactical matters I regarded as merely of secondary importance, at least wherever the strategic threads ceased to be visible." At first glance the conclusion seems paradoxical. One might expect that a historian who can no longer follow the strategic threads will give tactics a larger part in his account. The paradox disappears when we remember that for Clausewitz it is the strategic context that renders tactical episodes comprehensible and indeed subject to analysis in the first place. When he no longer understands the strategic thinking and decisions of the opposing sides, tactical matters become still less rather than more important in his histories.

Clausewitz seems to have felt it necessary to justify this position to Prince August, because he added: "Besides, the extremely poor sources did not permit even a relatively adequate tactical treatment." This was a diplomatic explanation rather than the plain truth. Even in his studies of such well-documented conflicts as the Seven Years' War and the spring campaign of 1814 he devotes most of his attention to the opposing strategies and their interaction. The battles themselves are usually passed over in a few sentences. This tendency persists even when he writes about events in which he himself took part—the campaign of 1812 in Russia, for example. Although his history of the invasion of Russia contains an extensive description and analysis of the battle of Borodino at which he was present, as a whole it is written from the strategic point of view. Few military historians have written as little about actual combat as Clausewitz. It is a different matter when he turns from history to theory. *On War* contains many discussions of tactical subjects. But again, his aim was descriptive and analytic, not didactic. He held firm views on the tactics of his day, but his purpose was not to tell his readers how to surprise the enemy or how to defend a river. His discussions of tactics have specifically theoretical functions. The inclusion of tactical phenomena in his theoretical texts turns war from an abstraction into a cluster of concrete forces; it helps explain how the military instrument of state policy, whose intellectual and political dynamics he seeks to interpret, operates in the real world of violence. Secondly, tactical episodes illustrate elements that Clausewitz believed were always present in war: "friction," for instance, or psychological factors; the whole multihinged indirect process by which strategic decisions are eventually implemented in the "resistant medium" of combat.

Clausewitz's letter to Prince August thus refers in compressed form to some of his basic ideas. The significance of the letter for his theories becomes even clearer when we recall his motives for writing about the Italian campaign. In 1827 he interrupted work on *On War* to pursue detailed historical studies that would help him clarify his ideas on the political nature of war and on the distinctions between limited and unlimited war. Three long manuscripts—one of them on the campaign of 1796—were the outcome, on the basis of which he planned to rewrite *On War*. By the time he left Berlin for Breslau, however, and then took up his new assignment on the Polish frontier, his revisions had not proceeded beyond the opening chapter and probably a few other chapters as well.

His letter contains one last hint that, as he was writing, the differences between his speculative, logical analysis and the doctrinaire, prescriptive formulas of some other theorists were consciously or unconsciously in the back of his mind. Before ending the letter he added as an afterthought: "I must also note that the descriptions of combat refer to the maps published by Jomini."[6] In conjunction with his earlier comment on the poor documentation of the campaign, this casual reference to his great rival in interpreting war may have struck Prince August—and may strike us today—as a flash of irony beneath the businesslike surface of his letter. With this incidental comment Clausewitz once more emphasizes the distance between his writings and the writings of Jomini, a difference that today as much as in the early nineteenth century defines and illuminates two radically opposed approaches to the historical and theoretical as well as to the policy-oriented study of war.

[6] Clausewitz's letter echoes his direct and indirect criticism of Jomini in the *History of the Campaign of 1796*. For example, on p. 226, at the end of his discussion of the Battle of Arcola, Clausewitz refers to the "barely adequate" map of General Jomini, "better suited to obscure than to explain the matter."

In an introductory paragraph of his *History of the Campaign of 1796*, p. 1, Clausewitz mentions the work of Jomini that served as one of his sources: the "second edition" of his "history of the revolutionary wars." But the complex publication history of Jomini's writings leaves uncertain which of several versions is meant. It may be either the eight-volume second edition of the *Histoire critique et militaire des campagnes de la révolution* (Paris, 1811–16), or the fifteen-volume "new edition," *Histoire critique et militaire des guerres de la révolution* (Paris, 1820–24), of which volumes seven through ten, supplemented by an atlas, cover the campaigns between 1795 and 1798. Although the earlier work is designated as the "second edition," it is probable that Clausewitz used the later work. The term "new edition" often meant and was thought to mean "second edition"; in its title the word "campaigns" had been changed to "wars," which agrees with Clausewitz's reference; and Clausewitz was likely to use the more recent and much expanded edition of Jomini's *History*, a set of which had been bought by the library of the War Academy.

PART THREE

THE HISTORY OF WAR

16

THE HISTORY OF WAR AND THE NEW

MILITARY HISTORY

IN 1970 FELIX GILBERT chaired a small conference on current trends in historical studies, at which he invited me to discuss the history of war. As might be expected of a meeting on such a subject at that time, social history and its methods assumed a dominant part in the program, and some participants took a dim view of a talk that addressed the past and present historiography of organized violence between states without exploring such other forms of violence as banditry, crime, and the class conflict. Still, I could not help notice that another paper, presented by Emmanuel le Roy Ladurie and Paul Dumont, quantified and interpreted French recruitment statistics of the 1820s. With a slight shift in perspective, their study might not only have added to our knowledge of French society in the Restoration, but also of its army. Their project seemed to suggest once again that hard and fast lines drawn between fields of research reflected academic fashions and convenience rather than historical reality. Felix Gilbert himself regretted the somewhat one-sided orientation of the conference, and for the published version, which appeared in *Daedalus*, asked several additional contributors to discuss such unfashionable topics as the history of diplomacy.

In my essay I expressed the hope that scholars would do more to trace the links between the actuality of war and its nonviolent context and speculated on ways of expanding research by adopting methods from other disciplines. I was of course far from alone in advocating such changes. Twenty years later, when I returned to the subject in a talk to the Society of Military Historians, an expanded sense of the field and borrowings from other disciplines had become commonplace. Today the history of war in this country is stronger than it has been in a century or more. Regrettably this advance is at times accompanied by exaggerated claims for the new approaches and by a disagreeable rejection of conventional work just because it is conventional. Consequently I gave my talk the title "The New Military History—an Appreciation and a Critique." The two papers, twenty years apart, seem to me to belong together. For this volume I have combined parts of both, an amalgamation that I hope bridges the two decades, and conveys my sense of where the history of war is today and how it got there.

શ.

Because wars, the institutions that make them possible, and the ideas that guide their conduct form an important part of the human experience, they ought to be a principal subject of historical study. In some respects they have been. From antiquity on, historians have devoted attention to organized violence, both to describe and analyze it for its own sake and as a constant of political history. And yet war has only intermittently been near the center of historical enquiry, and it has never been strongly represented as a field of academic specialization in colleges and universities. The following pages discuss some aspects of this contradictory condition. I begin with a look at European historiography, and then turn to the historical study of war in this country, as it has evolved since the Second World War.

I

Medieval accounts of armed conflict, especially of armed conflict in earlier times, were strongly marked by symbolic and mythic qualities. Gradually these faded, their place being taken by a greater interest in accounting and analyzing the actual course of events. By the eighteenth century, historians had become adept at employing a variety of sources in tracing the diplomatic exchanges preceding war, the course of military operations, and the negotiations leading to the reestablishment of peace. But their work still suffered from a failure to appreciate the differences in economic, social, and political conditions that might exist between antagonists—between Sweden and Russia, for instance, or the Hapsburg and Ottoman empires—or differences between former ages and their own times. On the whole they interpreted the military institutions and policies of earlier generations according to their own conditions and ideals. They regarded Caesar and Condé as contemporaries and judged both by the practices of Frederick the Great.

Nor did they inquire systematically into the relationship between military and political institutions or analyze the interaction of strategic policy and battle. Voltaire's history of Charles XII, for instance, devotes a great deal of attention to military events without ever departing far from a straight narrative whose only unifying principle appears to be the author's concern with the effect that a ruler's psychology may have on policy. Even the detailed description of a major encounter such as the battle of Poltava, though derived from eyewitness accounts and set down in paragraphs of elegant clarity, leaves the reader puzzled about much that occurred.

Toward the end of the Enlightenment this historiographical mold was broken. Frederick the Great's own histories of his wars had already demonstrated how an author with great inside knowledge could combine aspects of foreign policy, strategy, and operations into accounts that were both analytic and specific. Now the French Revolution enabled and compelled historians to pay at least some attention to the political and social realities of the belligerent states. In 1797 Gerhard Scharnhorst published a history of the War of the First Coalition whose purpose was to identify and understand the apparently crucial differences between the monarchies and revolutionary France. Unlike other writers who sought the key to the French successes in specific techniques, such as the *levée en masse* or skirmishing, Scharnhorst took note of the advantages that France enjoyed: a more favorable strategic position, superior numbers, unified political and military command, and greater incentive for the individual soldier. But he also analyzed the innovations in the French army's organization and methods, tried to trace their historical development, explained the strategy of the revolutionary commanders in light of the military and political situation, and pointed beyond military institutions to the greater energies that could be generated in a society that was more free than his own. "The reasons for the defeat of the allied powers must be deeply enmeshed in their internal conditions and in those of the French nation," he said, adding that he referred to psychological as well as physical elements.[1]

A few years later, his pupil Carl von Clausewitz extended the liberation of military history from the preconceptions of cabinet diplomacy and maneuver strategy to the study of earlier conflicts. In his work on the Thirty Years' War, written between 1803 and 1805, Clausewitz made a point of criticizing those scholars who could treat the war only with a sense of horror and superiority as a formless, brutish struggle, which they would have preferred to ignore altogether. The men of the early seventeenth century, Clausewitz wrote, acted in accordance with their economic and technological condition, their political and religious concerns, and their psychology. It may have been in anticipation of the conservative side of historicism for Clausewitz further to suggest that modern standards not only did not apply to the 1630s but that the energy and idealism of the

---

[1] Gerhard Scharnhorst, "Entwicklung der allgemeinen Ursachen des Glücks der Franzosen in dem Revolutionskriege," in *Militärische Schriften von Scharnhorst*, ed. C. v. d. Goltz (Dresden, 1891), 195, 203.

generation of Gustavus Adolphus and Wallenstein might well have been superior to that of their descendants.[2]

In the historiography of the nineteenth century, political and military elements were generally closely connected. Sir John Seeley's proposition that the degree of a state's internal freedom was determined in reverse proportion by the degree of military and political pressure on its borders illustrates the interpretive reach of the time, even if in our own day some have condemned his proposition as illiberal and therefore misleading. But detailed explorations of political and military interdependence were perhaps more often found in the work of continental scholars. Ranke, when he addressed himself to writing the history of Prussia during the French Revolution and the Napoleonic era, alternated as a matter of course between internal and foreign affairs, between the description of military planning and military action. Nor did historians whose work ordinarily lay in other fields hesitate to study themes that were predominantly military in character—as Friedrick Meinecke did in his biography of Boyen, when he integrated military history with the history of ideas and political attitudes. Toward the end of the century some scholars began to apply the speculations of the early sociologists about military elites and organized violence to their research into the nature and development of political institutions.

In the writings of Otto Hintze this fusion carried the history of war to a new level of methodological and interpretive significance. His long essays combined political, social, and economic history and the study of bureaucracies with comparative analysis; he firmly placed the military factor into a newly comprehensive approach to constitutional and institutional history. The armed forces served as a central element of his interpretations, not only in treatments of a particular episode ("Prussian Reform Attempts Before 1806," for instance) and in comparative explorations (such as "Military Organization and State Organization," which sought universal factors and regularities in the interaction of war and society over the course of Western civilization) but also in his many studies of such topics as feudalism, constitutional government, and imperialism. When Hintze wrote in 1906 that comparative history had established beyond question that "all state organization was originally military organization, organization for war," he was not alluding to a prime mover whose influence had dissipated, and which historians of later periods could safely ignore.[3] He was putting forward a programmatic state-

---

[2] Carl von Clausewitz, "Gustav Adolphs Feldzüge von 1630–1632," in *Hinterlassene Werke* (Berlin, 1837), 9:18, 19–21, 101–6.

[3] Otto Hintze, "Military Organization and State Organization," in *The Historical Essays of Otto Hintze*, ed. Felix Gilbert (New York, 1975), 181. Compare this to the statement in Sir Lewis Namier's book, *England in the Age of the American Revolution* (London: Mac-

ment. But although Hintze's work never lost its vitality—indeed, the strength of his method is only now becoming fully recognized—his immediate influence was limited.

Few historians took up his search for the specific links between institutional and constitutional development on the one hand and military force, its organization and employment, on the other. Nor can it be said that the historical profession in general was receptive to those scholars who wished to devote their work largely or exclusively to the study of the military theories, institutions, and policies of the past. History, as a discipline, continued to be dominated by political history, which, indeed, the epigoni of the idealistic school tended to treat more narrowly than had their masters. Efforts to develop new fields, such as social or economic history, met vigorous opposition; acceptable specialization was still limited to the auxiliary historical sciences, to philology, and to a few periods and national categories. Academics particularly interested in the study of war were further handicapped by the sizable organizations of historians dealing specifically with military affairs that had been established in France, Germany, Austria, Russia, and elsewhere in the historical sections of the various armed services. These official bodies to some extent preempted the field through their control of the archives and through their technical expertise, the importance of which was increasing with the industrialization of war. Their interpretations, particularly in Germany and France, came to exert a profound effect on civilian scholarship. Some of the official historians—for example, Jean Colin of the Section historique—were independent and original scholars; but too often the service publications had an apologetic or policy-oriented character that could only compromise the view in which the historical profession held the study of war. The antagonism that often existed between civilians and soldiers in Europe may also have played a part; it was simple enough to scoff at a professor as a *Zivilstratege* or, on the other hand, to dismiss the writings of nonacademic staff officers as the *Kultur der Kulturlosen*.

The failure of the European nation-state in our time has made the European historian more critical of his society's record of wars, without lessening his interest in it. Such works as Gerhard Ritter's *Staatskunst und Kriegshandwerk*, Rudolf Stadelmann's superb essays on Gerhard Scharnhorst, Emile Léonard's *L'armée et ses problèmes au xviiᵉ siècle*, or Raoul Girardet's *La société militaire dans la France contemporaine*, which take a synoptic view of political, military, intellectual, and social history, or apply economic data to the analysis of social and military development,

---

millan, 1930), 7: "The social history of nations is largely moulded by the forms and development of their armed forces, the primary aim of national organisation being common defence." The opening section of Namier's book, "The Social Foundations," seems to me to contain a number of direct reflections of Hintze's thought.

as Otto Büsch does in his *Militärsystem und Sozialleben im alten Preussen*, are exceptional for their level of achievement, but otherwise not unusual in modern French and German historiography. The years since 1945 have also brought increasing sophistication to the treatment of strategic decisions and actual operations. Two examples are Andreas Hillgruber's *Hitlers Strategie*, in which extensive interlocking studies explore the political, diplomatic, military, and psychological background of the Russo-German War, and the current project of a group of German historians of a multivolume history of Germany in the Second World War, which is particularly good on the organizational, economic, and technological context of the fighting.[4]

Equally innovative studies have been written by contemporary English historians, who in general seem less interested in treating ideas on war and their connection with political concepts than in exploring civil-military relations and the development and execution of strategy, operations, and tactics—a preference in which they may find themselves at one with American scholars. Their work, which has generated considerable new knowledge on how societies and governments arm themselves, and how they fight, is accompanied by a vast output of books that, in Michael Howard's description, skillfully blend reputable history with wide public appeal.[5] While this popular literature has little or nothing to say to the scholar, it appears to possess as much justification as do textbooks addressed to the college audience—indeed, the educational functions of the two genres are not dissimilar. Military history is, in fact, frequently popular history. It seems to respond to a demand for colorful gore and for the vicarious experience of crime and punishment—appetites whose apparent universality may have something to say about the intractability of the subject with which these books are concerned. Possibly the mass of historical belles lettres, which is as prevalent on the continent as it is in England, acts as a brake to change in the field, or at least limits the influence of innovation; but it does not prevent the history of war and of military institutions in general from occupying a secure if certainly not a major place in the writing and teaching of history in Europe today.

II

In the United States the historical study of war over the past fifty years has found itself in a more complex situation. The Second World War

---

[4] *Das Deutsche Reich und der zweite Weltkrieg* (Stuttgart, 1979–). The work is being translated into English: *Germany and the Second World War* (Oxford, 1990–).

[5] Michael Howard, "The Demand for Military History," *Times Literary Supplement*, 13 November 1969.

brought new energy to the field, and the impetus continued through the next decades, being carried further by the Korean War and the war in Vietnam. But already by the 1950s the history of war was shrinking into a marginal area of specialization, held in low regard by the discipline and in academic institutions.

One reason for this may be found in differences between academic history and the official history programs of the armed services. The stimulus to historical study provided by the recent wars benefited above all the government's research and publication projects on this country's military experience. They began with the publication in the last decades of the nineteenth century of the *Official Records of the Wars of the Rebellion* and with other documentary series on the Revolutionary War and on America's participation in the First World War. Subsequently emphasis shifted from the publication of records to scholarly interpretive history, which produced such important series as the *United States Army in World War II* and similar series on the wars in Korea and Vietnam. These projects have constituted the largest cooperative effort in historical writing yet undertaken in this country. They involved and often helped train many civilian scholars. One series, Samuel Morison's fifteen-volume history, *United States Naval Operations in World War II*, though sponsored by the Navy, was published commercially. Some of the research techniques used were innovative, and in general the quality of the official histories has been good.[6] At the very least they provide a reliable base line for the work of other scholars, as well as a backdrop and target for revisionist studies, which have been the second main beneficiary of the interest in the history of this country's recent wars.

On the other hand, certain characteristics often found in official histories have weakened their impact on the discipline and even have proved counterproductive. A noticeable lack in these works has been an adequate account of planning and decision-making at the highest levels—subjects, which, indeed, nearly always lie beyond their areas of responsibility. They are much better on organizational and operational issues; but even here their treatment is too often compromised by a pronounced utilitarian outlook: what can—or even, must—we learn from history? It is only logical that this orientation also affected the collection and selection of evidence. The historical teams that served in Vietnam, on whose work subsequent interpretations strongly depended, had as a primary duty the identification of evidence of tactical and operational lessons learned, which would help determine the validity of current service concepts and doctrine.

[6] The Army series on the Second World War readily accommodated different and even opposing points of view. Compare, for instance, the essays by Kent Roberts Greenfield and Robert R. Palmer in the first volume of the series (on the Army ground forces) or the respective volumes on the Mediterranean campaign by Maurice Matloff and R. M. Leighton.

Official history is written to provide a record, to fix the past firmly in our consciousness, but often also to lay bare the lessons for today and tomorrow that the past is thought to offer. The pedagogic mission combines with special expectations that are held by many potential readers of these works. Soldiers, Don Higginbotham has written, believe "history to be relevant. To study a famous battle is to simulate combat, to give officers a vivid sense of being present, of engaging vicariously in a meaningful tactical exercise."[7] This is not how most historians of nonmilitary subjects think of their work, and even if some of their readers are animated by vicarious motives, these are rarely of immediate professional relevance. Historians disagree on the purposes of history, but few would teach a course or write a book on the French Revolution or on McKinley's presidential campaign and conclude with a list of lessons learned. The utilitarian spirit, the faith in relevance, was a driving force in official histories—and probably remains so today—and certainly dominated the courses taught in ROTC programs, which for many college teachers represented military history as such.

A distinction must be drawn between the relevance of history—something that in one way or another many historians accept—and the kind of relevance that specifically seeks to strengthen the state and its armed instruments, which is regarded with far greater suspicion. Undoubtedly the policy orientation and the celebration of duty, sacrifice, and tradition that mark many service histories help account for the distrust of the history of war in general among American historians, which became widespread some years after 1945. As in Europe before 1914 and between the wars, the programmatic elements and scholarly shortcomings often found in official military history confirmed already existing doubts about the field in general, and validated prejudices and intellectual fashions. By and large, American historians seemed to consider war as something exceptional, a crisis—perhaps even a perversion—of the ordinary political and foreign policy processes, and therefore not suited to constitute one of the units in which research and teaching are organized in this country. The American Revolutionary War and above all the Civil War fell outside this taboo. These wars were clearly felt to be integral to the American experience, and scholars studied them without considering themselves—or being considered by others—to be military historians.

War is also a subject that cannot easily be understood from the outside. Its study may demand technical expertise and access to material difficult for the scholar to acquire—except in the very programs that many aca-

[7] Don Higginbotham, "George Washington and George Marshall: Some Reflections on the American Military Tradition," in *The Harmon Memorial Lectures in Military History*, ed. Harry R. Borowski (Washington, D.C., 1988), 157.

demics discounted as not fully part of the common scholarly enterprise, the history programs of the armed services. The isolation of military history was reinforced by another factor: whether official or unofficial, the literature contained much detailed reconstruction and some general hypotheses but relatively few middle-range propositions. It lacked the broad monographic base, offering hypotheses in a variety of contexts, that is needed to stimulate and structure discussion. The largely narrative, unanalytic treatment of military operations, which continued to make up the bulk of the literature, was not conducive to the development of creative historical hypotheses or to the closer integration of military history with other kinds of history.

These may be some of the explanations for the marginalization of the history of war in the American academic world in the 1950s and 1960s. In 1954, a survey of 493 colleges and universities showed that no more than thirty-seven institutions offered or intended to offer one or in a few cases two courses in military history.[8] Graduate study and tenure track appointments in the field were equally limited. Military historians seemed to have little to contribute to their colleagues in other fields. The profession in general ignored their work or looked on it with suspicion—out of disinterest, ignorance, or even from political or ideological motives, which the war in Vietnam was to reinforce. Had it not been for the service history programs and for a small number of scholars in colleges and universities—many of them teaching in the South—the history of war would scarcely have had a continuing institutional presence in American higher education.

III

Historians of war in the 1950s and 1960s could not be unaware of their less than favored, peripheral position in scholarship and the academy. In general they reacted in one of three ways. Many continued to write narrowly designed and conventionally executed history, often with a strong antiquarian bent: descriptive accounts of leading figures, particular units, campaigns, or climactic battles. Even if they uncovered significant new documentation, their traditionalist view of war as a cluster of ideas and activities that were largely self-contained and that they liked to study in isolation from the larger context made it difficult for their work to link up with the work of historians in other fields. Others tried to break through the artificial barriers between the categories of specialization that

[8] Louis Morton, "The Historian and the Study of War," *Mississippi Valley Historical Review* 48, no. 4 (March 1962): 601.

for a century have provided the framework for professional education and academic careers in this country. These historians had to fight simultaneously on two fronts: against the indifference or hostility of many of their colleagues, on the one hand; and against the narrowness of much of military history on the other. They insisted on the importance of studying and teaching the history of war while simultaneously arguing that it was made up of more than unit histories, narratives of battles and campaigns, and biographies of military heroes.

A third group sought to escape from the crisis in which the conventional history of war found itself by making it less military. A representative of this tendency was Walter Millis, whose study of the American military experience, *Arms and Men*, gained a wide audience in the 1950s. To a series of pamphlets on various fields of history, published by the American Historical Association, Millis contributed the pamphlet on military history. In it he divided American military literature into three categories: the literature of recall, with which he designated memoirs, unit histories, and personal reminiscences; the analytic study of war as an institution, by which, oddly enough, Millis meant strategic and operational analysis; and works such as Emory Upton's *The Military Policy of the United States*, in which military history was used "not simply to teach battlefield tactics but as a foundation for broad national policy."[9] It is suggestive that such an intelligent and able writer as Millis, whose contribution to our understanding of the American military past is considerable, could see military history as purely utilitarian—except for the instruction and vicarious pleasure that may be derived from reading the memoirs of General Sherman or General MacArthur.[10] His argument belongs, of course, to a vigorous tradition that is far from being exclusively American. When Sir Frederick Maurice, in his London inaugural lecture in 1929, spoke on "The Uses of the Study of War," he stated that the first use, "which most concerns the citizen, is to promote peace by promoting an understanding of the realities of war and of the problems which may lead to war. The second, which most concerns the professional, but also does or should concern the citizen, is to ensure that war, if it comes, is waged in the best possible way."[11] The desirability of these purposes need not be denied, but by themselves they are hardly adequate guides for research. They appear threadbare in their pragmatic exclusiveness when they are compared with Delbrück's nearly simultaneous statement in the

[9] Walter Millis, *Military History* (Washington, D.C., 1961), 5–7; see also ibid. 10–11.

[10] As Frank Craven pointed out in his lecture, "Why Military History?" *Harmon Memorial Lectures*, 13–14, Millis's own work takes a far broader approach than his policy-oriented categories would imply.

[11] Quoted in Michael Howard, "Military Power and International Order," *International Affairs* 40 (July 1964): 397.

introduction to the fourth volume of his *Geschichte der Kriegskunst im Rahmen der politischen Geschichte*:

> Recognition of the reciprocal effects of tactics, strategy, political institutions, and politics throws light on the interconnections in universal history, and has illuminated much that until now lay in darkness or was misunderstood. This work was not written for the sake of the art of war, but for the sake of world history. If soldiers should read it and find it stimulating, I shall be delighted and honored; but the book is written for friends of history by a historian.[12]

Once or twice, to be sure, Millis's pamphlet suggests that aspects of the military past might be studied for their own sake, but these are digressions that do not affect his main argument that the writing and study of military history has two functions: "to train professional military men in the exercise of their profession and on the other hand to educate governments and peoples in the military requirements of today." With this as his premise, Millis naturally enough concludes that since the strategy and tactics of the Civil War or even of the Second World War can no longer serve as models for the nuclear age, "military history as a specialty has largely lost its function." In a brief final paragraph, he urges military history, if it is to regain its usefulness, to "turn away from a study of past wars to the study of war itself in its broadest possible terms."[13]

IV

Millis's counsel of despair was not without influence on historians, the more so as demilitarized military history promised to be more acceptable to the profession at large. But his advice was based on a profoundly unscholarly, utilitarian view, which confused the effort to interpret the past with contemporary defense analysis, and time has proved false his prophecy that military history no longer has a future as a field of academic specialization. Nevertheless, his stress on a broad approach to the study of war pointed in the right direction, if not his reason for believing it necessary.

Millis was not alone in decrying the narrowness of much of military history then being written in this country. To mention only one other name, W. Frank Craven, a well-known historian of colonial America at Princeton and coeditor of the seven-volume series *The Army Air Forces in World War II*, made a similar point, but formulated in optimistic

---

[12] Hans Delbrück, *Geschichte der Kriegskunst im Rahmen der politischen Geschichte* (Berlin, 1962), vol. 4, unpaginated introduction.

[13] Millis, *Military History*, 16, 17–18.

terms, when he noted in 1959 that after the Second World War, many historians came to take a broader view of military history. "We recognize," he continued, "that the battle itself is no more than a part of the story. The central problem is man's continuing dependence on force as an instrument of policy, and we have come to see that every aspect of his social, economic, and political order . . . is pertinent to military history."[14] Today we might feel compelled to rephrase Craven's statement in non-gender-specific language, but his differentiation between two kinds of military history was valid when he made it thirty-two years ago, and it still holds true today.

It was in the 1960s, perhaps the nadir of American military history in this century, at least in professional recognition, that almost imperceptibly a change set in which now has gone far to raise interest in the historical interpretation of war and its attendant elements and placed it on a firmer, less contentious footing in American colleges and universities. In recent years this development has been generally associated with the *New Military History*—a term, incidentally, that has been with us for some time, at least since the late 1960s, and in slightly different formulations since the Second World War. Most intellectual activities that rise above a modest level of complexity do not lend themselves to definitions that are both unambiguous and accurate, and not surprisingly a confusion of favorable and less favorable meanings has been attached to the New Military History. Among the latter is the claim, frequently advanced by traditionalists, that it refers to histories of war that exclude combat. That description is, of course, inaccurate, and it is difficult to avoid the impression that it is motivated by the wish to maintain the core of war—violence—as the special preserve of conventional military historians, those scholars who are sometimes accused by unfriendly modernists of writing bugles and buttons history.

A more accurate characterization, with which many historians would probably agree, holds that the New Military History refers to a partial turning away from the great captains and from weapons, tactics, and operations as the main concerns of the historical exploration of war. Instead scholars and students are asked to pay greater attention to the interaction of war with society, economics, politics, and culture. The New Military History stands for an effort to integrate the study of military institutions and their actions more closely with other kinds of history. This very broad general movement includes a variety of specific approaches, which are not necessarily in agreement with one another. Some are defined by methodological interests—the application of social-scientific techniques is often mentioned. Others by ideological points of view—for instance,

[14] Craven, "Why Military History," 12.

interpretations patterned by the dogma of one or the other kind of Marxism. Others again are defined by their subject matter: the condition of the common soldier, for one; or, at the opposite end of the scale, the role of military institutions in the creation and maintenance of state power. These countless approaches are more or less closely related to the application of force, but tend to go beyond it. The New Military History asserts that the history of war is about much more than people killing each other, that it should look beyond the actual realization, the putting into practice, of man's organized inhumanity to man.

I have outlined a broad characterization; let me now suggest that we might draw three preliminary conclusions from it. First, despite the variety of subjects and methods encompassed by the term and the exaggerated claims sometimes made for it, the New Military History does represent a change in emphasis in the research and writing of many scholars that is important and to be welcomed. Second, the word *new* in the New Military History is inaccurate if it is used in an absolute sense to signify something that did not exist before. In this connection few people will take the word literally, but undoubtedly its use carries and is meant to carry powerful connotations. And finally, the New Military History is obviously related to other recent developments in the discipline of history: such movements as the New Cultural History, the New Narrative History, and above all the New Social History. We need to look more closely at each of these points, first at the positive changes that the New Military History represents.

The expansive, frequently more analytic approach that has become associated with the New Military History has helped to invigorate the history of war in this country. More good books and articles are appearing; the principal periodical in the field, the *Journal of Military History*, not only has raised its standards but has been able to maintain them. The former isolation of military history within history has diminished. Exchanges with other areas of specialization have become more frequent, an opening up that is also reflected in an increase in interdisciplinary and comparative approaches and topics. This has affected military history both in the services and in civilian institutions. Service programs have been broadened by such developments as the Air Force Academy's annual Harmon lectures and history symposia and by the visiting professorships held by academics at Carlisle Barracks. History departments seem to be showing a greater readiness to recognize the validity, even the necessity, of studying military thought, institutions, and policy in the past. Already in the mid-1970s a survey found more than 110 colleges and universities that offered courses in military history, not including ROTC courses.[15] I

[15] Maurice Matloff, "The Nature and Scope of Military History," in *New Dimensions in Military History*, ed. Russell F. Weigley (San Rafael, 1975), 406–7.

have the impression that the number of programs continues to grow—if often under the protective guise of "peace studies," a distorting label that signals how much of the old prejudice and failure to understand is still with us. Academic positions in the field may be increasing somewhat; at least a new Ph.D. who can point to a minor in military history may now seem a more attractive candidate to a greater number of search committees than formerly. These are modest changes, but compared to the way things used to be they signify an advance. They have helped create greater academic openness, have themselves benefited from it, and are enriching the study and teaching of history—not just of the history of war but history in general.

These are welcome developments. But not surprisingly some weaknesses are associated with them. One is the danger that too many historians will follow the advice Millis gave thirty years ago and not address the mass of tactical, operational, and organizational topics that have never been adequately studied. Whether the escape from war was a useful option for military history in 1961 or is today seems very questionable.

Another flaw relates to the assertion that the New Military History is new. Labels ought never be taken too seriously, but the naive or manipulative use of *new* may convey a mistaken and highly unprofessional sense of what the New Military History has and has not achieved so far. In responding to the claim of newness, two propositions might be put forward: First, the New Military History has not yet achieved a true methodological breakthrough. Its methods were developed long ago. Second, the New Military History has not yet been able to equal certain works written decades, or even generations ago, which if they were written today would certainly be considered part of the new wave. Put differently, the New Military History is a continuation, in some cases perhaps an expansion of what has gone before.

I feel free to say this because any serious reader of the history of war will have no difficulty in identifying historians of earlier periods, who took the broad, integrative view of their subject that is the core around which the New Military History has coalesced. To be sure, in reviewing our predecessors we must guard against being misled by the different, perhaps old-fashioned styles and terminologies they may have used. It is possible to write innovative history in traditional language, just as it happens that third-rate, derivative ideas are expressed in the most up-to-date, fashionable terms. Certainly the earlier scholars did not say all there is to be said. Historians writing today, who of course benefit from their work, often go beyond them, find new material, formulate new problems, even achieve methodological refinements. Reinterpretation, if based on genuine understanding and of an open acknowledgment of the intellectual debt that every reinterpretation owes, is one of the glories of history. But not a few of the scholars who wrote before the Second World War remain admirably contemporary, and to greater or lesser extent each asks questions and uses approaches with which the New Military History is identified. They are our ancestors; and, as is the habit of rich relatives, they stubbornly refuse to die.

An example of the many bonds that bind together the old and the New Military History is the presence of social history in each. Of course, social history itself is not unchanging, it comprises a variety of orientations and methods, and in recent years studies of the common people and the rank and file have undoubtedly played a much larger role than they did two generations ago, although they existed even then. Nevertheless, in the minds of many of its adherents—readers as well as writers—the New Military History is associated with studies that concentrate on history from below. That would suggest links with the New Social History, which raises the question of the relationship between the New Military History and recent developments in the discipline of history as a whole.

It is probably no accident that the New Military History is merely one among several kinds of historical study that in recent years have emerged as "new." These so-called new forms have several roots. They emerged in reaction to earlier conditions, and to the extent that they respond to new issues and questions they are products of scholarly development and change. They are also stimulated by intellectual developments elsewhere—that is, they are not only the outcome of a linear process but also of interdisciplinary changes. And as they grow they support each other. One borrows the concept of newness from the next, and together they soon present a front of the new against tradition and convention, a front that is made up of mutual sympathies and scholarly borrowings.

In this development, the New Social History has played an ambiguous role. By transmitting to other fields its faith in the methods of social science and its belief in the importance of studying the conditions and attitudes of the mass of the population, it has influenced the New Military History. But if we think back on the 1960s and 1970s, we will find that attitudes associated with or engendered by the New Social History strongly contributed to the hostile environment in which military history then existed.

Opposition to the historical study of war, which is not the same as indifference to it, has often been driven by political attitudes. These very attitudes were one of the forces—certainly, only one among several—that lent impetus to the New Social History: a critique by the left of American capitalism; of inequities of class, race, and gender; of the cold war, often interpreted as an expression of American imperialism—all intensified by opposition to the war in Vietnam. These political elements not only helped energize the New Social History, they fostered a certain intolerance in some of its followers. Some areas of study were dismissed as unimportant or even pernicious—among them military history—and efforts were made to impose standards of thematic and methodological correctness on our unruly discipline. Even if these efforts did not succeed, they had an impact. In his essay "The Influence of Air Power upon Historians," Noel Parrish recalls a session during the 1977 meetings of the American Historical Association at which two young professors announced that "history is not history unless it has social significance."[16] That degree of silliness was rare, but the statement does point to an attitude that in diluted form was widespread for a time. It gained further strength because graduate students and junior faculty on the hunt for jobs, grants, and tenure felt pressed to present their work in a certain manner. When fashions changed and the domination of the New Social History faded, many people, especially those just beginning their careers, were left poorly prepared for finding their way through the newly fragmented, more challenging academic landscape.

This phase in the recent past of historical studies in this country is worth recalling not only for its ironic twist by which the New Military History became indebted to the very force that had doubted the scholarly legitimacy of studying war, but also as a cautionary tale. It reminds us how people get hurt when mutual tolerance and the acceptance of many varieties of history are rejected in favor of a homogeneous, uniform standard: this is how history should be written. And, to repeat, it is particularly people at the beginning of their careers, in their precarious psychological and professional condition, who are victimized by the threat and promise of the absolute.

V

The history of war has traversed a difficult course in this country. My discussion tried to map some of the turns of the road it has taken, and with a few exceptions has concentrated on the surface features of the intellectual and institutional landscape. A thorough exploration of the motives of the various attitudes in the academic world that have been hostile to the study of war, or disinterested in it, would take us deep into the complex relationship between American society and violence since the days of the early settlers. That many works of military history have been poor history surely contributed to the isolation of the field but could not have been the only cause. Indeed, the weakness of the field was in large

[16] Noel F. Parrish, "The Influence of Air Power upon Historians," *Harmon Memorial Lectures*, 28.

part the result of its isolation. If recently academic history has become somewhat less dismissive of the history of war as an interesting area of research, it may reflect no more than the usual back and forth of scholarly fashion, a reaction against a vogue that has had its day. Possibly this development also expresses more general forces—a changing mood in the country, the collapse of communism and the fading of the cold war abroad. But perhaps no special explanation is needed for the long-overdue recognition of the self-evident truth that every aspect of the past is worth study.

The New Military History is associated with this change, and as I have tried to suggest it cannot well be discussed in isolation from the old. Put differently, the expansive view of the history of war is not a new achievement, it has existed for centuries, even if the ways in which this view was expressed took different forms. That is not surprising: regardless of scholarly fashion and of the concepts according to which the study of history was institutionalized, reality always demonstrated that war was more than drill and combat.

I am writing in the early spring of 1991, at a time when this truth is once again illustrated by events. The Gulf War is a particularly clear example of an interaction that is basic to all armed conflict, the interaction of society, politics, policy, armed forces, and the threat and use of violence. It will be difficult to write the history of this war from a purely military perspective. I am not saying there won't be such histories—there will be many of them—but they will leave out much that is of basic importance, without which the planning and fighting will make little sense. If they claim to be histories of the war, they will not be true histories. The Gulf War is the perfect subject for what some have come to call the New Military History—and for its many ancestors, going back to Clausewitz, who in 1827 wrote that "there can be no ... *purely military* evaluation of a great strategic issue, nor ... a purely military scheme to solve it."[17] The history of the Gulf War will have to take account of all the factors I have mentioned and many others besides. It will need to weave them together in a way that re-creates and makes comprehensible the dynamics of the conflict. There will also be hundreds of studies on parts of this great subject: the role of blacks, the role of women, the issue of the Scuds, the history of reporting the war, and so on. But also the history of the 101st Airborne Division's air assault, the account of the armored fight at Kuwait International Airport, the biography of an individual soldier. All these themes, however conventional or innovative they may be, are valid and represent issues that should be studied and interpreted. Equally valid is a broad range of methods, whether applied to research designs or to

---

[17] Carl von Clausewitz, quoted in "Two Letters on Strategy," above, 127.

narrative and analysis. The New Military History will prosper and best benefit history in general if its followers reject dogma and recognize that the greatest threat to historical scholarship remains where it always has been: in the coercive intent and power of orthodoxy, whether old or new.

INDEX